An Introduction To Russian Literature

AN INTRODUCTION TO

Russian

Literature

BY

HELEN MUCHNIC, Ph.D.

Professor of Russian Literature
Smith College

DOUBLEDAY & COMPANY, INC.

Garden City 1947 New York

PG
2951
M8

28032

Preface

THE PRESENT ESSAY IS WRITTEN NEITHER TO EXALT NOR TO condemn Russia, nor to apologize for her. Nor does it purport to define the "Russian soul," nor to be a history, nor even a full outline of Russian literature. It is an attempt to point out, in the productions of some of her greatest writers, certain traits that might be used toward an explanation of her art, and so, perhaps, of her people.

It does not take up the work of the Soviet Union, which carries on and modifies the great tradition of Russian letters in a development that is fascinating—and important not only in itself but also for what it contributes to the general theory of art. The questions that this new literature raises—how the moral and aesthetic preferences of a nation survive revolution and a changing ideology; what happens to art when it is required to follow an official program; how novel modes of perception are combined with the old, and what in them remains of the past, what is lost, and what is added—are too intricate to be dealt with briefly. The problem requires a separate study and is not touched on in this book.

Contents

An Introduction To Russian Literature

Introduction

GREAT WORK OF ART IS ONE OF THE MOST MYSTERIOUS products of the human spirit. The impulsion to it is obscure and its effects are incalculable. Its meaning is complex, and the greater it is, the more interpretations and debates is it likely to provoke. Bound to the place and moment of its origin, it is, nevertheless, international; and it becomes eternal, proving, as nothing else, that man's experience is both continuous and compressible. The illusion of actuality which it creates brings it immediate acclaim in its own country, but its wisdom, transcending boundaries of time and of geography, confers immortality upon it. For a great work of art contains some of humanity's most cherished aspirations; and mankind, delighted with this profound and ennobling treasure, refuses to be parted from it. That is why neither languages nor centuries can reduce in stature nor cast into oblivion a Sophocles, a Shakespeare, or a Dante.

An artist is a restless being, who is not satisfied to take

objects and events as they occur. His mind, yearning for a greater stability than they can offer, stretches out to meanings behind objects and events, and forms of them a mold for his observations. Thus he succeeds in making life more understandable, because, in the pattern of sound, line, or color through which he builds his structures, the details that have come to his notice are big with reference to the unseen.

The pictures he paints and the stories he tells are not, therefore, although they may appear "lifelike," reproductions of tangible reality but pointers to something beyond it. Yet because they give the impression of being exact copies, the nature of art is often misconceived. There is a tendency to overemphasize the importance of the more obvious and relatively superficial factors in it, to consider that an author's greatness depends on the degree of immediacy and clarity with which his work reflects the society of his day. But that is to mistake the values of art for the values of journalism. They are not the same, though art may perform some of the functions of journalism and journalism may sometimes be artistic. Today, especially, when literature is seldom accorded the status of independence and is, by and large, thought of in terms of utility, as a source either of instruction or of entertainment, this mistake is generally made. But a work of art is not simple. It cannot be accounted for by a catalogue of the facts to be gleaned from it. The meditative Hamlet was anything but literal-minded when he said that "the purpose of playing" was "to hold as 'twere the mirror up to nature." The "as 'twere" of his definition makes his figure of speech only a suggested comparison, not an accurate description of art. If art is a mirror at all, it is no usual, static one, but a kind of magic looking glass that moves, changes its focus, varies in the depth of its reflections—a combination of ordinary mirror, X-ray machine, and catalytic agent. And the man behind it, the artist, is not merely its porter but its master and its maker. He changes his instrument, sometimes knowing what he is about and sometimes hardly knowing at all. And he himself is part of the historical pageant which the glass reflects, for such is its nature that, turn it as he will, the range of its focus must include not only people and things outside him but also, and primarily, himself.

There has, indeed, been a reaction against the truism of literary criticism, that a work of art is a record of the age in which it was produced. In his *Aspects of the Novel,* for example, E. M. Forster attempted, some years ago, to "exorcise the demon of chronology," to reassert and demonstrate that art is timeless, and to exemplify the truth, admitting it to be a "partial truth," that History develops but Art stands still. By way of illustration, Mr. Forster pictured novelists of various centuries sitting side by side in a great, circular room, something like the Reading Room of the British Museum, working away at their books. There they were: Samuel Richardson with Henry James, H. G. Wells and Charles Dickens, Laurence Sterne and Virginia Woolf. Mr. Forster prowled about, peeping over their shoulders, and discovered that they were writing, in these pairs, passages of extraordinary similarity. What Mr. Forster was saying, in other words, was that time made little difference; that a man of the twentieth century might feel about life pretty much as did a man of the eighteenth; that, in short, temperament and talent—what Mr. Forster calls an author's "tone of voice"—were more important for art than chronology.

And yet, however just Mr. Forster's opinion may be, and however entertaining and startling his demonstration of it, there is no denying that an author's pitch is given by his generation no matter how familiarly the tone of his voice may sound in ages other than his own. We speak of something as "characteristically Renaissance" or as "characteristically eighteenth century," and it is no mere fantasy that leads us to these distinctions. What we do sometimes forget is the intricacy of the picture which we thus designate. The mind is more flexible than the "stubborn and irreducible" facts with which it must cope; it may, without realizing what it is about, turn these facts arbitrarily to its own use. We can be most clear, we think, when we are most dispassionate, most knowing as to what is farthest from us. We are content to hazard guesses concerning the chaos of our own lives, but ready to make dogmatic statements about the past. Yet it is not hard to twist some puzzling disharmony into a falsely simple pattern and to forget that in generalizing about centuries it is a blueprint, and not the building itself, that we are looking at.

This can be even more justly said of our conclusions with regard to nationalities. "French clarity," "English melancholy," "the Russian soul" are as true, and as false, as descriptive epithets like "Renaissance" or "eighteenth century." Probably there is greater similarity between men of different nations at a given time than between men of the same nation in different centuries, more in common between an American and a Russian of 1947 than between a Russian of 1647 and of today. And yet, though Englishmen, Americans, Russians may not exist in the abstract, they do, without question, look on life in somewhat different ways, and these ways are embodied in their literary tradition perhaps even more surely than in their institutions. For "it is in literature," as Alfred North Whitehead has said, "that the concrete outlook of humanity receives its expression. Accordingly it is to literature that we must look . . . if we hope to discover the inward thoughts of a generation." Now, the inward thoughts of a people are more fundamental and more complex than the way it acts, the way it dresses, and the way it builds its houses—though these outward signs, the labels by which an age is recognized, are often clear reflections of the deeper, hidden thoughts, just as, for example, in the landscape architecture of the eighteenth century, passing from the patterned classical garden to the wild and profuse "English" garden, was expressed the change in dominant ideas and tastes from the ordered design of rationalist systems to the unrestraint and abundance of romanticism.

Through the work of its many artists is built the artistic tradition of a nation. It expresses its culture, which is not some mystic quality that in an inexplicable way makes human beings of one land essentially different and of necessity forever alien to those of other lands, but an involved combination of attitudes and feelings that develop through the circumstances of history. The way a people responds to the events with which it must contend is determined by the nature of events and is formed by the tradition built up through a series of such responses over a long period of time, rather than by some predetermined, innate qualities of character. And a people's art is a record of how its attitudes and feelings are shaped in the historic process. No simple explanation can be given for a matter so complex. The materialist's view, eloquently proclaimed, for example, by Trotsky, that "in different epochs and in different social environments a man loves, hates, and hopes in different ways," that, "as through its roots, a tree feeds its blossoms and its fruit from the earth's substance, so the human being finds nourishment for his feelings and his thoughts, even those that are most 'lofty,' in the economic foundations of society"—even this view, with all that is convincing in it, seems too limited, unless "economic" can be taken in a very broad sense indeed. For the ways men love, hate, and hope are shown not only in what men do and what they say but in the very language they speak, which through changing cadences retains its basic sound and structure and is probably as important a factor in forming men's emotions as the environment in which it is built. But whatever the entangled and manifold reasons for them, the differences between the inhabitants of various countries are shown in their artistic traditions and are given labels, which are not false as labels; for example, one sees French culture as mainly classical, English as romantic, and Russian as realistic. In spite of the fact that there have been classical, romantic, and realistic movements in all these lands, the romanticism and the realism of the French have been dominated by a formality and a critical attitude that are in essence "classical"; the classicism and the realism of the English by an emotional subjectivity which is "romantic"; and the classicism and the romanticism of the Russians by a detached and dramatic apprehension of experience which is "realistic."

Russian literature differs, in certain fundamental respects, from others of Western Europe. Its development is more sudden and more violent. It gives the impression of leaping rather than of growing, just as the history itself of the country, by comparison with that of others, seems to be not a process of evolution but a series of upheavals that come to disturb sporadically a great, lethargic land—as if the nation dozed for centuries, then woke up, and, startled by its backwardness, tried in feverish zeal for self-improvement to catch up with, assimilate, and outstrip whatever civilization had brought it out of sleep. Not unlike other European literatures, the Russian begins after the introduction of Christianity into the country, is grafted on pagan folklore, is at first dominated by the Church, and then becomes gradually secularized. But whereas an English romance or lyric of, for example, the twelfth century cannot be mistaken for a fictional narrative or a poem of the sixth century or the eighth, and the spoken language is brilliantly adapted to literary use as early as the fourteenth century, and there is little, after the seventeenth, that English literature can do by way of innovation, in Russia, works of the twelfth century and the sixteenth, when they occur in a late manuscript, cannot be told apart except through study of internal evidence that might give clues as to their date of composition, the vernacular comes to be used for serious literary purposes only in the seventeenth century, is adapted to poetry in the eighteenth, and the great flowering of the national literature comes only in the nineteenth century.

The influence of Western culture, under which Russian literature may be said to begin in the seventeenth century, was neither the result of military conquest, when an alien civilization is gradually assimilated and a native language slowly modified, as was true, for example, of the Norman invasion of Britain; nor of official command, which affects a powerful small section of a population and then filters to the masses, as in the case of the Slavic importation of

Byzantine religion; nor that of an enriching supplement and extension of an indigenous culture, like the broad influence of ancient Greece on Renaissance Italy. The influence of Western culture on Russia was neither a long process of unconscious assimilation, nor an imposing by decree of beliefs and formal observances, nor a spontaneous and enthusiastic adoption of new modes of thinking and living. Russia did not pay tribute to the West, nor did she worship it, nor was she in love with it; she chose the West to be her teacher and went to school to it. Just as, according to ancient legend, certain Slavic tribes invited Scandinavians to rule over them, so the princes of Old Muscovy applied to Germany and France for education, preserving, while they learned, a critical attitude toward those who instructed them.

The shape of Russian literature is determined, in large part, by this consciously critical attitude toward foreign cultures, and also by the fact that its formative period culminated not in the Renaissance but at the end of the eighteenth century, under the influence of early romanticism and the Enlightenment. The echo of the Renaissance was faint in Russia, and the literature of its Middle Ages was not comparable in richness and variety to that of Europe. There was no worldly court here to foster the composition of lyrics and romances, and the formal, ritualistic character of Byzantine religion encouraged pictorial rather than verbal expression. The great achievement of Medieval Art in Russia is icons rather than verses. Furthermore, from the thirteenth century to the middle of the fifteenth, when great cathedrals were built in France and Italy, when chivalry flourished, and the *Divina Commedia* and *The Canterbury Tales* were written, Russia was silent beneath Tartar rule. Her written language was a Bulgarian dialect, used chiefly for ecclesiastical documents. It was known as Church Slavonic, and it was not the language that the people spoke.

That Russian literature is realistic is partly due, of course, to the fact that it came into its own in the nineteenth century, when all European art was experimenting with realism; but its special version of this mode of composition cannot be explained by the simple factor of chronology. The Russian novel became known abroad at the time French "naturalism" was making itself felt through the work of Zola and his followers, and the difference in tone of the two kinds of writing was noticed immediately. The naturalists were, on the whole, in disfavor: they were considered cold, indecent, and untruthful, with a perverse hankering for the ugly and the salacious. The Russian novel seemed to be an antidote for the "troughs of Zolaism." And Melchior de Vogüé, whose *Le roman russe* was one of the earliest, and remains among the best, discussions of the subject, saw in it the virtue not only of a "noble" view of life but of an artistic method that corresponded more closely than that of the French to the admirable objectivity of science. The French, he wrote, were impatient with all that was slow; they loved large, brilliant effects, whereas the Russians attained a truer view of reality through an accumulation of almost imperceptible, accurately noted details. It was a good thing to bring into the vague and prejudiced discussion of morals the more relevant matter of artistic procedure. But there is more to Russian realism than common sense, respect for science, and a well-developed technique. It comes of an attitude to life that is deeper than any of these and embraces them all. And the two factors in it that seem to me to be of primary importance are an absolute independence of judgment and a profound feeling for the primitive.

From the time when the romantic poets brought the problem to the consciousness of the literate, the value of the "primitive" has been in question in the West. The attitude toward it depends on certain emotional and philosophic predilections concerning the nature of man and his relation to the world, in which Christian concepts clash with pagan and rationality comes to grips with intuition. "Primitivism" is a concept broader than any school that has made use of it and rich enough to nourish a great variety of minds. Romantics themselves, whose attitude to life seems posited on admiration of it, differ as to what they find in it to admire, so that from Wordsworth and Coleridge, from Lamartine and de Musset, to Byron, Shelley, Victor Hugo, and Hoffman, love of the primitive ranges from gratitude for placid security to fascination with storm, nightmare, and all kinds of violence. But even the classicists of Greece had found in the apparent chaos of a senseless fate wisdom that was well worth their contemplation; they built their masterpieces on unreasoned myths, being adventurous enough to plunge into that undercurrent of unreason which the rationalists of a later epoch feared as a brute force that might engulf their clarity, and on the surface of which the romantics were sometimes pleased to float. When Voltaire told Rousseau that his philosophy made him want to crawl on all fours, he summed up the extremity of the rationalist's position. If reason distinguishes men from beasts, then to discard reason is to become a beast. Like Voltaire, Dr. Johnson saw no value in the "unreasonable" rhetoric of Thomas

Gray and, when asked whether he thought that any but
a great man could have written the cycle of Ossian, replied,
"Yes, many men, many women, and many children."

But it was Gray and Rousseau who won out in the
intellectual movement that followed the French Revolution,
for their romantic doctrine voiced a need that clearheaded
admirers of pure reason could not satisfy: the need of men
to be recognized as in themselves important, by virtue not
of their achievements but simply of their humanity. Romanticism was based on the proposition that man is by nature
good, that his unreflecting impulses are right, that he is
capable of distinguishing intuitively between good and
evil, right and wrong, truth and falsehood, beauty and ugli-
ness. It answered Hobbes's famous stricture on the
primitive—"man's life in a state of nature was nasty, solitary, poor, brutish, and short"—with Rousseau's belief that
the innate nobility of the savage had been corrupted by
civilization; and, proceeding with perfect logic from this
premise, declared the "natural" superior to the "artificial"
in every phase of life: the country was better than the city,
the "English garden" better than the formal garden, simple
dress, speech, manners better than the elaborate and
ceremonial, inspiration in art more valuable than hard
work, invention preferable to imitation, the folk song
greater than studied compositions, passion nobler than
restraint. Everything for which man's work and reason
could not be held responsible was, in short, considered
supremely good: lakes, mountains, trees and flowers, the
unexplained mysteries and dimnesses of religions, grander
than monuments and buildings or deistic explanations of
the universe. Romanticism substituted the limitation of
vagueness for the limitation of clarity, awe before the

Immeasurable for resignation to a hierarchical scheme of creation. But it encouraged man to be more proud of himself by assuming that his experiences were interesting, irrespective of his attainments, that he was important as an individual, not only as a type. Romanticism was essentially democratic, but its democracy left the door open wide to prejudice and cloudy mysticism. Realism, which grew out of it, attempted through a scientific attitude to correct these dangers; it followed classicism in daring, though not always in exquisiteness.

The battles about primitivism have been waged in the West more consciously than in Russia. The romantic movement as it developed in England and France could have been possible only in well-industrialized countries, where civilization was sharply divided between the urban and the rural and where the tendency was predominantly urban. The romantics were city dwellers who "discovered" the peasantry, collected their relics, studied their ways, introduced them, with a certain benign condescension, to their worldly-wise brothers, and made the imitation of their virtues an educational program. Neither Gray, nor Wordsworth and Coleridge, nor Scott, nor later Thomas Hardy, attained the kind of understanding of the simple that comes of complete identity. They thought about, admired, proclaimed the importance of untutored people, but never felt themselves genuinely part of them. There is always, therefore, a sense of duality in their treatment of the elemental, an interested, analytic curiosity, as of appreciative travelers in a foreign land. In Russia, where industrialization is very recent, the situation has been different. Writers there have not been burdened to the same extent with the necessity of proving that the primitive has value.

They have addressed themselves to a public that half believed it already.

Furthermore, folk tradition in Russia was from the beginning opposed to foreign influence, and so has always had the natural persuasiveness of something native, as against the alien and artificial. Throughout the eighteenth century the written word in Russia was dominated by the French; it was the discovery of folk tradition and the development of a colloquial idiom that made it independent. Whereas the literatures of the West were already autochthonous at the moment they took notice of folklore, Russian literature became itself only when its roots sank deep into the soil of the people's tongue and legends. Unlike, therefore, writing of the West, which tends to be strained, self-conscious, and decadent when it decides to be primitive, the Russian, Antaeus-like, loses its strength when it is torn from the soil; its finest, boldest, and most brilliant ventures have grown from unsophisticated modes of feeling and understanding; and whenever these roots have been cut, the resultant product has been dry and twisted. It is this that makes Russian realism different from that of the West. In the West this school of writing came as a corrective to romantic exaltation of simplicity; but Russian realism, without necessarily exalting it, is nourished on the simple. Its idiom, the ideals it upholds, the attitude to life which is implied in it—all are based on an ingrained respect for the unworldly. This is not a program, hardly even a tradition; it is the intellectual climate in which the art of Russia flourishes, the air breathed by its writers.

What I mean by the independence of judgment, which seems to me to be also characteristic of Russian realism, will, I hope, appear in the course of this essay. On the whole, Russian literature has not been so influenced by programs of cliques and aesthetic movements as the French and even the English. It has progressed as a more or less direct commentary on life rather than as an exercise in artistic method, and has for this reason followed social and philosophic thought more than the inclinations of a changing aesthetic. "Our literature," said a French poet to a Russian friend, "begins with beauty and ends with truth, but yours begins with truth and ends with beauty." By the circumstances of its development Russian literature has been fundamentally critical—critical of its own tradition, critical of other literatures, critical of theory. And this intellectual position has given it a detachment which is different in kind from the prescribed objectivity of "scientific" realism in France and England. Its integrated sense of life, which understands the "cultivated" without losing touch with the primitive, has endowed it with the directness and unity of drama, but with it has gone an aloof contemplation of the drama itself. In other countries realism was a distinct literary movement that came between romanticism and symbolism; from the first of these it gleaned respect for modes of thought that were not merely rationalist, and to the second it effected an introduction in its attempt to decide what precisely might be the relation between the thinker and the object of his thought. In Russia realism has been, with various modifications, the one and only literary school; it describes a traditional attitude to life, not a limited and temporary interest.

CHAPTER II

The Beginnings

PART I: LITERATURE OF THE FOLK

By THE TIME THE LITERATURE OF THE FOLK WAS FIRST
recorded by scholars in the eighteenth and the
nineteenth centuries, the vernacular in which it had origi-
nated must have undergone great changes. Almost nothing
is known of it until the seventeenth century, when the
language spoken by the masses of Russians was first used
for literary purposes; but that it had, from the first, been
understood by all classes of society we know from accounts of how medieval noblemen were soothed at night
by peasant recitations. And, although the forms of folk
literature have always been distinct, its substance and
spirit were incorporated in some of the earliest written
work, done in Church Slavonic. Great compilations of
folklore—proverbs; songs, which are mostly parts of such
rituals as weddings, harvest feasts, and burials; fairy tales;
"ballads," more like brief romances and fabliaux than the
ballads of the Scots; and a special genre, called *bylini*—
have been made since the nineteenth century; and the

store is constantly increased by fresh discoveries, as well as by new compositions, for folk literature continues to be produced in Russia.

Whatever may be the meaning of fairy tales, whether they are, as some maintain, symbols of Nature or, as others think, of sex, or whether they are simply dreams of wish-fulfillment, their method of combining narrative traits, of emphasizing certain qualities, their general tone indicate, perhaps better than anything else, the temper of a people. But it is easy to make false generalizations about them. Much depends on the circumstances in which tales are told and gathered, on the mood and character of the narrators. Each story has a thousand versions; there can be no certainty as to what others may still be found and no knowledge of how many have been irretrievably lost. The Russian fairy tales which are known to us are not unlike those of other countries in their childlike fantasies about man's struggle with adversity and his dreams of conquest and reward. But their tone is somewhat different.

"I remember vaguely," said William Butler Yeats, writing of his childhood, "that I liked Hans Andersen better than Grimm because he was less homely, but even he never gave me the knights and dragons and beautiful ladies that I longed for." Had Afanasiev been translated in his day, he might have been better satisfied, for there he would have found dragons and wizards, who made their appearance accompanied by storms at sea and claps of thunder; a Firebird, with eyes of oriental crystal and feathers of such radiant gold that one of them could illuminate a room as brilliantly as many candles; a wood spirit, Leyshi, an old man in peasant dress, with the right shoe on his left foot and his belt tied in a way nobody else tied it, with green eyes and a long beard, tall as the trees when he was in the woods but, out of them, short as the grass, who sang a song without words that was like wind howling in the forests into which he lured people to make them lose their way; Kostchey the Deathless, who tormented brave and merciful men, and whose death was hidden in an egg, which was inside a duck, which was inside a rabbit, which was in a trunk buried beneath an oak on an island in the ocean; the witch Baba Yaga, who lived in a hut that turned on hens' legs, with gateposts, hinges, and a lock that were human legs, hands, and a mouth with sharp teeth, who had a mortar and pestle to carry her through the air, ate human flesh, rolled in a meadow on the bones of her victims, was served by three pairs of mysterious hands that were too awesome for explanation and by three swift horsemen, white, black, and red, who were Day, Night, and Dawn. There is a free and wild imaginativeness in these tales and, often, grand emotional power. They have in them something of the color and rhetoric of the Orient, the sense of tragic destiny of Greek myths, and the European peasant's humorous acceptance of commonplace living. They give glimpses of windy plains, dense forests, and turbulent seas. And they seem to show a preference for relating entire lives rather than brief events, as if the narrators were more impressed by how the will of man and the chances of Fortune were interlaced over a span of years than by the sudden drama of a moment's duration. The characters in them behave in ways that are symbolic of Evil, Time, and the Forces of Nature.

The *bylini,* "that which has been," semihistoric narratives about national heroes, varying in length from thirty to nine hundred lines, are composed even today, with Lenin and Stalin as their subjects in place of legendary demigods and the early princes of Kiev. They are chanted to the accompaniment of a small, harplike instrument, called *gusli,* and are performed by gifted peasant narrators, who change and amplify the stories as they sing them. The best of these chanters—they are called *skaziteli,* i.e., "those who tell"—are as well known in Soviet Russia as great actors. They recite in cities before large audiences, and their tales are published in scholarly volumes.

The outstanding hero of the old *bylini* is Ilya of Murom, a *bogatyr,* or warrior-prince, who, like Lancelot or Gawain, is one of a company grouped about a ruler who is himself not so great as the members of his entourage; this monarch is Vladimir, Grand Prince of Kiev, who introduced Christianity to Russia and who, in the legends of his country, occupies a place similar to that of King Arthur in Western romance. Ilya's adventures are the most numerous, the most lovingly related; and in him, more clearly than elsewhere, is embodied the heroic ideal of the Russian people.

He is, according to tradition, the crippled child of a rich peasant of Murom. "He grew to be five years old, and he could not walk; he grew to be ten years old and he could not walk; he grew to be thirty years old and he could not walk." Then one day, when he is thirty, and his parents leave to work in the fields, admonishing him to sit quietly on the stove while they are away, some pilgrims come to the window and ask him for beer. Ilya invites them in and explains in tears that glad though he would be to serve them, he cannot, since he has never been able to walk. But at their command to try his legs, he finds, to his amazement, that he can move about, and the beer they give him makes him at once immensely strong. The pilgrims leave, instructing him to tell his father what has happened and to ask him for a warrior's equipment: a gray colt which he is to water with spring water, to feed on early wheat, and to exercise in green meadows, armor and a lance, a saddle made of cyprus, a silken whip, a sharp sword, and a steel knife. Ilya does as he is bid and is provided with what he has requested. His colt jumps higher than the forest, races beneath clouds, leaps over walls and towers, over streams and small lakes, over rivers and large lakes. With his parents' blessing, Ilya leaves for Kiev, where Prince Vladimir orders him to gather together a host of heroes and makes him their commander.

Other *bylini* have to do with Ilya's astonishing feats in slaying monsters, the most formidable of whom is Nightingale the Robber, a creature who lives in a nest that stretches over seven oaks, cries in a voice at which grass withers, flowers fade, trees bend to the earth, and all men die, and delights in wanton destruction. Ilya shoots him through the eye, ties him to his stirrup, drags him to Vladimir, and cuts off his head. Other times, loyal to his prince when others have abandoned him, Ilya conquers hosts of Tartars singlehanded, taking hold of a dead enemy by his feet and using him as a club to cut his way through a whole army. When he himself, on one occasion, is annoyed with Vladimir, who fails to invite him to a banquet, he wreaks his vengeance by knocking down church domes and steeples and gathering to his support a mob of drunkards from all the pothouses of the city, until the prince sends a messenger to lead him to the place of honor at his board. Ilya's revenge can be terrible, but his grudges are not lasting; he can forget personal slights in pity for the orphans and widows of his country.

One remarkable *bylina* tells the story of his death. In his old age he comes upon a crossroads marked by three stones: one points the way to riches, one to a wife, and one to death. Riches, Ilya reflects, are of no use to him, because he has no wife to spend them on; and, since he is now too old to get himself a wife, he chooses the road to death. He is set upon by forty thousand thieves, all of whom he kills; returns to the crossroads, writes on the stone that he had followed death but had not met it, takes the road to the wife, is enticed by an enchantress but eludes her wiles, frees a dozen warriors whom she has kept imprisoned, returns to the crossroads to change the second inscription, and takes the last road, which brings him to three cellars heaped with gold, silver, and jewels. This treasure he distributes among beggars and orphans, and meets his death only long after, turned to stone in the midst of battle.

How and by whom the *bylini* were first composed we do not know, nor why it happened that the stories of Kiev were forgotten in what must have been their place of origin but remained alive in the northern province of Olonetz, where modern scholars found them. They were probably transported there by those who fled the Tartars and survived among Cossacks and the inhabitants of Siberia who could understand the heroic nature of free warriors better than the Muscovites, among whom serfdom had developed. But they are loved by Russians with a fervor that is hardly understood in the West, where primitive epic tradition is no longer alive. In Russia the recitation of a *bylina* is an absorbing and moving occasion. One such performance related by a Russian student of folklore, Lyatski, is quoted by Mrs. N. K. Chadwick of Newnham in her *Russian Heroic Poetry:*

Utka coughed. Everybody became silent at once. He threw his head back and glanced around with a smile at those present, and seeing their impatient, eager, expectant expressions, he at once began to sing again. Little by little the face of the old singer changed; all its cunning disappeared, and it became childlike and naïve. Something inspired appeared in it; the dove-like eyes opened wide, and began to shine. Two little shining tears sparkled in them; a flush overspread the swarthiness of his cheeks; occasionally his nervous throat twitched.

He lived with his beloved bogatyrs; grieved in tears for the infirmity of Ilya of Murom, when he sat paralysed for thirty years, gloried with him in his triumph over Nightingale the Robber. Sometimes he broke off of his own accord, interpolating his own remarks. All the people present lived with the heroes of the byliny too. At times an exclamation of wonder involuntarily escaped from one of them; at times the laughter of another resounded through the room. From one fell tears which he involuntarily brushed away from his lashes. Everybody sat without winking an eye while the singing was going on. Every sound of this monotonous but wonderfully gentle tune they loved.

Gorky, in his novel of the Revolution, *The Life of Klim Samghin,* presents his hero as happening almost by accident, at the performance of Fedossova—a great, contemporary *skazitelnitza:*

Up to the stage there came, with tiny steps, swaying, a twisted little old woman, dressed in dark calico, her head tied in a bright-colored, worn kerchief, a funny, kind little witch, glued together in wrinkles and folds, with a rag-like round face and smiling childish eyes. . . .

From the stage poured forth an unusually sweet voice, there rang out weighty, ancient words. The voice was an old peasant woman's, but one could not believe that it was an old woman reading the verses. Apart from the solid beauty of the words there was in that voice something inhumanly tender and wise, a magic power that made Samghin stand numb with his watch in his hands. He wanted awfully to turn round, to see with what faces people listened to the twisted little old woman. But he could not keep his eyes off the play of wrinkles on the rumpled, kindly face, off the astonishing sparkle of the child-like eyes, which, eloquently completing every line of verse, gave the ancient words a live brilliance and an enchanting, soft ring.

Monotonously shaking her cotton-like hand, looking like a hideously sewn rag doll, the old woman from Olonetz told of how the mother of the bogatyr Dobryna bade him farewell, sending him off to the field on his heroic deeds. Samghin could see this corpulent mother, could hear her firm words, through which sounded both fear and grief; could see the broad-shouldered Dobryna: he kneels and holds the sword in his outstretched hands, looking with humble eyes into his mother's face . . .

Fedossova began to tell of the quarrel between the peasant of Ryazan, Ilya Murometz, and the Prince of Kiev, Vladimir. Samghin, charmed once more, caressed by the soft sparkle of the unquenchable eyes, looked on the bewitching face that spoke with all its wrinkles. With his mind he understood that, after all, it was not in that voice that the stout bogatyr from Karacharov, angered by the capricious prince, had talked, and, certainly, with keen eyes used to the steppe, it was not with such ironic mockery that he looked out. But . . . Samghin suddenly, and not with his mind, but with his whole being, acknowledged to himself that that badly sewn calico doll was actually the most authentic story of the truth of good and the truth of evil, which must and can speak of the past in just the way the twisted old woman from Olonetz spoke of it, speaking with equal love and wisdom of anger and of tenderness, of the unquenchable grief of mothers and the heroic dreams of children, of everything that is life.

Gorky's own grandmother was a fine *skazitelnitza*. So also was Pushkin's old nurse; and it is by these peasant artists that, time and again, the greatest Russian poets have been inspired.

But for those whose taste in art inclines to polish and rational design the *bylini* seem barbarous productions. "There is almost no poetry in them," wrote the classicist Derzhavin, "and, except in rare instances, neither pictorial nor rhythmic variety. They are colorless and monotonous. Monstrous and tasteless exaggeration alone rules in them: in the boasting, the hospitality, the battles of the bogatyri. They drink a pail of wine at a gulp, knock down thousands of pagans with a corpse they hold by his feet—and similar nonsense, giving evidence of barbarism and a crude disrespect for women." And L. A. Magnus, who, in spite of the evident love of his theme in *The Heroic Ballads of Russia,* one of the most complete and sympathetic books on the subject in English, remarks on the "uncouth and inartistic" genius of the Russians, who seem to him to lack a sense of the picturesque and a feeling for the lyrical. They have created nothing so "fascinating," he says, as the Lorelei; their fairies and ghouls are merely "vivid" and "ghostly"; and "where a Celt would have made a heart-rending horror of Ilya Murometz' death . . . the Russian states the bare fact. It would be almost ludicrous to contrast the scene of Cuchulain's death (in Lady Gregory's account), and this is a fair comparison, for the Irish verse is distinctly barbaric in tone. The great epics of Greece are on an infinitely higher level of compact true poetical compression."

Primitive in both thought and form, compound of myth, Christian legend, and history, these crude, simple narratives embody the ideals of an illiterate and subject population whose tales echo the emotions with which they are most familiar and whose standards of ethics have been formed independently of their masters. The colossal exaggeration in them is the rhetoric of rough men who love loud laughter and whose imaginations are free. Their humor is large. But it is not without slyness, as in the episode when Ilya, in the dress of a humble pilgrim, is confronted by the Monstrous Idol whom he is to fight. When the giant boasts of his tremendous prowess in eating and drinking and inquires about the champion he must encounter, the disguised Ilya retorts that this hero is no bigger than he is himself, that he eats and drinks no more than he does, but that his own father once had a cow which stuffed itself and burst. These ancient Russian heroes have the modesty of the supremely self-assured. The feeling of tacit strength in them is so great that they do not boast of their valor, for boasting would diminish it. There is also a kind of gross irony in the *bylini,* sometimes humorous and sometimes half somber, as in Ilya's search for death. And, though the lines are unadorned, they can be subtle in conveying shades of emotion. There are versions, for example, of Ilya's childhood which are admirable in tenderness and restraint: the anxious words of the parents to their son as they are about to leave; their lament over his fate, very touching in the music of long, melancholy vowels and loving diminutives; the calm scene, with its mood of speechless astonishment and joy, when the son walks up to them in the field—such passages have a directness and power that are often lost in more consciously skilled writing.

The structure of the *bylini* is primitive. Without assonance or alliteration, the narrative is held together through repetition of the most elementary kind, which links a series of incidents in a chain of *ands.* There is nothing here of that "incremental repetition," whereby in Scotch ballads a story is brought to its point through a surprise ending, by the change of a simple word in a recurrent line; nor anything of that urgent intensity of thought and feeling achieved by repetition in the Hebrew Psalms, where the intent is to stress the emotional logic of song or prayer. The general effect, by comparison with Scotch ballads and Hebrew Psalms, is of a more naïve absorption, a perpetual wonder at and pleasure in the narrated events; and this is true not only of *bylini* but also of other forms of Russian folk poetry. In the so-called Russian "ballads," for example, one often comes upon such lines as the following:

> *As over the mountains, mountains, high mountains,*
> *As over the meadows, meadows, wide meadows,*
> *And even along the blue sea shore,*
> *And over pastures, the green, good pastures,*
> *There walked, there wandered, a maiden fair.*
> *For roots she was searching, terrible poison.*
> *She washed the rootlets in the blue sea,*
> *She dried the rootlets in a glazed stove,*
> *She ground the roots in a silver cup,*
> *She mixed the rootlets with honey sweet,*
> *She stuffed the roots with sugar white.*
> *She wished to kill her enemy.*
> *By chance she killed her dear, good friend,*
> *By birth her own, her brother dear . . .*
>
> .   .   .   .
>
> *And over the youth the maiden wept.*
> *She weeps the maiden, weeps unto death,*
> *Laments the maiden, plaintively,*
> *"In vain has perished my dear one's head."*

The primitive lyric and rhetorical device of repeating a noun or adjective, or both, within a single line occurs constantly in the *bylini*—for example:

Razgorélos sérdtze bogatírskoye, bogatírskoye sérdtze molodétskoye
[Fired was the lordly heart, the lordly youthfully brave heart]

which combines, in a characteristically Russian measure, a sense of melancholy with admiration; or:

Iz—za gór bilo, gór vissókikh, iz-za léssov, léssov témnikh
[*From beyond mountains, mountains lofty, from beyond forests, forests dusky*].

Lines such as these—and they are typical—convey a quality that seems to me to be peculiarly Russian. In *Beowulf,* for example, in the characteristic Anglo-Saxon kennings— "wave-skimmer" for boat, "the whale's path" for sea— objects are called by an appropriate name which is discovered for them through analytic perception. Old Russian poetry is both more simple and more mature—more simple, because in it an object is named whole, unbroken into its ingredients; more mature, because the thing named and the feeling of the namer remain distinct. The mountains stand by themselves; no epithet is attached to modify their uniqueness, and the observer's love of them shows only through the cadence of his line.

In 1795 a well-known Russian antiquary, Count Mussin-Pushkin, discovered in a sixteenth-century manuscript, at the monastery of Spasso-Yaroslavl, a narrative poem, which he published in 1800 from a copy he had made of it. It is very fortunate that this was done, for both the original and the copy were destroyed in the Moscow fire of 1812, so that in this printed version alone has been preserved the only epic of the Slavs. It is known as *The Lay* (or, literally translated, *The Word,* in the sense of "discourse," from the Greek *logos*) *of the Host of Igor;* and it has to do with a campaign waged in 1185 by Igor, a prince of Novgorod, his brother Vsevolod, his son Vladimir, and his nephew Svyatoslav, against the Polovtsi, a

Turkish tribe that occupied the southern steppe from the Volga to the Danube and made constant raids upon the Russians. In the first encounter Igor's host was victorious, but the Polovtsi rallied and, in a bloody three-day battle on the river Kayala, defeated the Russians and took Igor into captivity. One night he managed to escape and returned home. Although there is an account of this event in *The Kiev Chronicle,* the most important of Old Russian annals, it does not appear to have been of great historical consequence, and it has become memorable only through *The Lay,* where a fine poet has made it the symbol of his nation's heroism.

Because its theme is national and its quality heroic, this poem is called "epic," and yet it lacks many of the traits characteristic of epic poetry. It is brief, is written not in verse but in a kind of rhythmic prose, and it has nothing of the slow-paced dignity, the high decorum of Homer or of *Beowulf.* It is romantic in tone, more lyric and intense than *The Song of Roland,* with which it is sometimes compared; and its structure of rapidly succeeding images and elliptical symbols follows the logic of emotional conviction rather than the consecutiveness of rationality. "Shall we not, brothers," it opens, "begin in ancient words of warlike legend, the tale of Igor's armament, of Igor, son of Svyatoslav?"; and, in keeping with this secular address to the poet's comrades, his *druzhina,* rather than to God or a goddess, it proceeds not to invoke a deity but to criticize an ancient bard. His story, the poet declares, must be told just as it happened, not in the manner of Boyan, the eloquent, who would "soar in the trees with his thought, would race as a gray wolf on the ground, as a dark eagle beneath the clouds," who "would lay his fingers on the strings and they themselves would warble the praise of princes." For he will speak according to the truthful accounts of the times. Here, then, is a deliberate artist, who makes a conscious choice of methods, prefers realism to fantasy, but shows, in the tacit appreciation of his very censure, that he admires the legendary bard whose way of writing he purports to reject.

There follows a somewhat more circumstantial restatement of the theme, and then the poem proper begins abruptly: "Then Igor looked at the bright sun, and saw that it covered all his warriors with darkness." "Brothers and comrades!" he says to them, "it is better to be dead than captive. Mount we our swift steeds that we may see the blue Don." The eclipse of the sun mentioned here is historic, but in the record of *The Kiev Chronicle* it occurs when Igor is already on his way. Here the time is changed for artistic effect and also to emphasize the hero's fearlessness. Igor might have put off the expedition until the omens were better, but he prefers to scorn danger; and the poem gains immeasurably in this early premonition of disaster, which is echoed all through, until Igor's fortunes take a better turn.

A great desire possesses the mind of the prince, and the thirst to visit the great Don overcomes the omen. "I want," he says, "to break my lance at the end of the steppe of the Polovtsi; with you, Russians, I want to lay down my head, that I may drink from my helmet the water of the Don." And the poet remembers again his legendary predecessor, "Boyan, nightingale of ancient times." If he were praising these warriors, flitting in the tree of thought, soaring in mind beneath clouds, weaving through praise the past and the present, racing over Trajan's road, over the steppes to the mountains, he would have sung in this wise: "It is not falcons that a storm has driven over the wide steppe; a flock of crows races to the mighty Don." Or he might have sung: "Horses neigh beyond the Sula, praise resounds in Kiev; trumpets blare in Novgorod; banners rise in Putivl." Our artist has an ironic sense of the discrepancy between the expression at his command and the glory of the occasion he must celebrate; he knows the allusive and figurative method of ancient poetry; he thinks it inadequate for what he has to say, and he treats it with a mournful and gentle scorn that pays tribute to its beauty; and, in effect, thus, subtly, he handles his theme in two ways, in both the old form and the new.

Then, without transition, a few tense lines: "Igor awaits his dear brother Vsevolod. And speaks to him the great warrior Vsevolod: 'My only brother, you, Igor, are my only light. We are both sons of Svyatoslav. Saddle your swift steeds, brother; mine are ready.'" And after a tribute to the swiftness and wisdom of the steeds comes a somber description of Igor galloping across the steppe. He puts his foot into the golden stirrup and—in a line of which the sound in Russian gives a feeling of space and distance, swiftness, and of reins let loose—races over the plain. The sun darkens his way; the night is stormy, its moaning awakens the birds; there is the screech of wild beasts; and Div, the bird of ill omen, cries from the top of a tree, commanding foreign lands to hear the news. The Polovtsi race toward the Don, their wagons creaking at midnight like frightened swans. Suddenly a sharp little sentence: "Igor leads his army to the Don," which, in the midst of the description, strikes a note of foreboding. Carrion fowl, wild animals, wolves and foxes, await his misfortune. "O

Russian land, you are already beyond the hill." Through a brief passage of transition, which begins, "Long is the darkness of night," we are brought to the next morning, which opens on a day of victory for the Russians, who spread like arrows over the plain, seize Polovts girls, carry off gold and costly stuffs, and make bridges of robes and cloaks over bogs and marshes.

Very early the following day bloody rays proclaim the dawn, black clouds come from the sea, seeking to cover "the four suns"—that is, the four great Russian warriors—and blue lightning quivers in them. There shall be mighty thunder. Rain shall fall in arrows from the Don. And a brief allusive verse of defeat ends again with the refrain: "O Russian land, you are already beyond the hill." The winds howl, shaking arrows from the sea on Igor's brave army; earth wails, rivers flow murkily, dust covers the fields. And banners speak: the Polovtsi come from the Don and from the sea, surrounding the Russians on all sides. Now comes an apostrophe to Vsevolod. He fights bravely, forgets honors and riches and his city Chernigov, his father's golden board, the love and tenderness of his dear wife. And this praise of his fighting recalls past battles, the ancient times of Oleg and of Yaroslav. At that time seldom did plowmen call to each other over the Russian land, but crows would caw, dividing corpses among them, and ravens croaked. Such were the campaigns and battles of those days; but such a war as this had never been known! Our poet returns to the present fight. It goes on all day, and the black earth is sown with bones and watered with blood.

But what is the noise, what the ringing which I hear from afar, early before dawn? Igor is turning back his army;

he feels pity for his dear brother Vsevolod. They fought one day, they fought another; on the third at noon the banners of Igor had fallen. Here parted the two brothers on the banks of the river Kayala. Here there was not enough of bloody wine; here the brave Russians ended their feast, gave the matchmakers their fill of drink, and themselves lay down for the Russian land. "The grass bows in pity, and the tree bends in sorrow to the earth." Unhappy days, brothers, have now arrived. Mischief comes as a maiden to Troyan's land, beats her swan's wings on the blue sea, and, splashing on the Don, drives away happy times. The enemy gallops over the land. The Russian wives lament, saying they will not see their husbands again. And Kiev groans in mourning, and Chernigov in its misfortune. Grief has flooded Russia, abundant sorrow has flown in the midst of it. The brothers Igor and Vsevolod have quarreled and have brought disaster to the land. There is a verse of reproof for them and of praise for their father, Svyatoslav. Svyatoslav has a troubled dream, in which he sees himself enveloped in a shroud, blue wine poured over him, and gems thrown on his chest from the empty quivers of pagan foreigners. That night ravens croak and forest serpents are carried out to sea. Svyatoslav grieves for his country. And the poet calls upon the other warriors of Russia to come to the rescue, recalling ancient heroes of whom Boyan had sung.

Then comes the most famous part of the poem, the lament of Yaroslavna, Igor's wife. She will fly, she says, as a bird, as a cuckoo, along the Don, will dip her beaver sleeve in the river Kayala, will wipe with it the wounds on the mighty body of her prince. Yaroslavna weeps upon the walls of Putivl town. She calls upon the wind: why does it blow so fierce, sending hostile spears upon her dear one's army? Yaroslavna weeps upon the walls of Putivl town. And calls upon the river Dnieper which has pierced, she says, the mountains of the Polovts land, has rocked the ships of Svyatoslav. "Sir," she addresses it, "shelter my dear one, too, bring him back, that I may not send forth my tears to him so soon upon the sea." Yaroslavna weeps upon the walls of Putivl town. And calls upon the sun, the bright, the brightest of suns: "You are warm and beautiful for everyone," she says. "Why then, O Sir, have you spread your scorching rays upon the warriors of my dear one?"

It has been pointed out that there is great artistry in placing this lament just where it comes. That of all the other Russian women had been spoken of before, but not Yaroslavna's. Directly after it the poet tells of how Igor escapes from captivity and comes back to Russia. And so, coming where it does, it has the force of a magic incantation, so that Igor seems to have been brought back through the strength of her love. Masterly also is the use here of folk-song motifs. In the wedding songs of the people the bride always calls upon her father, her mother, and her brother. Here the wind, the river, and the sun are substituted for the relatives, which gives Yaroslavna's dulcet lament something of the tragic majesty of King Lear calling upon the Heavens for sympathy when the world holds no comfort great enough to assuage his grief.

Igor's escape also is echoed in Nature: the sea is troubled at midnight, mists bring darkness, the river Donets addresses the hero. The poem ends with his return. The sun shines, maidens sing by the river, the town rejoices. And now Boyan is mentioned again. He had sung the praise of ancient princes. But it is now right to sing the glory of the young: of Igor, son of Svyatoslav, of the warrior Vsevolod, of Vladimir, son of Igor. Glory to the princes and the *druzhina,* fighting for Christianity against pagan hosts. Glory to the princes and the *druzhina.* Amen.

From the poem itself we must draw conclusions as to its author; there are no other clues. But the text yields enough for a fairly clear picture. He was a contemporary of the events he recorded. In fact, he must have written the poem not later than 1187, for he mentions as alive a prince who is known to have died in that year. He was a partisan of Svyatoslav, for he writes in praise of him and in pity of Igor, whose defeat had undone his father's victory over the Polovtsi in 1184. It is a matter of historic record that after Igor's defeat Svyatoslav sought to bring the Russian princes together in an organization to war against the Polovtsi—and Karl Marx saw the poem as a piece of propaganda in favor of this attempt. He might have been a warrior, one of Svyatoslav's *druzhina.* That he was not a cleric we may be sure, for although his poem ends on a conventionally Christian note, it breathes throughout the spirit of paganism. Whereas in *The Kiev Chronicle,* for example, Igor praises God for his first victory, explains his defeat as the Lord's punishment for his sins, and, confronted by the eclipse, at the outset of his campaign, reflects: "Nobody knows God's mystery, and God is the creator of mystery as well as of all His world . . . we shall find out in time whether God means our good or our evil," and his *druzhina* advance, "placing their faith in God," the Igor of the poem has no such piety in him. He does not commit himself to the hand of God and makes no reflections either on God's mysterious ways or on

His power to forgive and punish. When he looks "up to the bright sun" and sees that it "had covered all his warriors in darkness," it is better, he says, "to be cut to pieces than to be made a captive," and proceeds into battle without thought of possible salvation, but only because he wishes "to break a spear on the borders of the Polovts land and to drink from his helmet the water of the blue Don."

Whatever his profession, he was a serious, well-read, and sensitive poet, as conscious as Pushkin or Milton of the craft of poetry and of the high destiny of his verse. He knew the written literature of his day: his work reflects at times early historians and catches the cadences of Byzantine rhetoric. But, above all, he was steeped in the stories, traditions, and songs of the folk. His epithets and symbols are those of folk poetry, and he shares the peasant's feeling for the land, for the slow, ageless processes of peaceful life, for the primary emotions of fury and of love. He is not interested in giving a simple transcript of events. What he means by "truth" is something more poetic. *The Kiev Chronicle* records:

In the year 6693 (1185). At that time Igor, the son of Svyatoslav, the grandson of Oleg, rode out of Novgorod on the 23d of April, which was on a Tuesday, having taken with him his brother Vsevolod from Trubetsk, and Svyatoslav Olgovich, his nephew, from Rylsk, and Vladimir, his son, from Putivl, and Yaroslav sent him, at his request, Olstin Oleksich, the grandson of Prokhor, with Kovuans (a Finnish tribe) from Chernigov. They proceeded slowly, collecting their druzhina, for their horses were very fat [and so on].

But our poet tells the story in snatches of dramatic action, of lyric comment, song, and allusive imagery, not with the supposed wildness of Boyan but with some of his devices. He knows how to give suffering its due, to sympathize with grief, anxiety, devotion; and he has a sense of deep-lying contrasts, so that through his picture of war in the images of peace, through his account of disaster in terms of grandeur, and in his view of men's moods as symbols of Nature and the moods of Nature as symbols of men, one gets a vision of complex existence, in which present moments are linked to the past and violent deeds are framed in the grave circle of historic sequence.

Generally speaking, then, Russian folk literature is distinguished by certain predispositions toward life which are not usually ascribed by Westerners to the "Russian soul": an unpretentious, warm understanding of emotions; a happy assumption that all men, great and small, are united in a community of human experience; a humor that is ironic in a good-natured way, more kind than the French, more subtle than the German, less visionary than the Irish: a wild and primitive imaginativeness which is held in check by reverence for the earthy—its flights to unreality, controlled by a sense of the appropriate, an amused awareness of where fantasy belongs; an intelligent, middle-road attitude, with much generous affection in it, without the brooding melancholy of the Anglo-Saxons, the stark, sharply controlled response to tragedy of the Scots, or the intellectual exquisiteness of the ancient Greeks. There is solidity here, without dullness, and emotional balance, which comes not of resignation but of an active and pliant acceptance of brute fact; there is a love of love, of kindness, and of shrewdness, and admiration neither of dominance nor servility but of heroic usefulness. Russian heroes act as they do because the authors who sing of them are imbued with a sense of eternal struggle, and each of their accomplished tasks appears one only in an unending series. There is nothing definitive in the wonderful feats performed by Ilya of Murom. His services are admirable and necessary, but they do not rid his nation of trouble for all time. Success and failure both are temporary, and evil is deathless. Igor's defeat comes between a past victory and the hope of a future one, but neither Kostchey nor Baba Yaga can be permanently killed. There seems to be an ingrained sensitiveness to history in the Russian mind, a feeling for continuous progression, in which every known event, however important, is sensed to be a fragment. The plaintive but vigorous lines of the heroic narratives, full of humor to contradict their sadness; the fairy tales, even the ritual laments, are the chant of a sturdy people who have come to terms with hardship and in quiet detachment preserve their own ideals and the knowledge of their latent strength. And these qualities were early appreciated by the literate, one of whom, at least, wove them into a great work of sophisticated poetry.

CHAPTER III

The Beginnings

PART II: THE WRITTEN TRADITION

The Lay of the Host of Igor IS THE ONLY EXTANT WORK of Medieval Russia which is based on the tradition of the spoken word. Church Slavonic was mostly used for ecclesiastical documents and translations from the Byzantine: Greek liturgies, monastic chronicles, sermons, saints' legends, church history, pilgrims' records of journeys to holy places. The Church condemned secular art and frowned on all learning.

Impious unto God [one reads in an old "book of instruction"] is every man who loveth geometry, and a spiritual sin it is to study astronomy and the books of Greece; for, according unto his reason, will the true believer readily fall into diverse errors. Love thou simplicity rather than wisdom, and seek not that which is above thee, nor attempt that which is over-deep for thy understanding. Whatsoever is given thee of God shall be meet for learning, and cleave thou fast unto it.

There were effective physical means of knocking intellectual pride out of monks who read too much, being fond of the kind of learning not "given of God." The strength of the Church lay in a gorgeous ritual, which awed people without enlightening them.

The story of the Christianization of Russia is told in *The Kiev Chronicle,* which relates how in 987, Vladimir I, Grand Prince of Kiev, sent ten trusted men to investigate the religions of various countries from which emissaries had previously come to convert him. The following year his messengers

. . . came back to their country, and their Prince called together his boyars and old men. Said Vladimir: "The men we have sent away have come back. Let us hear what has happened!" And he said: "Speak before the druzhina!" and they spoke: "When we were in Bulgaria, we saw them worshipping in the temple, where they talk in the shrine and stand without their girdles. Having made their obeisance, they sit down and look around hither and thither like madmen, and there is no joy among them, only sadness and a great stench: their religion is not good. And we came to Germany, and we saw many ceremonies in their temples, but of beauty we saw none. We went to Greece, and they took us where they worship their God, and we do not know whether we were in heaven or upon earth, for there is not upon earth such sight or beauty. We were perplexed, but this much we know that there God lives among men, and their service is better than in any other country. We cannot forget that beauty, for every man that has partaken of sweetness will not afterwards accept bitterness, and thus we cannot longer remain in our former condition."

One should compare this report with that in *The Ecclesiastical History of the Venerable Bede,* where under entry for the year 627 we are given the following well-known account of how King Edwin of Northumbria was converted:

. . . he asked of every one in particular what he thought of the new doctrine and the new worship that was preached. To which the chief of his own priests, Coifi, immediately answered, ". . . the religion which we have hitherto professed has, as far as I can learn, no virtue in it. For none of your people has applied himself more diligently to the worship of our gods than I; and yet there are many who receive greater favours from you, and are more preferred than I, and are more prosperous in all their undertakings . . ."

Another of the king's chief men, approving of his words and exhortations, presently added: "The present life of man, O King, seems to me, in comparison of that time which is unknown to us, like to the swift flight of a sparrow through the room wherein you sit at supper in winter, with your commanders and ministers, and a good fire in the midst, while the storms of rain and snow prevail abroad; the sparrow, I say, flying in at one door, and immediately out at another, whilst he is within, is safe from the wintry storm; but after a short space of fair weather, he immediately vanishes out of your sight, into the dark winter from which he emerged. So this life of man appears for a short space, but of what went before, or what is to follow, we are utterly ignorant. If, therefore, this new doctrine contains something more certain, it seems justly to deserve to be followed."

We can be pretty sure, of course, that events did not occur as they are related in either of these stories, but legends have a truth of their own that sometimes explains the history they seem to falsify. So here, whatever may have actually taken place, the symbol of the tales is fairly clear, and the difference between them is an important one. On the one hand, we are told of a religion adopted to satisfy philosophic questionings in the hope that it might allay somewhat the terror of existence; on the other, of one expected to do no more than, through ritual, to gratify a love of the aesthetic. It was the picturesque aspect of Byzantine religion which appealed to the pagan Slavs, who were unprepared for anything else. But its beauty was not sufficient to offset in popular imagination the rigid forms and brutal punishments which it brought. The people took to it reluctantly, and Russia remained down to modern times the nation of the "twin-faith," *dvoevérie*. It may be that the formlessness itself of native literature was due to the ceremonial obscurity of the church service. All that the peasants were able to carry away from the elaborate observances was the memory of chants and a superstitious wonder at rites which they could not understand; and when they came upon their own symbols for life, they built them up to resemble the shapeless reality they knew without the awesome structure of formal pattern.

Sometimes Church Slavonic was used for secular or semi-secular purposes, of which the outstanding instances are the twelfth-century *Instruction to his Children* by the pious Grand Prince of Kiev, Vladimir Monomakh, and the sixteenth-century correspondence between Ivan the Terrible and his recalcitrant subject, Prince Kurbsky. But in the seventeenth century, literary productions begin to show unmistakably the influence of the unwritten tradition; and there is one remarkable poem, composed it may be two hundred years earlier, which is unique, inasmuch as it reproduces not only the substance but the meter of narrative folk poetry. This is *The Legend of Woe-Misfortune,* the story of a prodigal son who slights the good advice of his loving parents and, under the influence of evil friends, gets drunk, is robbed, and, ashamed to return home, wanders away to foreign lands, where he no sooner gains wealth, chooses a bride, and learns to live wisely than he comes under the power of Woe-Misfortune, who has heard him boast of his happiness and determines to bring him to ruin in punishment for his sins and his disobedience. Appearing in a dream as the Archangel Gabriel, he persuades the youth to give up his bride and his riches and hounds him almost to death. In vain does the poor fellow change his shape:

> *The fine lad soared, a radiant falcon,*
> *But Woe went after, a white gerfalcon.*
> *As dove-gray pigeon the brave lad flew;*
> *As sparrow-hawk did Woe pursue.*
> *As a gray wolf to fields he bounds,*
> *Woe to the chase, with borzoi-hounds.*
> *In field he stood as feather-grass,*
> *But Woe came with a sharpened scythe.*

Not satisfied with giving his victim no quarter, Woe taunts him about his helplessness—until the young man, bethinking himself of the one sure path to salvation, enters a monastery, and Woe-Misfortune is left standing at the gate. The poem is written very simply and with grave sympathy for the temptations and sufferings of the whole perverse and fallen race of man, of whom the youth is but an illustration, its tone of edification and its emotional depth reminding one of *Everyman*.

It was also in the seventeenth century that the vernacular was used for the first time in a literary work. This was the autobiography of the Archpriest Avvakum, the most colorful figure in the great schism which tore the Church apart between the years 1642 and 1687. The controversy concerned points of church ritual—whether the sign of the cross should be made in a two-fingered or a three-fingered position and whether the Alleluia should be double or triple—which, in spite of their apparent triviality, involved the very nature of Orthodox religion and the position of Holy Russia as repository of the true Christian faith. In fighting for the Old Belief, Avvakum was upholding Muscovy as the Third Rome. The innovations proposed by Nikon, Archbishop of Novgorod, seemed to him the device of the devil, and he opposed him with an inflexible outspokenness that led to torture, exile, and, ultimately, the stake. His *Life* is blunt and eloquent; his ardent idiom is as bold as his opinions. Gorky called it "the fiery speech of a warrior"; Turgenev thought that every serious artist should study it; D. S. Mirsky, in his *History of Russian Literature,* compared him to Tolstoy.

Of old the Devil did say [he writes, for example],
"I shall erect my throne in heaven and I shall be equal

unto the Almighty"; and likewise do the almanac-mongers say: "We understand the things of heaven and earth, and who is equal unto us?" But what Christians achieve is not external wisdom, nor the understanding of the movements of the moon, but they mount to heaven itself by their humility and their bodies remain incorrupt on earth. Look then, proud almanac-monger, where are thy Pythagorases and Platos: they have all been eaten by worms, like so many swine. But my Saints, for the sake of their humility, have been glorified by God . . . Pigs and cows know more than you do: before bad weather they grunt and they low, and hurry to their sties and pens, and then the rain comes. And you rational pigs, you measure the face of earth and heaven, but cannot foretell your own hour when you shall die. It's a hopeless job with you, fat steers that you are.

Such vituperation is tempered by a stalwart humor, the scorn of a man so detached and secure in himself that he can disdain the torments he must suffer and deride his captors. On one of the many occasions when his sadistic keeper was preparing to torture him, "I was repeating prayers for my latter end," he remarks, "for I knew what manner of cook he was and that few came out alive from his roasting." "For ten years," he writes of the same man, "he had tormented me, or I him—I know not which . . ." And once when he is led to the Cathedral Church to be anathematized: ". . . after the Elevation of the Host they sheared me and the deacon Theodor, and then they cursed us, and I cursed them back." He is troubled only when he fears that he has given way to spiritual presumption, and his self-reproaches are very touching. After one terrific beating, for example, he complains to God: "Why didst Thou permit them to beat me so sorely," and then blames himself for his complaint: ". . . another dung-faced Pharisee, wishing, forsooth, to judge the Almighty! If Job spoke in that fashion it was because he was a perfect and an upright man; and, moreover, he knew not the Scriptures."

The first serious work of Russian literature, then, to be done in the vernacular is the protest of a passionate man against what he believes to be imported artificialities, harmful to his nation. For his faith in the moral grandeur of Russia, Avvakum has been called the earliest of the Slavophiles; and his heroic self-abnegation, his courage to stand on principle without compromise make him the first in a line of rebellious writers, from Pushkin to Mayakovsky, the great poet of the Soviet Revolution, who shape the main tradition of Russian letters.

While the issue of Byzantine culture was thus debated, and long before it had eventuated in the drama of the Great Schism, another foreign influence, that of Western Europe, was infiltrating into Russia to become dominant there in the next century. From the time of Ivan the Terrible, foreign artists, soldiers, and craftsmen were invited to enter Russia, and when Russian ambassadors were sent abroad they were instructed to observe with care the ways of foreign courts. They returned with delighted accounts of what they had seen and took over what they found, in the true manner of barbarians. One prince, for example, was so enchanted with clocks that he filled his rooms with them; another built a coach "upholstered in gold brocade, lined with costly sable, and hooped in pure silver in place of iron." The government hired German soldiers, placed the army under the instruction of German officers, obtained equipment from Holland and Sweden, imported engineers from Holland and England, invited German actors and German scholars to enter the Imperial Service, and, imbued with zeal for education, formed an Academy of Sciences near Moscow, setting up a school in the Kremlin in 1667 for the imparting of "cunning in letters and the Slavonic, Greek, and Latin tongues, and other free teachings." During the time of Ivan the Terrible there were enough Germans in Moscow to form a community of their own, which was called the German Quarter; and Peter the Great continued to borrow soldiers and technicians from Europe. What Russia took from the West was useful knowledge and practical schemes to make life more safe and comfortable. Western influence was, therefore, primarily secular; and, as regards its effect on the people, the reverse of the churchly Byzantine. The West introduced new political concepts, new ideas of civic relations, new provinces of knowledge, and changes in customs, manners, and beliefs. It affected the day-to-day existence of men in all spheres of life but did not provide a universal language of formal theories and observances. And so, whereas the Byzantine Church embraced the entire community but hardly touched the lives of individuals, the Westernized state affected the individual but not the community as a whole. These two conflicting tendencies, the Churchly East, representing nationalism and tradition, the old, the native, a unique Holy Russia, and the secular West, standing for intellectual enterprise, social progress, and the promotion of political organizations along European lines, are the root of the intellectual debate which in the nineteenth century evolved into the controversy between the Slavophiles and the Westernizers and which down to the twentieth century dominated Russian thought. These two foreign influences were grafted on an indigenous civilization which neither of them expressed; and the cultivation of native modes within the orbit of those consciously acquired shapes the character of Russian literature.

In the eighteenth century, especially through Catherine the Great's interest in French theories of the Enlightenment, Europe began to exercise a philosophic influence on Russia. Catherine the Great corresponded with Voltaire, bought Diderot's library and made him keeper of it, invited d'Alembert to be tutor to her son, modeled the laws, at the beginning of her reign, on the principles of Rousseau and Montesquieu, and wrote her own memoirs in their tongue. French during her reign was overwhelmingly in fashion. The manners of France were adopted by the court, French tutors brought up Russian children, and the French language was spoken by the aristocracy almost to the exclusion of Russian. It was under these auspices that Russian literature came into its own.

The language was shaped to poetic use by Mikhail Vassilievich Lomonosov and Gavrilo Romanovich Derzhavin, both of whom began with stiff imitations of French and German classics but developed an original prosody that brought forth the latent variousness, flexibility, and magnificence of the native idiom. Lomonosov has been called the "father" and the "Peter the Great" of Russian literature. A peasant's son, who put himself through the Academy in Moscow, he was one of the young men chosen by Catherine to study in Germany, was subsequently appointed Professor of Chemistry at the Academy of Sciences, and did important work not only in literature but also in history, astronomy, meteorology, and in physics and chemistry, in which he achieved eminence, advancing theories about the structure of matter and the composition of gases which were some one hundred and fifty years ahead of their time. In literature he was both innovator and lawgiver. He wrote a rhetoric and a grammar, which established the modern Russian literary language, and produced verse which, in spite of its being also something of a scientific demonstration in the field of prosody, served as a model for poets who followed and surpassed him. He urged elimination of foreign terms, Latin, Polish, Dutch, English, French—which had been adopted along with technical knowledge—in favor of ordinary Russian expressions; and although he thought that Church Slavonic was still appropriate to the "high" and "middle" styles proper to orations and scholarly articles, the vernacular alone, he said, should be used for the "low" style of informal writing. His comment on the Russian language is famous:

The Russian language, the sovereign of so many others, is superior to all the other languages of Europe, not only in the extent of the regions where it reigns, but also in its peculiar comprehensiveness and abundance. Charles V, the (Holy) Roman emperor, used to say that one ought to talk Spanish with God, French with one's friends, German with one's enemies, and Italian with the ladies. But if he had learned Russian, he would certainly have added that one could speak it appropriately to all of them. For he would have found in it the majesty of Spanish, the vivacity of French, the strength of German, the tenderness of Italian, and, besides these, the richness and the concision, so vigorous in its imagery, of the Greek and Latin tongues.

His poems—versions of the Psalms, odes to God and to various empresses, done mostly to order for state occasions—are "elevated" in tone, abstract in diction, ornate, magniloquent, but swift-paced and robust; his lyrics have often a delicate music, and his satiric pieces, a fresh, colloquial ease.

On these prosodic experiments the greatest of his eighteenth-century successors, Derzhavin, built his "grand" style, which combines the dignity of classical writers and the wildness of the early romantics. Influenced by Young and Ossian, as well as by Fénélon and Lomonosov, and, above all, expressing his own crude self, "his classicism," as Mirsky put it, "was that of a barbarian." He was a genuine and original poet, who wrote with something of Avvakum's bluntness, "bending the word to its knees," in epigrams that beat rather than point home. Take, for example, a passage in his *Ode on the Death of Prince Meschersky* which derives from the first of Young's *Night Thoughts*. Young had written:

> *Death! Great proprietor of all! 'Tis thine*
> *To tread out empire, and to quench the stars.*
> *The sun himself by thy permission shines*
> *And, one day, thou shalt pluck him from his sphere.*

Derzhavin's lines express virtually the same idea:

> *Unpitying Death annuls all things:*
> *And stars are quenched by her,*
> *And suns put out by her,*
> *And doom to all the worlds is threatened.*

But they are abrupt by comparison:

> *Béz zhálosti vsё Smért razít:*
> *I zvézdi iéyu sokrushátsya,*
> *I sólntzi iéyu potushátsya,*
> *I vsém mirám oná grozít.*

The music of Young's threnody, the melancholy reflectiveness which inspires it, have become, with Derzhavin, a
rounded drumbeat to accompany a fact. Other lines recall
Sir Philip Sidney's "cradled in their graves," in the way
they pack all life into a phrase; and others, for amusing
cruelty, remind one of Voltaire:

> *The ass will still remain an ass*
> *Though you may heap the stars upon him.*

A great, crude, stubborn, rebellious, impatient, pleasure-
loving man, Derzhavin produced poetry in his own image,
sublime and rough. The spirit in it "breathes mighty and
deep," Vladimir Khodasevich—a too-little-known poet of
the twentieth century—writes of it in a beautiful study.
"His language," he says, "is primitive, original. There is in
it absolute creative freedom, the gift of savages and
geniuses"; and Gogol had written that in his *Waterfall* a
"whole epic seems to have flown into a single rushing ode,"
that other poets were "pigmies beside him," that Nature in
that Ode "appears grander than the nature we see, people
mightier than the people we know, and our ordinary life
there presented, like an anthill which swarms somewhere
far beneath."

No sooner had Russian become a literary language than
controversies arose as to its nature and proper use. By the
end of the century and the beginning of the next, writers

were divided into those who wished to eliminate, however uncouth the result might be, all, even thoroughly Russified, foreign words in favor of the Slavic and those who advocated urbane, Westernized diction. But whatever their stand on linguistics, the thinking of all writers was at this time influenced, though in various ways, by the intellectual attitudes of the Enlightenment and by the events of the French Revolution. The conservative Karamzin and the gentle Zhukovsky, leaders of the "Western" school, were attracted by the sentimental implications of eighteenth-century liberalism; their chief opponents, Krylov, Griboyedov, and Radishchev, were interested in how the new concepts might affect the actual conduct of human lives.

Both Karamzin and Zhukovsky began their literary careers with translations. And it was English, not French, works they chose—Karamzin, Shakespeare's *Julius Caesar* and Thomson's *Seasons,* Zhukovsky, Gray's *Elegy.* They addressed themselves to a class of nobles, whose power, ever since the days of Peter the Great, had increased in proportion as their obligations to the state diminished; who, living on the labor of serfs, oblivious of the realities of their world's social and economic structure, dabbled in theories of Liberty, Equality, and Fraternity, were proud of knowing French better than Russian, loved to weep over tender verse and touching stories—and beat their servants as a matter of course. They had lived through the ominous peasant uprising of Pugachev, which seemed to them to be no more than the wild outbreak of a lawless Robin Hood; and they adopted as verbal cloaks for their sensitive consciences the high-sounding ideals in the name of which the bloody events they had observed at a comfortable distance had been perpetrated in France. Their sensibilities were exquisitely developed, and their ear became attuned to the delicate cadences of subtly harmonious styles. The purity and flawlessness of Karamzin's and Zhukovsky's work appealed to them; and all those who love stylistic perfection are in their debt for encouraging it. Vasili Andreyevich Zhukovsky's versions of Dryden, Scott, Campbell, Byron, set a standard for translations that, to my knowledge, has never been surpassed; Nickolay Mikhaylovich Karamzin's *History of the Russian State,* without bothering about the people, gave magnificently dramatic portraits of their sovereigns, and, in inspiring Pushkin, came to occupy in Russian literature the place held in English by North's *Plutarch,* on whom Shakespeare drew; the subjective lyrics of both opened vistas to reflectiveness and gave momentum to a whole literature of melodious introspection; and Karamzin's story, *Poor Liza,* has had probably as great an influence in its country as *Werther* had in Germany.

Poor Liza is written in the first person. Our author loves to wander about Moscow, he tells us, and to stop at a certain favorite spot of his, on the outskirts of the great city, where there is a little hill with a ruined Gothic monastery and a splendid view. Here he likes to sit, leaning against the ruins, harkening to the "hollow moaning of centuries, consumed in the abyss of the past." He meditates on the history of the monastery, but most of all he takes pleasure in recalling the melancholy tale of Liza. "Ah! I love those things which touch my heart and make me shed tears of tender sorrow," he sighs. About thirty years earlier lovely Liza had lived with her old mother not far from the monastery wall. Her father, a well-to-do farmer, had died and the two women fell upon hard times. The poor widow wept almost constantly, for "even peasant women know how to love," and fifteen-year-old Liza tried to cheer her and worked day and night to make a living for them both. She wove cloth, knit stockings, and picked flowers and fruit which she sold in town. Once, about two years after her father's death, Liza went into the city. A well-dressed, handsome young man came up to her, charmed and flattered her with gallantry and pretty speeches, and, before leaving, induced her to tell him where she lived. Next day she waited until evening, refusing to sell her flowers, and threw them away, at last, because the young man had not appeared. But the day after that, he himself came to her cottage, asked for a glass of milk, and offered to buy all that she made, so that she would no longer have to journey so often into town. And he began to come regularly. He was a rich nobleman, Erast by name, with a lively imagination and a love of romances. He liked to picture himself living in those far-off days when people "always walked in meadows, bathed in clear springs, kissed like doves, rested beneath roses and myrtles and spent all their days in happy idleness." And in this romantic way he fell in love with Liza. They saw each other every day; Liza was happy and finally gave herself to him, whereupon, as might have been expected, Erast grew tired of her, let several days go by without coming, then reappeared to announce that he must be off to the wars. He bade Liza farewell at dawn. "What a touching picture!" exclaims our author, as he describes the tall oak under which Erast stands, holding his pale friend in his arms, while all Nature is silent around them. Two months go by. Then, in town one day, Liza sees her lover in a magnificent carriage. She runs after it as it drives into the courtyard of a splendid mansion and throws herself upon him. Erast brings her into the house, shuts the door, and explains to her coolly that he is about to be married and that she must leave him alone. "I loved you," he says, "I still love you, that is, I wish you well." He gives her a hundred rubles and asks a servant to show her out. "My heart bleeds at this moment," says Karamzin; "I forget that Erast is a human being. I am ready to curse him, but my tongue will not move. I look at the sky and a tear rolls down my cheek. Ah! Why am I not writing a romance, instead of the sad truth?" Stupefied, Liza goes away, comes to the brink of a stream, gives the hundred rubles to a girl who is passing by, to take to her mother, and drowns herself. She is buried near the stream by a dark oak, with a wooden cross above her grave. Her mother dies when she hears of her fate. And Erast is never happy again: he considers himself a murderer, and it is he who had brought the author to Liza's grave and had told him her story.

In 1790, two years before the publication of the restrained, urbane, and elegant *Poor Liza,* so clearly influenced by the fashion in the West for Samuel Richardson and the literature of easy tears, a young man printed on his private printing press a very different kind of book about the lowly. He gave twenty-five copies of it to a bookseller; one of them reached the Empress Catherine, who wrote angry notes in its margins and condemned the author to death, commuting the sentence, however, to exile in Siberia. This young man was the son of a wealthy and benevolent landowner, who at the time of the Pugachev rebellion had been concealed from harm by his own serfs. He had been brought up at court, had completed his education in Germany, and had just returned from a journey through France. His name was Alexander Nicholaevich Radishchev, and his book was innocently entitled *A Journey from Petersburg to Moscow*.

The traveler on this journey makes twenty-two stops between the new and the old capitals of Russia; and at each one an incident or a discussion reveals to him some phase of Russian life. In one place, it develops, horses cannot be had without a large bribe, which is accepted by the posting clerk as a matter of course; in another, he hears about an official who, on the grounds that it was not his job, refused to help save a boatload of drowning men; in a third, a peasant discloses the inhumane conditions under which he must labor; in a fourth, a discussion of justice leads to a story of serfs murdering their master in rightful and warrantable vengeance for the way they had been treated—and so on.

> I looked about me [the *Journey* begins], my heart was rent by the sufferings of humanity. I turned my gaze into my inmost self—and saw that the misfortunes of man proceed from man, and often only because he looks obliquely on the objects that surround him. Can it be, I discoursed with myself, that Nature is so miserly with her children that from the innocently errant she has forever concealed Truth? Can it be that this severe stepmother created us to undergo only misfortunes and no felicity at all? My reason trembled at the thought, and my heart thrust it far off. I found man's consoler in himself.

Radishchev believes that man's fate is in his own hands, that all men are born equal, that God is the same everywhere and by whatever name He may be called, that civic law is a wise restriction of natural rights; and he says so in impassioned rhetoric. His style is awkwardly weighted with uncouth Slavophilisms, but it is eloquent through the despair that rings in it, the exasperation of a just man whose reason cannot lift him above the foulness he has uncovered. He writes from a somewhat idyllic, but genuine, love of simple people. The sketch of a country girl, honest, unaffected, dignified, is fresh and serious, and passages about the nature of the Russian muzhik indicate the kind of insight which Gogol and Dostoevsky were later to corroborate and amplify:

My horses carry me along; the driver intones a song, a mournful one as usual. He who knows the tunes of Russian popular songs will admit that there is that in them which indicates heart's sorrow. Nearly all the tunes of these songs are in the minor key. In this musical predisposition of the popular ear, search out the soil of government. In it will be discovered the groundwork of our people's soul. Look at the Russian. You will find him reflective. If he wants to chase off weariness, or, as he himself calls it, if he wants to have a good time, he goes to the pub. When drunk, he is impulsive, rash, quarrelsome. If anything occurs that is not to his liking, he starts a brawl or a fight. The rustic going to the inn, his head cast down, and coming out again bloody from blows, can explain a great deal that has hitherto seemed puzzling in the history of Russia . . .

I have observed in numerous instances that the Russian people are very patient and will endure to the farthest limit; but when their patience is at an end, then nothing will keep them from resorting to cruelty.

A splendid peasantry oppressed by legally protected tyrants must lead, Radishchev sees, to revolution; and he not only prophesies it but exhorts men to it:

Free people, who have committed no crime, are in chains, are sold like cattle! Oh, laws! Your great wisdom lies often only in your style! Is not the mockery of this clear to you? But even more, the mockery of the holy name of freedom? Oh! if the slaves, burdened by heavy shackles, raging in their despair, would smash, with iron, these heads of ours which obstruct their freedom, the heads of their inhuman masters, and with our blood would incarnadine their fields! What would the government lose thereby? Soon from their midst great men would be delivered to defend the beaten tribe, but they would have other notions about themselves and would be deprived of the right to oppress. This is no dream; my gaze pierces the dense curtain of time, which conceals the future from our eyes; I see through an entire century.

In the few poems that he wrote, Radishchev displayed the same independence. "Let others fawn," he said, "before authority, exalt in praises, power and might. We shall sing to celebrate the merits of society." The Empress Catherine declared that his *Ode to Freedom,* with its clear advocacy of rebellion, was criminal in design. Later Pushkin praised it and in an early version of his *Monument* mentioned its author as one whom he himself had followed in extolling liberty. The *Ode* was written in the iambic tetrameter which Lomonosov, whom the revolutionary poet greatly admired, had sought to establish as the meter most suited to majestic utterance in Russian; but some of his other poems were experiments with less familiar measures, such as Sapphics and dactyls.

After the death of Catherine he was permitted to return from Siberia. On the way back his wife, who had followed him into exile, fell ill and died. Radishchev found himself lonely, prematurely old, burdened with debts he could not meet. In 1802 he committed suicide. *A Journey from Petersburg to Moscow* was not published until after the Revolution of 1905.

In their reactions to the Russian scene and to the humanitarian doctrines of the late eighteenth century, Karamzin, Zhukovsky, and their followers were suave, conservative, urbane; Radishchev, passionately serious; Krylov and Griboyedov, quietly amused or derisive. Ivan Andreyevich Krylov began by writing outspoken satires that got him in trouble with the government, and since his temper was anything but bellicose, he changed his tactics, after a lapse of silence, and invested his criticism with a form that seemed innocuous and entertaining to everybody. His fables were the product of a sedately ironic spirit which looked on folly with a common sense that bordered on complacency. Their language was the colloquial idiom of the middle class whom he knew well; and they turned to wit the plodding morality of a plain bourgeoisie, honestly susceptible to hypocrisies and scoffing at pretensions and artificiality. Krylov sometimes pointed to obvious flaws in a bureaucracy-ridden government, but, for the most part, he treated men's moral deficiencies as defects of Nature, which had no relation to social structures.

The great period of Russian literature may be said to begin with Alexander Sergeyevich Griboyedov's play *Gore ot Uma,* literally *Woe from Wit,* or *The Misfortune of Being Clever,* as it has been translated. With the possible exception of Gogol's *The Inspector General,* it remains to this day the greatest Russian comedy. Its verse is untranslatably fluid, producing, for all its polish, the effect of natural and racy speech; and its characterization is of the kind that gives permanence to period pieces. The action takes place in the home of Famusov, a government official in Moscow, and concerns the discoveries which Chatsky, a young friend of his, makes about him, his household, and his friends one day when he returns from a three years' trip abroad. He had gone away in the first place because he was bored with the life he was obliged to lead among the people he knew; but he is in love with Famusov's daughter Sophia, whom he has known from childhood; his absence has confirmed and strengthened his attachment, and he returns with great hopes of happiness. But he is to be so disillusioned and disgusted that, at the end of a day, he flies from Moscow, never to return.

The curtain goes up on the servant, Lizanka, drowsily complaining of the inconsiderateness of masters. For two nights she has not had a chance to sleep, keeping guard by the room of her young mistress who has till dawn played flute-and-piano duets with her father's secretary, Molchalin. But Liza is a loyal soul, and now that day has come, she tries to warn Sophia of danger from an awakened household. While she is at this task, turning the clock ahead to make it strike, Famusov himself comes upon her, and when he tries to make love to her, she shakes him off by telling him he might rouse Sophia, who has only now gone to sleep after a night spent in reading French out loud.

> *Tell her* [says Famusov] *she must not ruin her eyes,*
> *That there is scanty good in reading.*
> *It is French books keep her awake*
> *And Russian ones keep me from sleeping.*

At last, after Liza shouts loudly enough to wake up everybody, he leaves:

> *He's gone* [she sighs], *from all these masters, save us,*
>   *Lord, I pray!*
> *Or else there's always trouble brewing from above.*
> *More than all sorrows may we keep away*
> *Our lordships' anger—and our lordships' love.*

But he returns directly, runs into Molchalin and Sophia, and lectures them both, complacently and garrulously, on their frivolousness. It comes, he says, of endless reading and of French influence: "Eternal Frenchmen, from whom we get our fashions, authors, muses—debauchers of our pockets and our hearts." Molchalin, whose very name derives from *molchat,* "to be still," has little but *yes* and *no* to say for himself, but Sophia shows herself to be a resourceful girl. She knows that her father wants her to marry a rich man, and she tries to kill two birds with one stone: to give a plausible excuse for being up at crack of dawn, and to reveal her love for the secretary. This she does by inventing a dream on the spur of the moment, in which, in a setting that changes from the pastoral to the gothic, she sees herself separated from the man she loves by groaning, laughing half-human monsters. She wakes up. Someone is talking. It is her father. "Why so early?" she thinks. "Yes," says Famusov, not wishing to discuss what he was doing up at that unseasonable hour, "an evil dream. There is everything in it: devils and love and fears and flowers. You searched for grass and stumbled on a friend. You'd better knock this nonsense from your head. Where there are marvels there is little meaning. Go on, lie down, and go to sleep again."

He leaves with Molchalin, and while Liza is upbraiding Sophia for her fickleness to Chatsky and Sophia is defending her preference for Molchalin, who, she says, is not conceited, does not make fun of everyone, hates impertinence, and can spend a whole night just holding her hand and gazing on her, Chatsky is announced. He has come straight from abroad, without having even stopped at home. He bursts in, falls at Sophia's feet, kisses her hands, makes a passionate speech—and receives in reply: "Oh, Chatsky! I am very glad to see you."

> *You're glad! I'm glad of that—But who,*
> *sincerely, is made happy in this fashion?*

He tells her she is beautiful, asks her about herself and about their Moscow acquaintances, whom he characterizes in dazzling, pitiless epigrams. And what of life in general —of education, and the reigning tone? Are teachers still invited in whole squadrons, as many and as cheap as possible, and does the language mixture still continue, the French combined with Novgorodian? To Liza's impertinent remark that it would be difficult to carve his tongue out of any language,

At any rate [he says], *it's not inflated.*
Here's news! I'm making most of every minute.
Excited now by seeing you again,
I'm talkative. But am I not at times
More stupid even than Molchalin? How is he, by the way,
Has he not broken yet the seal of silence?

Sophia departs in irritation. "How beautiful your Sophia has become" is all that Chatsky can think of saying when Famusov comes to pester him with questions about his travels. "How beautiful she is," he murmurs, leaving.

Later that day he speaks at greater length with Famusov and has a chance to observe him, Sophia, and Molchalin. He is gradually forced to believe the incredible, that Sophia has learned to prefer to him a mean-minded cad, a stupid nonentity; and he is goaded by Famusov's toadyism to a magnificent speech on the corruption of the times. "Everything is new in Russia," he exclaims, "except prejudices, and they are old. Neither years, nor fashions, nor fires will destroy them." Where are the elders whom a young man might respect? Those who have got rich through robbery? Who have found refuge from justice with relatives and friends, who have erected splendid palaces where they expend themselves in orgies? Such Nestors as the one who one day exchanged, for three greyhounds, the faithful servants who had more than once saved his life and his honor? Or the one who tore serf children from their parents and made them serve in a ballet which all Moscow admired, until he sold them one by one to put off creditors? A young man who loves science or art and desires neither position nor rank, has no place in this society. Should some such individual appear, he would pass for a dreamer, a dangerous man, and would be hounded by cries of "Thieves!" and "Fire!"

Chatsky's prophecy is proved on himself. Sophia, annoyed with him, says casually at a party that evening: "He's crazy!" The word is taken up. Everyone is sure that he is. Most say that they had already noticed it in one way or another. They talk of how it happened. Some say he drank too much. But Famusov insists that he knows the real reason: it is that he has read too much. One ought to gather up all books and burn them. Chatsky, having once seen the company he is thrown with, runs away from Moscow. And so, he says, the day is done, and with it all his visions and his hopes. What had he, after all, expected? The charm of welcome, some real feeling of people one for another. Instead of which he found empty shouts, embraces, faithless creatures full of hate, traitors, gossips, malicious simpletons, evil-tongued old women, stupid old men. He dreams again of traveling, of sitting idly in a carriage and driving all day long, over endless plains, when there is always something blue, light, varied in the distance. After a final tirade, in which he sums up all his disappointments and censures, he calls for his carriage: "Away from Moscow! And never back again. I'll run without a glance behind, and search out in the world some corner where an injured soul may hide. My carriage! Bring my carriage!" And so off goes the only genuine, surehearted, and clearheaded man in Moscow society, the first of many famous wanderers, the "superfluous men" of Russian literature. "Well, see, of course, he's crazy. What stuff he talked. And how severely about Moscow! Dear me, dear me, what will the Princess Maria Alekseyevna say?" mumbles Famusov as the curtain goes down.

This play was finished in 1823. Naturally it could not be acted, nor even published; but it circulated widely in manuscript and created a sensation. The same year Pushkin finished the first chapter of *Evgenyi Onegin*. Chatsky has been called the "elder brother" of Onegin.

CHAPTER IV

Alexander Sergeyevich Pushkin

1799–1837

READERS OF THE WEST HAVE BEEN INCLINED TO THINK THAT Russians exaggerate Pushkin's value. What, after all, can his work show comparable to Dante's or Milton's philosophic insight, to Shakespeare's comprehension of the individual, or Goethe's vision of man's ethical struggle, or Cervantes's of his ideals? And yet it is with the greatest that he is ranked by his countrymen. He is the despair of anyone who wants to explain him to those who cannot read Russian, for although some creditable translations of him have been made, few so far have been adequate. The beauty of his work depends so much on a rare exactitude in the use of words, it is to such a degree a matter of verbal magic that he is almost impossible to render in another tongue, and so by those who cannot read him in the original his excellence must be taken on faith. This understandably raises skepticism. It is more than command of words that we demand of first-rate poetry, more than music, however perfect that music may be. To say of a poet that he is a pure artist is likely, in fact, to make him seem not very important. It calls up the image of a delicate aesthete; it suggests effeminacy and preciousness. But this is precisely what one must begin by saying of Pushkin. He is the purest of artists. And also one of the most vigorous and most deep. Like Shakespeare in English literature, he stands alone and supreme in Russian, Russia's national poet, worshiped by all her great artists, all of whom are his followers but none his successor.

When Pushkin was born, in 1799, the Russian language, although refined by Karamzin and dignified by Derzhavin, was stiltedly used by writers to amuse a Frenchified court. Pushkin was to make it more supple and poetic, and he was also to integrate the foreign and the native elements of Russian culture by writing such work as could rouse not only the interest of a Europeanized aristocracy but the feelings of those masses of Russians who had not yet found themselves and their hopes so fully and so appreciatively expressed. This was, perhaps, his greatest achievement. What made it possible was his extraordinary sensitiveness to all literatures and cultures, foreign and domestic, living and dead—which in turn may have been due to a deep-seated division in his own nature, a hardly recognized craving for integration that achieved through poetry a synthesis of wide divergencies. He was able, at any rate, to identify himself with modes of feeling that were not his own, a quality of which Dostoevsky made much in his famous speech at the unveiling of the Pushkin memorial in 1880. Pushkin's Italians, Germans, Egyptians, he said, were convincingly themselves, not like Shakespeare's foreigners, for instance, who always remained Englishmen in essence; and this capacity to be "universal" was, he declared, peculiarly Russian. However that may be, it was as a citizen of the world that Pushkin became the poet of Russia, for although he never left his country, he could, as perhaps no one else, grasp the core of an alien civilization, just as he was able to understand intricacies of personality and paradoxes of intellectual systems.

Born into an ancient family of somewhat impoverished boyars, and on his mother's side descended from Peter the Great's favorite Negro, Abraham Hannibal, Pushkin, by the very circumstances of his heritage, felt himself a divided being, equally proud of his honored name and of his African blood, which had to be defended against the prejudice of snobs. The two strains accounted, perhaps, for a temperamental dualism that shows deeply in his work: on the one hand, marmoreal poise, on the other, violent passion. He himself ascribed his intensity to the African in him; and when, in a symbolic fragment of 1830, he speaks of how in school he would flee from the frightening dignity, the sweet, quiet, holy speech of the severely beautiful, clear-eyed Woman who admonished the youngsters and gave them difficult advice, away to a shady garden, where he would dream, lulled by the sound of leaves and water and fascinated by two demon statues, one an idol of pride and anger, the other, feminine and sensual, a magic, doubtful, lying, beautiful ideal, he sums up the Apollonian-Dionysiac war of which his short life was the battleground, with a Fate he never lost sight of always standing guard. The primary battle of his life was between the events that engaged his emotions and the genius that claimed all of him.

His education, the usual one for a young nobleman of his day, must have added another enriching element of division. The language spoken at home was French; and Russian was somehow haphazardly picked up, mostly from servants. His father's library was stocked with French books, and these the boy devoured and imitated, writing comedies on the model of Molière, fables after La Fontaine, and even a Voltairian epic, all before he was sent to school at the age of twelve. The school was at Tsarskoe Selo, just opened under the patronage of the then liberal-minded Alexander I. There Pushkin continued his studies of language and history, becoming as much a gentleman of eighteenth-century Enlightenment as a citizen of nineteenth-century Russia. And he wrote so well that before his graduation, in 1817, he was already a recognized poet. His early verse, love lyrics, drinking songs, short satires, epigrams are somewhat straitened in eighteenth-century mannerisms, but already masterful in form and sounding now and then a note of genuine experience and a view of life's brevity that are more than mere youthful variations on the *carpe diem* theme. There is a joyous paganism in these early things—playfulness, geniality, mischief—and an aesthetic seriousness that has already learned to subdue events to perfect form.

After graduation, Pushkin, holding a nominal official post that left ample free time, plunged into a life of dissipation. His love affairs, which had begun in school, now multiplied; but although he complained that he was unsuccessful in love and that women interfered with his work, it is hard to take his complaints seriously. He wrote some of the greatest love lyrics that have ever been written, and those who are interested can read his amorous biography in them, open and direct as they are. Their story is plain, but not the deeper tale of the complex nature which created both them and the occasion for them. Pushkin's life was never completely revealed in his work; it shows itself glimpsewise, in unmistakable evidence that the poet knew what he was talking about, that he had no need, for instance, to feign a passion or to draw his knowledge of society from books, but what may have been chaotic in his life never blurs the objective clarity of even his most intimate lyrics. On Pushkin's stage Apollo and Dionysus are reconciled, whatever may have gone on behind the scenes. "We always feel in reading Pushkin," writes Edmund Wilson in an essay that is one of the finest I have seen on the subject, "that there is something behind and beyond, something we can only guess at; and this makes his peculiar fascination—a fascination which has something in common with the inexhaustible interest of Shakespeare, who seems to be giving us his sonnets and *Hamlet* and *Lear* and the rest as the moods and dreams of some drama the actuality of which we never touch."

Pushkin's first important work, *Ruslan and Ludmila,* is a fairy tale about a princess who is abducted on her wedding night by a wicked enchanter, is sought in strange lands through perilous adventures by her prince and his three rivals, and is ultimately found and brought back by the right man, with everything ending happily as the wicked magicians are discomfited and a besieging army is defeated. But although there are genuine elements of folklore in this poem—such, for example, as the episode of the enchanted giant's head, roused from its sleep of centuries only to die through the wound that woke it up —and though critics of the classical school objected to its childish primitivism, *Ruslan and Ludmila* is really an eighteenth-century romance, modeled on Ariosto, and not a simple folk tale at all. It sparkles with sophisticated wit. Its fantasy is steeped in ironic amusement. It is the work of a carefree young genius who is playing with his gift. It holds the place in Pushkin's work that Shakespeare's first gay comedies hold in his—and just as *Love's Labour's Lost* and *A Comedy of Errors* deal lightly with complexities of human attachments which were to become the theme of all Shakespeare's subsequent dramas, so *Ruslan and Ludmila* indicates Pushkin's fundamental interests: his delight in the erotic, his love of a story as a story, his fascination with mystery. But what is perhaps its most bewitching quality is the way it pins wildest fantasy to earth. When, for example, in the darkness of the bedchamber, after an interminable wedding feast, Ruslan is about to embrace his Ludmila and she is snatched from him at that very moment, it is to a barnyard tragedy that Pushkin, without a shade of cynicism, compares the situation. Just so, he says, having described the cloudy whirl through which Ludmila is carried off and Ruslan's helpless astonishment, just so, from his own cottage door, on a summer's day, he had watched the sultan of the barnyard run in pursuit of a frightened hen and encircle her in his passionate wings, when over them with destructive intent there floated a gray kite, and swooped like lightning on the yard, and swirled up again and flew away, leaving the grief-stricken cock to call in vain for his beloved, with no more of her to be seen than a bit of fluff carried by the wind. Neither the rooster nor Ruslan loses dignity in this comparison. Such is the fate of bliss in this world of chance! This is a realistic view of life that comes of a love of it in all its phases, and it is most deeply Pushkin's. Other evidence of it is his tolerantly amused view of people's characters and of their fortunes. Ludmila, for example, appears no less charming nor less real when, a prisoner in the enchanter's garden, she meditates gloomily on suicide but, having caught her reflection in a pool, decides against it. Pushkin deals with her as he will later deal with his Tatiana, as he will deal, in fact, with nearly all the women of his tales, tenderly, smilingly, affectionately. Or when the friendly old hermit tells Ruslan the story of how he had spent forty years studying witchcraft to gain a woman's love and succeeded at last when the beautiful enchantress had become a monstrous old hag, we get another glimpse of Pushkin's laughingly ironic attitude toward love and circumstance and time as tyrants over lives. There is in *Ruslan and Ludmila* the ebullience of a young epicurean to whom neither hardship nor disappointment nor terror is unknown, but whose pagan strength will not allow any kind of tragedy to shake the pleasure he takes in living. Aware of possible frustration, of the certainty of change, the likelihood of evil chance, he enjoys life, realistically, without substituting what might be for what is.

Ruslan and Ludmila was a new venture in Russian poetry. It roused a storm of criticism from diehards of the classical school. But other of Pushkin's verses called forth more ominous opposition. By the time he finished *Ruslan and Ludmila,* in 1820, Pushkin had written a few poems that brought him the censure of the government. There was, for example, an *Ode to Freedom,* in which he declared that wherever he looked he saw only whips and fetters, destructive shame of laws, impotent tears of captivity. He warned tyrants to tremble and called on "fallen slaves" to rise. "Despotic villain," he addressed the Czar, "I despise you and your throne and with a cruel joy look forward to your destruction and the death of your children; upon your brow I read the people's curse; you are the horror of the world, the shame of nature, a reproach to God and earth." It was not that he condemned czarism itself, but only those czars who forgot that their power was derived not from Nature but from Law. Neither punishments nor rewards, nor dungeons nor altars, nor sure protection would save them. But if they bowed their heads before Law, their subjects' peace and freedom would become eternally the guardian of their throne. Or there was the verse, *Noël,* in which the Virgin Mary tries to terrorize into silence the loudly wailing Christ child with the threat of the Czar's arrival. The Czar comes in and proclaims magnificently: "Let the Russian people know, let the whole world know, that I have had a uniform made. And let the populace rejoice; I am well fed, healthy, stout," and let them know further that through his imperial goodness the Czar will give people all their rights. At this glad news the Christ child jumps up and down for joy, but his mother quiets him: "Hush, hush, go to sleep. That was only papa Czar telling you some fairy tales." Or *The Village,* in which the poet's delight in a secluded corner of earth, where he can find quiet for his work, a magnificent solitude away from laziness and envy and troublesome, officious eyes, is offset by "the frightful thought," oppressing the soul "of one who loves humanity" that here "gaunt slavery crawls in the reins of a pitiless master." The poem ends with a despairing question: why was he given fruitless fire without a prophet's vision? Will he ever see his people freed from slavery; will the beautiful dawn of enlightened liberty ever rise over his land? These poems were circulated among Pushkin's liberal friends; they came to the attention of the higher authorities, the last one to that of the Czar himself, who gave instructions that Pushkin be thanked for the good thoughts in it, but also that he be sent away from Petersburg. The banishment was not formal; Pushkin was simply transferred to an office in Ekaterinoslav (now Dniepropetrovsk), but from now on for the rest of his short life he was to be under governmental surveillance.

Thus, before his departure for the Caucasus, Pushkin was already familiar with doctrines of French Enlightenment, and with the contrast between them and the state of society in Russia, with the relative merits of the "world" and of solitude, with the strength and joy of passion and the restraints imposed by conventionality. In the Caucasus he spent some happy months traveling with the family of Nikolay Raevsky, a school friend of his. It was a family of liberals. General Raevsky was a hero of the War of 1812; his two sons were associated with radical groups; one of his daughters was married to General Orlov, an influential leader of the Liberal party; the other daughter later married the Decembrist Prince Sergey Volkonsky and followed him into exile in Siberia. Through them Pushkin became increasingly interested in advanced political movements and was introduced to the poetry of Byron, whose influence is evident in his work for the next ten years.

Mistakenly Pushkin has been called the Russian Byron, mistakenly because, although, like everybody else at the time, he went through a phase of admiration for the romantic rebel and although, in common with Byron, he had a love of the free and the unconventional, there was nothing in him of the English lord's narcissistic posturing

nor of his naïve interest in exhibiting himself and his
soul. Pushkin's nature was more generous, more quiet,
and deeper, his view of life more mature, and his poetry
infinitely more exquisite and restrained. He admired Byron
but was never dominated by him, and wrote his most important work, *Evgenyi Onegin,* in criticism of the Byronic
pose. But between 1820 and 1823 several of his poems, *The
Prisoner of the Caucasus, The Brother Robbers,* and *The
Fountain of Backhchisarai,* in their exotic setting, their
themes of violence, outlawry, and desperate love, are super-
ficially reminiscent of Byron. The similarity goes no deeper.
The magnificent descriptions in them that re-create an
atmosphere foreign to Europeans make the distant and
unusual seem understandable and close, rather than exotic.
What in Byron is endowed with the glamour of the strange
has with Pushkin the clear-cut splendor of the actually
known. Furthermore, these are not merely colorful, emotional stories; they are symbolic examinations of a problem
with which Pushkin was preoccupied and which Byron
took for granted. The prisoner, disillusioned with friends,
with love, tired of the hypocrisy and slander of civilized
society, flees to the Caucasus in search of the natural and
the free. But he is captured there, held now in chains of
iron instead of in the less tangible chains of an obnoxiously
artificial environment; and when he is set free by the
Circassian girl who loves him, he is still a prisoner, in
the bonds of an earlier unhappy attachment from which
he has vainly tried to escape. In *The Brother Robbers* a
murderous outlaw is gnawed by a feeling of guilt, which
his brother, in the delirium before he died, had imposed
on him. The brother had been freed by death; the robber
himself is free in the happy company of fellow robbers, but

he is the captive of his conscience. In *The Fountain of Bachchisarai* a sultan executes the girl, who through jealousy has either murdered or had only desired the death of his newly captured mistress. All are prisoners of unsatisfied love. It is the problem of freedom with which Pushkin is here concerned. Does it, can it exist? And what is physical imprisonment to the various chains of love, guilt, habit, desire, by which a man is held captive? To single out in this way what seems to be their hidden meaning is, of course, to destroy the special quality of these poems. They are not problem pieces done to illustrate or to analyze. They are swiftly moving narratives, and what is impressive in them is their quick passion, their pictures, their sounds and silences, and especially a certain wonderful effect of contrast that brings out events in a kind of relief—like the tumultuous storm seen by the lonely prisoner from a mountaintop, or like his calling in a vast stillness that has no echo, or like the faint tramping of horses that sounds from a great distance, where everything is asleep; or like the robber telling the story of his life to his noisy companions, the quietness of recollection drowned in their shouting, and the agony of his sense of guilt quite lost to their unawakened consciences; or like the sad and peaceful fountain that stands as a memorial to violent, tragic love.

Before Pushkin had finished these poems he was at work on *Evgenyi Onegin,* where the problem of freedom is seen in a new light. This novel in verse has to do with a young man about town, a shallow, foppish, unimaginative Don Juan who inspires the devoted love of an inexperienced girl, rejects it, and discovers too late that he has missed his chance for happiness. Evgenyi's prison is not that of passion but of its absence, that *Weltschmerz* which was the characteristic disease of the Romantics, induced by a suddenly rediscovered individualism that had lost the directive of impersonal ideals. It was a loss of feeling, hope, desire, of which Pushkin was himself complaining:

> *I've lived to bury my desires,*
> *And seen my dreams corrode with rust;*
> *Now all that's left are fruitless fires*
> *That burn my empty heart to dust.*
>
> *Struck by the storms of cruel Fate*
> *My crown of summer bloom is sere;*
> *Alone and sad I watch and wait,*
> *And wonder if the end is near.*
>
> *As conquered by the last cold air,*
> *When winter whistles in the wind,*
> *Alone upon a branch that's bare*
> *A trembling leaf is left behind.*
>
> (Translated by MAURICE BARING)

Evgenyi is a dilettante, brought up in foreign ways. He knows French perfectly, dresses like a London dandy, is learned enough to chat wittily about Juvenal, to write *vale* at the end of a letter, to quote a couple of verses from *The Aeneid* with only a few mistakes, and to recall spicy anecdotes of history from the times of Romulus to the present. The society he moves in thinks him brilliant but a bit pedantic. His rooms are decorated with a picture of Byron and a bust of Napoleon and are filled "with all that London and Paris ship to Russia across the Baltic in exchange for land and lumber: amber, porcelain, bronze, perfume in cut glass, combs, nail files, scissors, brushes of thirty different varieties." His one interest in life is the "science of the tender passion which Ovid sang," and in that science he has, through practice and a natural gift, achieved something like perfection. No woman can resist his charms. From innocent girls to experienced coquettes, he can seduce them all, and such is his mastery that even the men he deceives remain his friends. This Europeanized product of the Russian beau monde, this parody of Byron, comes in contact with two other embodiments of Romanticism. One of them is Lensky, just returned from studying in Germany, his mind steeped in Kant and Schiller, an idealistic, poetic soul who loves as men no longer love, "as only a poet can still love, pursued by one and only one thought always, which neither distance, nor years, nor work can dispel." Onegin thinks him a fool, provokes him to a duel through sheer irritation, and kills him out of secret envy for the very qualities which he ridicules. The other Romantic is the lonely and dreamy Tatiana, who reads Richardson and Rousseau and believes their lies because they express what she feels or wants to feel. But whatever she may read, Tatiana does not borrow her emotions from anyone. She remains entirely herself, a stranger even in her own home, among people whose ways of feeling are different from hers: a mother whose heart had once been set on a "Grandison" of her fancy but had grown used to the man she married for convenience; an easygoing father, content with his wife's habit of affection; a younger sister whose attachments are so slight that within a year after his death she can forget the man she loved and marry another. These people speak a language Tatiana does not understand. Her real companion is her old peasant nurse, who has the earthy sympathies of humble, undemanding creatures and whose mind is nourished on the human depths of superstition. Onegin murders Lensky and kills all possibility of happiness for Tatiana. She comes out, of course, morally triumphant. But it is a cold triumph, which has been won at disproportionate sacrifice. Here is Pushkin's implicit answer to the classical heroes of French tragedy. Tatiana's nobility is not compensation for what she has been made to suffer and to lose. The tragedy of the poem—and it is a tragedy in spite of its seeming lightness and the subdued tones with which it paints emotional conflicts—is neither that Lensky is killed nor that Onegin ends up with as empty a soul as ever, but that Tatiana's unaffected, concentrated strength is misunderstood and dissipated in an artificial world. Pushkin's best-known, and in some ways greatest, work is, then, a critical epic of romanticism, which damns the Byronic as perniciously shallow, the Schilleresque as sentimental, but defends that primitivism which is the basis of Rousseau's philosophy. Only here, Pushkin seems to be saying, can the individual find a measure of freedom. Tatiana alone is free, because her simplicity makes her strong enough to remain herself. It is not from anything external, neither from liberal ideas—Evgenyi had actually begun to institute reforms on his estate—nor from a partly theoretic emotionalism like Lensky's, that a man can throw off constraints, but only through an unpretentious acceptance of his plain humanity. Pushkin is realist enough to understand the power of ideas in actual living, to see human beings in both their physical and their mental environment, and so to give, in what is ostensibly a somewhat trite love story, a view of people that yields to no one in penetration and an analysis of his epoch that is no less profound for being presented as a simple drama of individuals' emotions.

It was not, of course, study of Rousseau that led Pushkin to advocate the primitive. His own experience convinced him that human nature is made free when it is given a chance to be simple. He himself was always pained by the constraints of society, was charmed by the liberty of rural seclusion and of the Caucasus, and, finally, was enchanted by his discovery of Russian folklore. It was shortly after he had begun to work on *Evgenyi Onegin* that he was banished to his father's estate, Mihailovskoe, in the province of Pskov, where he stayed, in comparative seclusion, between 1824 and 1826. Arina Rodionovna, his old nurse, who has become famous in the history of Russian literature, was there. Pushkin, already familiar with folk tales from collections that were becoming popular at the time, heard more of them from Arina Rodionovna, who was a gifted *skazitelnitza,* and got from her what he had not had before—the characteristic sound and tone of folk speech. He listened to her many hours, writing down some of the things she told. It was probably her he drew in Tatiana's nurse; and it is under her influence that in 1828 he wrote the prologue to *Ruslan and Ludmila,* eight years after the completion of the poem itself. The difference between this prologue, with its brooding sense of wonder, and the sharp, gay poem shows how much Pushkin's work gained in depth from knowledge of folk legend. He did no more with folklore for a while; his wonderful fairy tales were written six or seven years after his evenings with Arina Rodionovna. He described the effect of primitivism before he reproduced it, and allowed the cadences of folk speech and the ways of folk thought to sink deep into his consciousness before he dealt with them directly.

While he listened to his old nurse, he was more actively engaged not only on *Evgenyi Onegin* but also on a study of Shakespeare, of history, and of various foreign literatures. The lyrics of this time include translations and adaptations from *Orlando Furioso, The Song of Songs,* the *Koran;* and he now wrote *Boris Godunov* as an exercise in Shakespearean drama; *Graf Nulin,* a facetious tale inspired by Shakespeare's *Lucrece,* in which ordinary provincial people parody the historic episode, to show, Pushkin said, that "had Lucrece slapped Tarquin's face instead of yielding to him the course of history would have been changed"; and *The Gypsies.* His historical studies he used later in *A History of Peter the Great* and *A History of the Pugachev Rebellion.* But apart from the direct use he made of his studies, his widening knowledge lends his work a sage perspective just as his sense of the primitive gives it greater emotional depth. *The Gypsies* must be classed with his Caucasian narratives. Here Aleko, another bored wanderer from civilization, like the prisoner of the Caucasus, is taken into a tribe of gypsies, loves one of their girls and is loved by her, but murders both her and her lover when she proves unfaithful to him. He has not been able to understand her old father's explanation of the gypsies' unrestrained and open life, their view that love can be neither commanded nor curbed. "She loves another," the old man tells him, "let her go," and, after the murder, orders him to leave. "You want power only for yourself," he says, "you have no idea of freedom; you are not one of us." The egotistic, corrupt man of civilization is really incapable and unworthy of liberty. Like the prisoner of the Caucasus, like Evgenyi Onegin, Aleko goes back to his miserably artificial life, a perpetual wanderer, trying in vain to find happiness outside himself.

The Gypsies was written the year before the Decembrist uprising of 1825, and although it cannot be taken as a satisfactory explanation of Pushkin's ambiguous position in this revolt, it can, perhaps, provide something of a clue. That Pushkin, with his liberal views and his loyalty, should have failed his friends at the critical moment, starting out to join them and then turning back—the story went, because of evil omens, a priest meeting him and a hare crossing his path—has puzzled his biographers. After the revolt he continued to correspond with those of his friends who had been exiled to Siberia and, when he was officially questioned, declared unequivocally that had he been in Petersburg on December 15, he would have stood with the rebels; and yet the fact remains that he burned incriminating papers in his possession and soon accepted the Czar's patronage. Whether he had been really frightened, or whether he could not have taken part, since, after all, although he had many friends among their members, he was never admitted to any revolutionary group, or whether he thought he could serve the cause best by not being actively involved in it—his narrative poems, as well as various notes, indicate how little store he set by formal means to social improvement. He lived at a time of disillusionment with the French Revolution, when hopes for democracy in Europe remained unfulfilled and in America were suppressed by a new kind of tyranny:

Everything noble, disinterested [Pushkin wrote], everything that elevates the soul of man is crushed by pitiless egoism and passion for comfort . . . negro slaves in the midst of education and freedom; pursuit of genealogies by people who have no aristocracy; among electors greed and envy, among employers timidity and servility; talent, through respect for equality forced into self-imposed ostracism; the rich man on the street wearing a ragged coat so as not to offend arrogant poverty which he secretly despises; such is the picture of the United States recently placed before us.

Real freedom, the kind that mattered, was to be won only by an individual for himself.

That, of course, was by no means the whole story; and as time went on Pushkin became more and more entangled in a mesh of hypocrisy, unfulfilled promises, and intrigue that made even honesty with oneself extremely difficult. After the revolt, in 1826, the new Czar invited him back to Petersburg with cordial promises of liberty. Pushkin was grateful and elated. The Czar had proved generous and understanding. He could appreciate poetic merit; he would allow the poet to come and go; he saved him from oppressive loneliness. Pushkin compared him to Peter the Great and called on him, in several lyrics, to follow his glorious predecessor in pardoning his enemies. But he soon discovered that the Czar's patronage was another form of imprisonment. His work was subject to stupid censorship, and he could not move without the permission of the chief of police. He wanted to join the army in the war with Turkey and was denied; he requested to go abroad and was refused. His difficulties with the government were complicated by the tragedy of his marriage, in 1831, to a beautiful, frivolous young girl who forced him into the affected court life which he hated and finally involved him in a scandalous intrigue that culminated in the duel in which he was killed on February 10, 1837.

After 1825 a sinister note enters Pushkin's writing. The work continues to be graceful, witty, exquisite as ever, but the themes are darker. Between 1830 and 1834 Pushkin wrote, among other things, three apparently very different pieces: a farcical narrative in verse, *The Little House in Kolomna,* a tragic poem, *The Bronze Horseman,* and a prose tale, *The Queen of Spades,* which, in spite of their differences, have always been classed together, because of their common setting, as the "Petersburg Tales." But they are linked by something more than their city background and are all derived from a common source, as was brilliantly shown in an essay of 1917 by Vladimir Khodasevich. The original story Pushkin himself, one evening in 1829 in the home of Karamzin, told to a group of friends and permitted one of them to publish under his own name. This story is of how the devil, pretending to be the friend of a young man, gains power over his fiancée, causes her death and the death of her mother, and so drives the young man insane. In the humorous *The Little House in Kolomna* an old lady hires a cook who, to the dismay of the lady's sweet young daughter, turns out to be a man in disguise. He is discovered one Sunday morning sitting before his mirror, shaving; and he takes to his heels, the story ending no more tragically than that. *The Bronze Horseman* is about a flood that wipes out the home and family of the girl whom a poor clerk loves and is about to marry. The clerk goes mad. And in *The Queen of Spades* an insignificant army officer is given by the ghost of an old woman, whom he had literally frightened to death in an attempt to wrest it from her, the secret of her lucky play at cards. But the secret he gets is false; it makes him lose a fortune instead of gaining one. And he, too, goes mad. Certain details of narrative and description show that these stories derive, without question, from the original tale of 1829; but, as Khodasevich points out, they are held together by something more than these details. All three have to do with "little, ordinary people" who are deprived of life by "unknown, unexpected, hostile powers." Their common theme is man's struggle with these unknown and hostile forces, which lie beyond the range of his control. In one of them only is the solution comic, and in one of them only is the initiative of the struggle taken not by the dark powers but by man. The original story ends with the question: "And why is it that devils want to get mixed up in human affairs, when nobody asks them?" And this question is applicable to all the tales but one. Only in *The Queen of Spades* are the forces of evil roused by man; in the other stories demons enter human lives without provocation. A lyric written in 1830 gives the simplest image of the experience of terror implicit in all these works. It is called *Demons,* and it pictures a night of racing clouds, with whirls of snow lighted by a tiny moon. The tinkle of the sleigh bell is muffled; the horses can hardly move; the way is lost. The driver cannot see. "What must we do?" he asks. "The devil leads us, the devil spins us round about. He is playing; blowing, spitting on me." The horses stop, the bell is silent, the tempest sobs and rages. And all at once the horses race again, through swirling, squealing demons, thick as leaves on a November day. The heart is rent by their piteous moaning. In the original version of the Petersburg Tales there was also an episode of a mysterious drive through the night, at the end of which, when the coachman turns to him, the passenger finds himself confronting a death's-head. Another prose tale of this period, called *The Snow Storm,* although it ends happily, uses again the image of people driven through hostile darkness and lost in it. Two other stories must be added to these eerie ones, that of Don Juan's last hours, *The Stone Guest,* and its humorous prose duplicate, *The Coffin Maker,* in which dead men also rise from graves to confute the one who has summoned them. But although fear of mysterious evil is implicit in all these works, they are not gruesome and creepy like even the best Gothic tales. Their tone is light, as in the farcical *The Little House in Kolomna,* which begins with a long, playful disquisition on the use of words and the language of poetry, and as in *The Coffin Maker,* which makes fun of ghostly things; or it is matter-of-fact, almost sedate, as that of *The Queen of Spades;* or it is a mixture of the ominous and the joking, as in *The Stone Guest.* Only *The Bronze Horseman* is tragic, but its restrained majesty makes one feel not so much the horror of an accident as the severity of Fate itself.

In such compositions as these Pushkin wrote down his despair. In others he dramatized his hatreds: greed in *The Covetous Knight,* envy, not only in the Lensky episode of *Evgenyi Onegin,* but also in *Mozart and Salieri,* which, with its drama of a genius poisoned by a limited academician who with enough understanding to know the greatness of the man he kills is not sufficiently high-minded to surmount his hurt vanity, is a symbolic intimation of Pushkin's own fate. Even of the fairy tales which he now wrote, two—*Snow White* and *Czar Saltan*—are stories of envy;

two others—*The Tale of the Pope and of his Workman Balda* and *The Tale of the Fisherman and the Fish*—are tales of greed; and one—*The Tale of the Golden Cockerel,* which has a siren theme—is the counterpart of the unfinished *Russalka,* in which the enchantress strain that had been heard already in *The Prisoner of the Caucasus* sounds more ominous and deeper. Incidentally, it is perhaps a sign of Pushkin's generosity that when he dealt with envy, from which he himself had had to endure so much, he saw it best in the humorous wisdom of folklore. Otherwise he could be scarcely bothered with it. His happy, openhearted Mozart is more convincing than Salieri, and in *Evgenyi Onegin* the theme of envy is only implied.

The intellectually rough and impatient Belinsky considered Pushkin greater as a poet than as a thinker. Enchanted, of course, by the technical perfection of his work, he missed its subtlety and naturally, therefore, saw nothing of its depth. It is true that Pushkin's beauty, loveliness, grandeur, and diversity exhaust one's store of praise—

He is one of the few writers [says Edmund Wilson, in the essay from which I have already quoted] who never seem to fall—from the point where he has outgrown his early models—into formulas of expression. He finds a special shape and a special style for every successive subject; and, even without looking for the moment at his dramatic and narrative poems, one is amazed at the variety of his range. You have lyrics in regular quatrains that are as pointed and spare as Greek epigrams or as forceful and repercussive as the *Concord Hymn,* and you have lyrics in broken accents: soliloquies that rise out of sleep or trail off in unspoken longings—where the modulated meter follows the thought; you have the balladry and jingling of folk-songs, and you have set-pieces like *To a Noble* (in the meter and rhyme-scheme of Boileau's epistles) of a rhetorical solidity and brilliance that equals anything in Pope or the Romans; you have airy little ribaldries like the *Tsar Nikita,* informal discursive poems like *Autumn* that are like going to visit Pushkin for a week-end in the country, and forgings of fierce energetic language, now metallic and malleable, now molten and flowing like *The Upas Tree* and *The Prophet.* You have, finally, dramatic lyrics like *The Fiends* and *Winter Evening,* for which it is hard to find phrases or comparisons because they are as purely and intensely Pushkin as *Furi et Aureli, comites Catulli*—is purely and intensely Catullus or *Sweeney among the Nightingales* Eliot.

It is not, of course, a good ear and a clever pen alone that can account for so much variousness and splendor and so much grace—but also, and primarily, the timbre of a mind that ear and pen have caught. If ever a poet was born, not made, that poet was Pushkin; and although it might be wrong to say that he lived in order to write, to think of him living and not writing would be as preposterous as to imagine our world without changes of seasons or without alternations of day and night. He always wrote. Like Pope, he "lisped in numbers, for the numbers came," and from the beginning he wrote perfectly. He began with what most writers take years to acquire, a flawless sense of form, and this he developed into the astonishing plasticity of which Mr. Wilson speaks. The apparent effortlessness with which he gives us an infinity of thoughts and moods is, of course, the deceptive simplicity of very great art. But for Pushkin this was not only a matter of acquired skill, but an expression of his very mode of experiencing life. The words he uses are more than strokes to paint flat images, but the musical score, as well, of what the pictures mean; they imitate not sounds actually heard, but the imagined harmony of moods and thoughts, and, for this reason, are not onomatopoetic, except in a figurative sense. In the prologue to *The Bronze Horseman*, for example, the full vowels and quiet consonants of the opening lines—

> *Na beregú, pustínnikh vóln*
> *Stoyál ón dúm velíkih póln,*
> *I vdál glyadél,*

—which suggest the largeness of Peter's meditations as he stands on the desert shore of the Neva, presently change with the description of the city he created—

> *Liublú tebá, Petrá tvorénye;*
> *Liublú tvóyi strógyi, stróyniyi víd,*
> *Neví derzhávoye techéniye,*
> *Berégovóyi yeá granít,*

—to stern, perpendicular *r*s, with little vowels rippling in and out of them, like the sinuous river splashing softly between its granite banks. Only direct experience of an initial unity of words and their objects can create such deep and subtle effects.

Khodasevich has remarked that Pushkin was born sage and remained the youngest of all Russians. Had he lived to be a hundred he would have been young still; and had he died ten years before he did, we would even so have known him wise. What one gets in all his work is a young man's joy and boldness, all things freshly seen and eagerly lived, but—and this is his uniqueness—always perfectly controlled. Pushkin is never chaotic. His poetry has that impersonal quality which comes not of indifference but of passion, of which T. S. Eliot speaks in discussing the nature of poets as those who have "personality and emotions" and so know "what it means to want to escape from these things." This it is that makes for the atmosphere of epic poise in which his turbulent themes unfold. There is nothing resigned in Pushkin's view of life, but in his work, with all that is mysterious and evil in it, there is serenity. And this sense of chaos in the framework of limitless peace, which takes account of all that is human but which nothing human can disturb, is like the peace of *The Iliad,* where alone perhaps one gets a similar effect of calm. This is realism of the deepest kind, a perfect example of that Spirit of Comedy which Meredith saw as presiding over art. With Pushkin it comes of mastery that, based upon love of life itself, not on a program for living, can give each thing its due—what D. H. Lawrence once called "the aristocratic principle," a respectful attitude for the independence of all creatures and an appreciation of that which makes each of them a being apart. That is why, like Homer's Ajax and Achilles, Pushkin's Mozart, Onegin, and Tatiana are individuals who establish types. They are not abstractions, but they have the stuff of myth in them. The strict and difficult Epicureanism by which Pushkin lived, with its assuredness that each individual thing and every separate moment has its own reality, was thoroughly undogmatic. Theories in themselves did not interest him, but he could see them exemplified in people's lives, as he did, for example, with Tatiana, who might have been suggested by Rousseau but is by no means a symbol of his philosophy.

As is true of all great artists, Pushkin has no fellow, but there is something in him of Shakespeare and of Chaucer. In common with Shakespeare, he reveres humanity and, through an inborn sympathy with native ways, like Shakespeare, he is a nationalist poet, the difference between them being that Pushkin's nationalism had to take into account a population three-fourths slave; that whereas Shakespeare could joke and play with the people he felt with and wrote about, Pushkin, who never spoke to them directly, could show his understanding of them only by retelling their legends. The measure of his appreciation is the beauty with which he performs this task. With Chaucer he has in common a laughing delight in the world. In point of subtle humor that all but spills over into satire, in sharp detail, in Renaissance humanism, *Troilus and Criseyde,* the first English novel, might be compared, as Professor Ernest Simmons suggests in his biography of Pushkin, to *Evgenyi Onegin,* the first Russian novel. They are different, above all, because their ages are different, Chaucer writing at a time when most assumptions at the root of human behavior were taken for granted, Pushkin when the most elementary problems of life were in question. It was all right for Chaucer to play sophistically with individuals' emotions according to the rules prescribed by the Court of Love, because both he and his audience shared certain assumptions about them; but Pushkin's generation was trying to reassert and reappraise the value of man's affections after a long period of rationalism that had all but denied their existence. And so, whereas Chaucer could use sentiments as counters in an elaborate game, Pushkin had to be fairly serious about them when their value was in question. He made game of situations in which emotions were involved, but feelings themselves he accepted as real, simple, and important. There is also, one suspects, a greater innate restlessness in the Russian author than in the comparatively placid Englishman. *Evgenyi Onegin* is more critical and revolutionary than *Troilus and Criseyde*. And it is tempting to see them as patterns on which the two literatures were to shape themselves, the English chiefly affirmative and comfortable, the Russian rebellious in the main and only now and then falling into quiescence. But such fancies must not be pressed too far.

Pushkin, at any rate, is a poet of division, whose work reconciles conflicts raised by a civilization changing from formalized eighteenth-century modes of life and thought to the nascent individualism of the early nineteenth century. It is as the poet of a world wavering between democracy and tyranny that he thinks in terms of such conflicts as inner and outward freedom, the ego's desires and the community's demands, insubordination and obedience, restraint and liberty, simplicity and artifice, primitivism and civilization; and it is as a man of great intensity and one for whom aesthetic values matter as much as anything on earth that he must create order without diluting passion and reconcile romantic feeling with classical restraint.

Because he cares genuinely for things and people outside himself, Pushkin is always adequate to the subject he treats. There is discrimination and appropriateness in what he does. He is melancholy without whining, appreciative without rhetoric, tender without sentimentality, angry without loss of reason. And his clear-eyed view of life makes him modest. No more than the significance of feelings does he exaggerate the importance of situations. He sees them all in relation to an implicit standard whereby each event may be variously judged. It is as if he were a mathematician using the same terms to work out different equations. Thus he will show you the power of evil lodged in the hideous ghost of a greedy old woman or appearing in the guise of a harmless, masquerading cook; the dead rising to drag to hell the most enchanting seducer of all legend or to frighten in a dream a silly man who has got drunk at a party; envy murdering a genius or confounding a vain, fairy-tale beauty—and so on. Neither evil, nor mystery, nor human baseness can be formulated in any one way or be seen in any one mood. The Russian critic Zhirmunsky has pointed to Pushkin's unusually frequent and very splendid use of oxymoron—such expressions as "bitter kisses," "distant fatherland," which Pushkin loves not for their epigrammatic wit but as a means of emphasizing emotional complexity. This is the method of one for whom contradiction is at the root of thought, who sees life always as shadowed by death, feeling on the verge of extinction, strength limited to experience of sense. It is the quality that makes for that detachment of which I have already spoken, the balanced analysis and the intimation of mystery—as if life were painted on a screen of the Ununderstood. With Shakespeare one also gets this pervasive suggestion of "the behind and the beyond," but more explicitly than with Pushkin; and this makes Shakespeare's work fundamentally tragic but Pushkin's comic. Shakespeare's tragedies are presented as symbols of life's deficiencies in a scheme of the ideal that makes them exceptions, but Pushkin's seem to give the norm rather than the exception. An aloof and comic sadness comes of this, not passionate despair. And with it goes a hunger for elemental processes, a leaning toward a wordless and uncharted truth—of the kind which, with another emphasis, will appear later in Tolstoy. Such, then, is Pushkin's realism, not a literal-minded transcript of concrete objects and actual events, but an imaginative use of them as symbols of what they mean to a mature contemplativeness.

CHAPTER V

Nikolay Vasilievich Gogol

1809–52

PUSHKIN'S ABILITY TO CARE INTENSELY FOR EXPERIENCE, the tacit assumption of all he did and thought that the immediate is all-important, that—to use terms of which he himself would never have been guilty—universals are deductions from concrete instances and not the other way round, is the artist's assumption *par excellence*. It is the attitude which Pater was to formulate, but not exemplify, in his doctrinaire prescription for undogmatic living, and which Santayana has described with greater scope and depth. As distinguished from ethical, pragmatic, or theological positions, it might be called "aesthetic." And if it is thoroughgoing it must also be realistic, as was the case with Pushkin. But Pushkin's attitude is extremely rare. The writers who followed him are realists of another kind.

Gogol, for example, seems to be as unlike Pushkin as it is possible for a writer to be: in temperament, in the circumstances of his life, in artistic method, in intellectual direction. Yet they have certain qualities in common, and it was to Pushkin that Gogol looked for guidance. It was he who gave him the themes for his greatest works, *The Inspector General* and *Dead Souls;* it was he, Gogol said, who alone understood him fully; and when he died, Gogol felt lost. He had never written a line, he said, without having him before his eyes, without asking himself what Pushkin might say. The poet's judgment and advice alone mattered to him. And yet, close though they were to one another, and though Gogol was only ten years younger than Pushkin, a century seems to separate them. Intellectually, Pushkin belongs to the eighteenth century, Gogol to the nineteenth.

Both the atmosphere in which Gogol grew up and his own emotional predisposition inclined him to romantic and idealistic modes of thought that were becoming popular in the early nineteenth century. Brought up in the easygoing, semireligious household of a comfortable, dilettante landed proprietor of the Ukraine and in an equally easygoing school, Gogol had, to begin with, nothing of Pushkin's training in the rigorous, clearheaded intellectualism of eighteenth-century French thought. So that when, as a young man, he came in contact with German idealism, he was not equipped to examine it critically as Pushkin had done. Besides, his nature made him more at home in ways of thinking that emphasized sentiment rather than clearheadedness. From the first he showed himself a highly emotional but repressed being. In school he displayed an extraordinary gift for acting and mimicry with which he entertained his classmates, but they nicknamed him, just the same, "the mysterious dwarf." Later on his secretive soul, the buried intensity of his nature, must have found release in philosophies that gave sanction to an imaginative riot of sentiments. All his work was marked by the exaggerated rhetoric of frustrated passion and the bitterness of disillusioned idealism.

He was not so sure of his vocation as Pushkin had always been. At the start he did not know what he would do with himself. His lifework would be important, he was convinced, and would bring him fame, but he thought that government service might be his way to glory. Directly he finished school, in 1828, he went to Petersburg to make his fortune. His father had died three years earlier, and he took his responsibilities as head of the family very seriously. He was nineteen and his hopes were vague but high. They were dashed immediately. The city was more expensive than he had imagined. He had to live in a squalid part of town, and even to spend a whole winter in his summer overcoat. He failed to get a job either in the theater or in government service. And his first piece of writing, a romantic idyl which he published at his own expense, was ridiculed; he bought up all copies and burned them. He was not discouraged. "If one fails in one thing, one can try another, and then another—then a third, and so on. The smallest bit sometimes helps a great deal," he wrote, a trifle sententiously, to his mother; but the disappointment to his sheltered, ambitious, secretly chaotic self was probably deeper than he knew. His next plan was to write up some of the folk tales of the Ukraine, since people in Petersburg were interested in that part of the country. He asked his mother to collect stories for him, and while she was busy at it, he himself decided on a trip abroad. The history of that trip is psychologically revealing. He thought he might go to America, but he got only as far as Hamburg and then returned again to Petersburg. Years later, in his *Confession,* he wrote of this abortive trip as follows:

I have never felt attraction and passion for foreign lands. Nor have I ever had that vague curiosity which often devours young men who are avid for impressions. But, strangely enough, even in childhood, even during my school days, even at the time I thought only of government service and not of writing, it always seemed to me that in my life there was to be some great self-sacrifice and that, precisely for the sake of my country, I should have to be educated somewhere away from her. I knew neither how this was to be, nor why it had to be; I didn't dwell on the idea, but I saw myself so vividly in some foreign country longing for my fatherland, this image so often pursued me, that it made me sad . . . Whatever the reason, I hadn't been in Petersburg five months, when I went aboard a ship, unable to resist the feeling which I myself couldn't understand. The plan and goal of my journey were entirely unclear. All I knew was that I would not at all enjoy foreign lands, but would endure them rather, as if I foresaw that I should come to know the value of Russia at a distance from Russia, and learn to love her away from her. Scarcely had I found myself at sea, on a strange boat, among strange people (it was an English ship, and there was not a Russian on board), than I became gloomy; I regretted so much the friends and comrades of my childhood, whom I had left and whom I had always loved, that even before I landed, I had made plans to return. I spent three days only on foreign soil, and despite the fact that the novelty of things began to interest me, I hastened to return on the same boat, fearing that otherwise I might not have a chance to get back.

This account may, of course, have been somewhat falsified in the light of subsequent events; but what it shows of fear, of masochism and self-pity, of helplessness before mysterious and overwhelming forces, is the root of Gogol's nature, a distressed uncertainty about himself, a dread of loneliness, an imperative need for protection and, with it, pathetic awareness that he must always live in isolation. All his life he found it difficult to come to terms with the world; he could not be at home with people and with ordinary facts of life; he hated them because they demolished his dreams; and he had to struggle to maintain his integrity in an apparently hostile land among people who seemed always foreign. Pretending to be like everybody else, he was in reality a ghost who wandered out of his own world into that other one in which people moved and which was strange to him. It was a mad, uneasy life. He gave way under it, but before he succumbed to mental illness he felt and saw such monstrous truths as men of less troubled vision must do without. The dark splendor of his work depends on this.

When he returned from his futile voyage he published a few essays, got work teaching history in a school and tutoring in private families, made some important literary friendships, notably with Zhukovsky and Pushkin, and set to work on the Ukrainian stories which his mother had collected. He published them in 1831, *Evenings on a Farm near Dikanka,* and was immediately recognized as an important author. It was at just this time that Pushkin was writing his fairy tales. And there is probably nothing that shows better the difference between him and Gogol than their treatment of folk themes. Pushkin loved in them their purity and calm, the wisdom which in simple humility accepts the inexplicable and resolves experience in the symbol of the wonderful and fabulous. Gogol saw turbulence in them, all that is distressingly uncanny. His tales are filled with gruesome incidents; devils and witches figure in them prominently. The feeling of terror is as deep as Pushkin's calm. They are chaotic and dark, not unlike Poe's stories, and, like Poe's, consciously poetic. Much in them also is humorous, but the humor too is boisterous. It is not, as with Pushkin, the smile of sharp wit and subtle understanding, but an easy, rough, sardonic playfulness, which reminds one sometimes of Dickens, as, for example, the comment on the gypsy in *The Fair at Sorochinsk:* "with but a glance at him, a man would readily admit that in that splendid soul seethed qualities of great magnificence for which, however, there is but one reward on earth—the gallows"; or bits of ludicrous whimsy, such as that at the end of *St. John's Eve,* when the roast lamb, really the devil, lifts up its head, moves its whiskers significantly at the tavern company who are prepared to eat him, and looks as if he might ask for vodka; or quietly amused accounts of people's speech and actions. It was this in the stories that Pushkin, to whom Gogol would read them, specially enjoyed. He listened to them and roared with laughter.

There is probably nothing else in the world's literature to compare with this book. The narrative method is a remarkable combination of colloquial ease and rhetorical lyricism. Passages in it, of which it is difficult to render the luxuriance and the music, are unexcelled in Russian prose. The one, for example, with which *The Fair at Sorochinsk* begins:

> How intoxicating, how magnificent a summer day in Little Russia! How languishingly warm those hours when noonday shines in quiet and in heat, and the blue, unfathomable ocean, a cupola voluptuously bending to the earth, seems sleeping, sunk in languor, holding the beauty encircled close in his ethereal embrace. No cloud upon it; no sound in the plain. It is as if all things had died; only above, in depths of heaven, quavers a lark and silver songs, along ethereal steps, fly down to the adoring earth; and now and then a gull's cry or quail's resounding note rings through the steppe. Lazy and unthinking, as if they wandered without aim, stand towering oaks, and blinding shots of the sun's rays set fire to whole masses of bright leaves, casting on others shadows black as night which only a strong wind may fleck with gold. The emerald, topaz, ruby of airy insects pour down on gorgeous kitchen gardens, which stately sunflowers shade. Gray haystacks and golden sheaves of corn camp in the plain and rove on its immensity. Bent with the weight of fruit are the broad branches of cherry, plum, apple and pear trees; the sky and its clear mirror, the river in green, proudly lifted frame . . . how full of languor and voluptuousness is summer in Little Russia!

Or that other famous one, about the Ukrainian night:

> Have you ever known a Ukrainian night? Oh, you do not know the Ukrainian night. Look into it: from the

sky's center the moon looks out; the boundless dome of heaven has given way, has stretched to greater boundlessness; it glows and breathes. All earth is in a silver light; and the wonderful air is sultry-cool and full of languor and stirs an ocean of sweet odours. O divine night! Enchanting night! Motionless, inspired, the woods stand, full of gloom, and cast enormous shadows. Still and quiet are the ponds, the cold and darkness of their waters grimly enclosed by gardens' dark-green walls. Virgin thickets of wild berries and cherries have timorously stretched their roots to the coldness of the spring and murmur in their leaves from time to time, as if angry and indignant, when the brave rascal, the night wind, stealing up suddenly, kisses them. The whole country-side now sleeps. But above it all is breathing; all is marvelous, all triumphant. And in one's soul there is immensity and wonder and crowds of silver visions rise straight within its depths. O divine night! Enchanting night! And suddenly all comes to life: the woods, the ponds, the steppes. Now there pours forth majestic thunder, the Ukrainian nightingale, and, it would seem, the moon itself has stopped to listen in the midst of heaven. As if enchanted the hamlet on the upland sleeps. Even more white, more fair in the moonlight shine clumps of huts; even more dazzling their low walls, cut out of darkness. The songs have ceased. All is still. God-fearing people are asleep. Few and far between, a light in narrow windows. And only here and there before the threshold of some cottage, belatedly, a family is ending its late supper.

Constance Garnett's version of these lines is somewhat too literal; mine is too stilted. Neither conveys the gorgeousness, the lush, sonorous quality, and the subtly delicate rhythm of the original. The music of such passages is the ground swell stirred up by all the distant, suppressed tenderness of Gogol's nature. Pushkin's descriptions of even quiet scenes are given by means of active verbs in subdued tones that restrain and counteract their movement. His pictures are alive within unstirring cadences. Of Gogol the opposite is true. His paintings are static, but the solid details of which they are composed seem blown to action by the restless notes in which they are sung. Incidents, aspects of life are tangible, ordinary, and concrete; but behind them is the motion and the music of the unattainable. And now and then one comes upon lyric lines of infinite sadness:

Clamour, laughter, songs grew quiet and more quiet. The bowing died away, grown weaker, its wavering notes lost in the empty air. Stamping somewhere could still be heard, somewhat like the murmur of a distant sea, and soon all became empty and mute.

In such a way, does not happiness, beautiful and inconstant guest, fly from us, and a solitary sound thinks in vain to express mirth? In its own echo it hears already sorrow and empty waste, and hearkens to it wildly. In such a way, do not the lively friends of one's stormy and free youth, one by one, one after the other, lose themselves throughout the world, and leave alone, at last, their one-time brother? Dreary is it for the one who remains! Heavy grows the heart and sad, and nothing can give it help!

—as if from some flat shore Gogol suddenly looked on himself, or as if he had been startled from a dream into the dreariness of his real life.

Yet this first book was as objective as anything Gogol wrote subsequently. His own nature comes out in it in his tone of voice and in occasional subjective interpolations; but, on the whole, he is here given over quite completely to material that is not of his own creation. Hereafter he was to be inventor and creator, not instrument or medium, becoming increasingly conscious of his experience as usable stuff for art, and of his world as a source of adequate illustration for what he lived through. His compositions were of three kinds: tales based on folk legends, historic tales, and those that purport to deal with everyday life. To the first belongs, beside the *Evenings on a Farm near Dikanka*, the vampire tale *Viy;* to the second, *Taras Bulba;* to the third, such stories as *The Portrait, The Nose, Old-World Landowners, The Tale of How Ivan Ivanovich Quarreled with Ivan Nikiforovich, The Cloak, The Inspector General,* and *Dead Souls*. And, paradoxically, it is the most fantastic of Gogol's work that must be considered the most "real."

For example, *Viy,* the story of a vampire witch who lures and kills, in frightful fashion, a young student of theology, is not, as Gogol announced, exactly the story he had heard from Ukrainian peasants. He adds episodes to it and changes the originally happy ending to a tragic one. Nor could any unsophisticated teller give the complex depths of apprehension one finds here. The voluptuous, uncanny witch's gallop over the land at night, the mounting terror of the three nights' vigil over the corpse in the bare and lonely chapel, have an oppressive meaning that is Gogol's own. The folk tale had an echo for Gogol of something

intimate and obscure that he himself had lived, and he used
it as a symbol for his experience of powerlessness and guilt
and of his fear that in the struggle between the good and
the bad in him the bad would triumph. It is for this reason one of the world's deep, poetic tales, concerned with
the quality itself of horror and extreme anxiety in the way
Wuthering Heights is concerned with the quality itself
of passion. These works are abstracts of feeling, of which
actual events might be the visible samples. They are fantastic inasmuch as they do not deal with people and situations one usually encounters, but they are profoundly real
in their imaginative grasp of the very structure of emotion.

Viy belongs obviously to the literature of mystery. But
Gogol was master of another kind of story that on the face
of it seems humorous and ordinary and only by implica-
tion shows itself also to be a tale of horror. Such, for example, is the brief sketch called *The Carriage*. A bleak provincial town is enlivened by the arrival of a regiment which
is quartered there. The general one day gives a sumptuous
dinner to which he invites, among others, one of the pil-
lars of the town's society, a rich merchant and successful
politician, who for some mysterious reason had at one time
been cashiered from the army. The merchant stays at the
party longer than he had intended, drinks a good deal, and
in his expansive mood invites the general and a number
of his officers to dinner, so they may see an expensive carriage he has recently bought. But at noon the next day,
when the guests arrive, he is still sleeping off his drunkenness. Nothing, of course, has been said or done about dinner. He tells his wife to hide, leaves orders to the servants
to announce that he has left for the day, and crouches in
the carriage, where no one can see him. The guests are

nonplused and angry. They prepare to turn back, but decide to take a look at the vehicle before they go. "So— you're there!" says the general, opening the door. And leaves. A droll little episode—but sardonic at bottom, a tale of weakness tracked to its lair. In *Viy* Gogol found a symbol to express his terror of women, here, one to show his uneasiness at all that was sham and showy in his nature. So also *Nevsky Prospect,* a story of the different ways in which two friends, a shy, idealistic artist and a commonplace, pleasure-loving officer, pursue two girls who strike their fancy, the artist killing himself for love of his girl, although she turns out to be an ordinary prostitute, the other man getting away with no more than a thrashing for his chase of another's virtuous wife—is not only an ironic sketch of differences in men's intensity, of, on the one hand, the tragic passion and pain of unfulfillment, and, on the other, the ridiculous aspects of it, but also a dramatic poem on the importance of ideals no matter how far below them reality might fall, and on life's unfairness in serving human needs. These stories take place on city streets; the poetry of primitive legend has been replaced in them by observation of the ordinary. It is as if Gogol had determined to stop lying about his own unhappiness, as if he had decided to look upon it in terms of understandable experience and to treat what was unusual in it as fantastically absurd. The symbol of the fairy tale has yielded to the no less horrifying but more realistic nightmare of psychological illness, which Gogol schools himself to see in a humorous light. Partly on his own account, partly through Pushkin's influence, he develops his gift of ridicule.

The Nose is a fine instance of how he makes the weirdly humorous serve to represent the morbid. It has to do with the discomfiture of a government official who wakes up one morning to find his face a flat surface, the nose quite gone; and who then encounters his nose, arrayed in a splendid uniform, going about his business in the city and refusing absolutely to pay any attention to him. "There can be nothing in common between us," says the Nose in a lofty way when the noseless owner approaches him; "judging by the buttons on your uniform, you must be serving in another department." All ends well. The Nose in uniform escapes with a false passport, without creating any trouble, and the original one is retrieved and, with little difficulty, made to stay on the face where it belongs. Nor does anything drastic happen to the poor little barber who seems to have been responsible for the removal of the nose in the first place. But nothing is very clear in all this. It is all bewildering and very strange. What nonsense comes into the heads of authors, Gogol concludes. "There is neither rhyme nor reason, nor any benefit to the nation in the things they decide to scribble." And yet, "Say what you will, such events do occur in the world—rarely, but they do." This story, obviously a castration fantasy of a kind not uncommon in the humorous writing of the time, is, with Gogol, more than a simple joke. There is in it too strong a sense of the uncanny, too sharp a note of distress, which the comedy does not conceal. To Dostoevsky, who saw its deeper implications, it provided a clue for understanding pathological duality.

Dostoevsky was even more influenced by another of Gogol's stories. "We have all sprung from Gogol's *Cloak*," he said of Russian writers. This, one of the greatest short stories ever written, has to do with a government clerk whose very name, Akakyi Akakiyevich Baschmatchkin (the last name, from *bashmack*, "shoe," suggests someone who is stepped on or kicked around), is pathetically ridiculous. His business is to copy documents, and although he has worked in the same office for years, no one pays any attention to him, except to laugh at him. When he is given a new paper to copy no one says even so much to him as: "Write this out," or "Here's a little job for you." They simply stick the paper under his nose. Young clerks make fun of him. He never answers them until their teasing becomes unbearable and is in danger of interfering with his work; then he says, "Leave me alone, why are you bothering me?" And there is something so strange, something so pitiful in the tone of voice in which he utters this plea that one young man, new in the office, egged on by the others to torment him, stops short one day, and long afterward, in the midst of even his gayest moments, remembers the little clerk with the bald spot saying: "Leave me alone, why are you bothering me?" Akakyi Akakiyevich is completely absorbed in his work. His face is blissful as he traces his letters. Some of them are special favorites of his, and he chortles and winks and smacks his lips when he comes to them. Home, at night, he eats hurriedly, not noticing what he eats, and then proceeds to do a little more copying; then goes to bed, smiling at the thought that tomorrow will be another lovely day with copying to do. Akakyi Akakiyevich makes four hundred rubles a year. And in Petersburg those who make only four hundred rubles have a bitter enemy to contend with—the winter frost. Akakyi Akakiyevich finds one winter that his old, patched, unshapely overcoat, which the young clerks in the office call his "kimono," must be mended. He takes it to his tailor, who announces that nothing can be done with it: it is full of holes like a piece of canvas; impossible to sew on a patch. Akakyi Akakiyevich is overwhelmed. He must have a new cloak. And so he begins to save: he goes without food at night, without candles, and, to preserve shoe-leather, walks on tiptoe. Every month he consults the tailor; together they visit stores, choosing materials, discussing patterns. Life takes on a new interest for Akakyi Akakiyevich; it is as if he had got married, had chosen himself a companion for life. Finally the cloak is made. Akakyi Akakiyevich wears it to his office, smiling festively, and one of the clerks decides to give a party in its honor. So he has a chance to wear it again that evening. But on his way back from the party, when he is crossing a vast, dark square, he is set upon by thieves who rob him of his cloak. Distracted, disheveled, covered with snow, he reaches home; and next morning, on the advice of his landlady, goes to the commissioner of police. "He is asleep," they tell him, "come back at ten." At ten o'clock he is still asleep; at eleven he is not at home. Akakyi Akakiyevich addresses himself to a High and Mighty Personage, who keeps him waiting and then terrifies and humiliates him. As a result of all his running about, he comes down with a bad cold, grows feverish, delirious, and dies. For some time afterward a ghost wanders about Petersburg, terrifying its inhabitants, snatching away their cloaks, until he gets the High and Mighty Official's—after which he is pacified, and the city is quiet once more. And so here is another story of frustration, of the impossibility of a man's fulfilling the most elementary demands of his nature.

If the background of Pushkin's creations is a tacit appreciation of life itself that lends solidity to things, the background of Gogol's work is acute mental suffering that casts what is apparently light and commonplace in tragic shadow. If Pushkin's work resolves dualities, Gogol's presents them lyrically and dramatically. Gogol gives you on the one hand tales of fantasy or pathos, such as *The Nose* and *The Cloak;* then others of exalted rhetoric, such as *Taras Bulba,* a historic tale of Cossacks in the fifteenth century, fighting against the Poles and the Tartars on the lower reaches of the Dnieper. But just as the concrete details of *The Nose* and *The Cloak* are embroideries of states of misery, so the historic elements of *Taras Bulba* are only an occasion for grandiloquent romance. With both there is mystification. Gogol pretends, with the falsehood of a man who is always taking vengeance on a world he hates. Just as *The Nose* is implicitly a savage joke on ordinary life and *The Cloak* a condemnation of its cruelty, so *Taras Bulba* is a joke on history. There is no attempt in it at historic accuracy, although the episode is historic. It is an ecstatic lyric on the theme of heroism. For the details of history, like the actualities of life, were repulsive to Gogol, and he took joy in disregarding the one and in twisting the other. There was, of course, the arrogance of madness in all this, but there was also the genius of wild and absolutely original creativity. *Taras Bulba* is a romantic prose poem, and as such it is magnificent.

It is the imaginative result of Gogol's one unfortunate venture with the academic, his brief professorship in medieval history at the University of St. Petersburg, which Pushkin had obtained for him in 1834 and which he should never have accepted, for he neither knew enough nor had the disinterested curiosity and patience requisite for historical research. He began with brilliant, showy lectures, could not keep them up, resigned in 1835, and published

Mirgorod, which contains *Taras Bulba, Viy,* and two stories of a different kind—*Old-World Landowners* and *The Tale of How Ivan Ivanovich Quarreled with Ivan Nikiforovich. Old-World Landowners* is a sketch of a simple, hospitable old couple who live comfortably on their little piece of property and spend most of their time eating: coffee in the morning, followed by cakes and pies, vodka and a snack an hour before dinner, dinner at noon "with all kinds of appetizing dishes," fruit after a brief nap, dumplings a bit later, another snack before supper, bed directly after supper, and perhaps something to eat even in the course of the night. They are touchingly devoted to one another, these old people. Their love is a long habit of mutual solicitude. But presently the old lady dies. Her husband lets the property fall into disorder. Upon his death, a few years later, it is taken over by a modern absentee landlord who cares nothing about it, and everything goes to rack and ruin. It is a passing social order that Gogol presents here with amused affection but without hope. *The Tale of How Ivan Ivanovich Quarreled with Ivan Nikiforovich,* about two silly old friends who quarrel over the possession of a gun and spend their lives in litigation, is even more hopeless, though it is one of Gogol's funniest productions. At the end the narrator, disheartened by his visit to Mirgorod, where the two ancient men are still excitedly awaiting from day to day the verdict in their lawsuit, climbs into a cab to get away:

The scrawny horses, known in Mirgorod as "couriers" pulled on, their hoofs making an unpleasant sound as they sank into gray masses of mud. Rain poured in torrents on the Jew who, covered with a mat, sat up on the coach-box. Dampness chilled me through and through. The melancholy town-gates with the sentry-box in which an Invalid mended his gray accoutrements, ran past me slowly. Again the same field, dug up in places, black; in places turning green; wet daws and crows, monotonous rain, tearful, unbroken sky. It is dreary in this world, my masters!

Petty, laughable, wearisome, drab commonplace—such is the modern world to Gogol. For poetry and color it is to history or legend one must turn; in history resides the heroic, in legend the grandeur of the soul's experience.

Gogol's greatest works—which followed *Mirgorod*—*The Inspector General* and *Dead Souls,* masterpieces of comedy, one in dramatic the other in epic form, are more elaborate statements of this view of the world and more direct animadversions upon society. Up to the time he wrote them, Gogol tells in his *Author's Confession,* he had been laughing just to pull himself out of fits of depression which occurred frequently and which he could not explain. To distract himself he "would imagine all the humorous things that could be thought of . . . would invent funny characters and place them in the funniest situations." But now Pushkin made him see that he was "laughing to no purpose" and that if one laughed one had "better laugh hard at those things which should be laughed at generally." And so Gogol began to laugh at all about him which was an objective equivalent of what he hated in himself. The scene of *The Inspector General* is—like his inmost self— "a provincial town so far away from everything that you would have to gallop three years before you reached the frontier"; the people are types of money-grabbing, vain officials; and the plot is of how they are outdone by a lively young rogue who goes them one better in villainy. This rascal, Hlestakov, is one of the great characters of Russian literature, an irresponsible fop who gets on in the world only because he knows perfectly on which side his bread is buttered. He is impudent, shallow, and stupid; and his one glory is that the people he encounters are a shade more stupid than he. He makes fools of all the townspeople who have taken him for the government inspector, robs them, and, adding insult to injury, describes them minutely in a devastating letter which they discover after he has given them the slip. "Well, he's scolded everybody and I got the worst of it," Czar Nicholas I was reported to have said, in mighty amusement, at the opening. The reason he could take the play good-humoredly was that it made fun not of the system of government but of its administrators. Petty officialdom is here satirized with merciless, blunt humor that is farcical rather than witty, but is poetically and philosophically important, because it is not malicious. Malice would have been inappropriate to Gogol's theme, for it was not human foibles he was ridiculing nor even immorality, but the flat, mean state of soul in which all that is immoral and petty can flourish best. The Russian word for it is *poshlust,* and it has no equivalent in English. Gogol's prodigies of meanness, with their one uncomplicated desire—to have wealth and social standing—exude a poison that permeates the atmosphere they live in, making even the glimmer of an idea or an ideal unthinkable in it. And so they can be laughed at but not laughed off. In *Old-World Landowners* harmless sweetness endowed the hoarding instinct with something like charm; the squabbling of Ivan Ivanovich and Ivan Nikiforovich was only vain and silly; and the unimaginative life of Petersburg officialdom could reduce individuals like Akakyi Aka-kiyevich to pathetic nonentities—but all this has now become in Gogol's view a condition of life that only derision saves from loathsomeness.

Dead Souls is *The Inspector General* extended. It is an epic of *poshlust*. *The Inspector General* was circumscribed within the boundaries of one isolated town, but *Dead Souls* has a geographic sweep that suggests the whole of Russia. And it breathes an atmosphere of stupid fuss, of empty forms, of provincial snobbery, of inhumanity, of the dreariness of the land itself, of an all-pervading paltriness. The large, the generous, the noble, the grand are absent. They exist only, the work implies, in a youthful dream that has died and in the hidden potentiality of the nation's strength. What actually exists is premature old age, will-lessness, decay, greed, and thievery. The very structure of the book, which is patterned on the picaresque novel, makes it a parody, for its hero's "adventures," instead of being spicy and hazardous, are dull in the extreme. This hero, Chichikov, is a middle-aged, middle-class, and in every way middling bachelor, who travels with two casual, disrespectful, very Russian servants, buying up serfs, or "souls," who are actually dead but still listed as living since the previous census. Their owners must pay taxes on them, and Chichikov proceeds on the assumption that it would be to their advantage to have the names crossed off. Once he owns them on paper, he proposes to pawn them, acquiring thus a considerable sum of money. This cynical scheme is in itself an implicit indictment of a system that reduces human beings to the status of chattels, but Chichikov's adventures and Chichikov himself are an indictment of a good deal more than a system. Chichikov is an ingratiating, hypocritical, self-seeking scoundrel who has been imbued from childhood with the notion of accumulating wealth by fair means or foul, and who, when other schemes have failed, hits upon the idea of buying up the dead. And the landowners he visits are grotesques, ranged in a mounting gradation of evil, from deficiency of good to positive corruption: from the sugary, lazy, do-nothing, sentimental fool Manilov, who spends his time dreaming, piling up little heaps of tobacco, and tenderly kissing his wife; the greedy, mistrustful, shrewd little old Korobotchka, who, before she sells her dead, wants to find out what their market price might be; the liar and impudent brute Nozdryeov, who the better he knows, the worse he will cheat you; the grasping, substantial, suspicious, ill-tempered, egotistic Sobakevich, who drives a hard bargain and slips into the list a female soul, which is not negotiable; to Plyushkin, a kind of Harpagon or Volpone, who is sinister rather than funny—a disgusting old miser, owner of over a thousand serfs, with mountains of his estate's produce, which he is too stingy to sell, rotting in his lofts, while he himself, dressed in filthy rags, lives in two rooms of his dank house, surrounded by heaps of moldy junk, in which old silver and Chinese porcelain are thrown together with the rusty nails and the old soles he picks off the streets, and a yellow toothbrush which antedates the Napoleonic invasion. The sum of Gogol's hatreds is in this book. The devil of his early stories has here become a contemporary type, the rootless man, whose single aim in life is to accumulate. Chichikov is the man of property for whom the kind of wealth on which he thrives does not count, for

whom quantity alone matters. When Pushkin gave Gogol
the theme of *Dead Souls,* he reminded him that had not
Cervantes written *Don Quixote,* he would not have attained his full stature as a writer. Gogol must have remembered Cervantes, for his Chichikov is Don Quixote in
reverse, traveling about his native land having adventures,
but, unlike his Spanish prototype, knowing all too well
what he is after, in direct opposition to the idealistic Don,
the incarnation of sordid practicality.

Pushkin, who remarked that no one else had been able
to convey the full horror of *poshlust,* was alone, Gogol said,
in understanding what his work was about. When he
heard the first part, as Gogol read it to him—so runs a
popular story—he stopped abruptly in his laughter and
commented gloomily: "Yes, what a sad country our Russia is!" For although *Dead Souls* must be classed with
Don Quixote and *Gulliver's Travels* as one of the world's
great comic epics, its comedy is a mournful nightmare of
the damned. It is as much of himself as of Russia that
Gogol is writing here. It is for his own insane dreariness
of soul that he has found a faithful image in a nation's
and an epoch's evil. Emotionally the book is of illimitable
flatness, brightened up now and then by something tense
and brilliant that is like the opium dream of the frustrated youth in *Nevsky Prospect.* Or it is like a vision of
hell where uncanny laughter takes the place of wailing.
As a matter of fact, Gogol had intended to make his
work a kind of *Divine Comedy.* He had planned a second and a third part which were to correspond to Dante's
Purgatorio and *Paradiso.* Of the third part he completed
an outline only; the second he had almost finished but in
fits of disgust destroyed most of the manuscript, so that

we have it now in fragments only. But even if the plan had been carried out, the chances are that the first part would have remained the best. The fragments that remain are an indication of this. Gogol was on surer ground when he dealt with evil than with good, since, half consciously, it was of his own deficiencies that he was most sharply and most consistently aware. The first part of *Dead Souls,* Gogol's Inferno, is his most important work and his last great one.

When, at last, filled with self-loathing, Gogol attempted to reform his unfortunate nature, he succumbed to extravagant mysticism, made a holy pilgrimage to Jerusalem, and published his *Selected Passages from Correspondence with Friends*—brief essays that sought in impassioned argument to explain his "message" about the regeneration of Russia. It drew Belinsky's famous condemnation, and this in turn elicited, by way of self-justification, *An Author's Confession.* Although Gogol lived to be fifty-three years old, his important work was done in the space of eleven years, between the ages of twenty-one and thirty-two, from 1830 to 1841—which corresponds almost exactly to the period of his friendship with Pushkin. The last decade of his life is a tragic story of increasing isolation and mental decline. After the production of *The Inspector General* in 1836, Gogol left for Italy. He was in ill-health and bitterly hurt by the reception given his play, for along with praise there was a good deal of condemnation, and he was one to exaggerate morbidly any unfavorable criticism. "My God," he complained, "if only one or two had bawled me out. But everybody, everybody!" In Italy he stayed seven years, returning to Russia in 1841 with the first part of *Dead Souls,* which—because the censor objected to all kinds of

things in it, including the title: he said the soul was immortal—he had a hard time getting published. Directly
after its publication he went back to Italy, where, with
occasional trips to Russia, he spent his last unhappy years,
weaving and unraveling the continuation of *Dead Souls*.
He died on February 21, 1852.

Because of the ferocity of his satire, Gogol has been
called the Russian Swift. But it seems to me that among
writers of other countries it is to Flaubert that he can be
most appropriately compared. They were not unlike tem-
peramentally. Both of them solitary men, nurtured on the
literature of romanticism, cherishing the experience of
dreams as more true and more noble than what the world
they knew could offer, bitter in contemplation of everything that in modern life made human aspirations seem
futile and ridiculous. The greatest work of both is work of
hatred, but whereas Flaubert pounced with detestation
upon the dream itself and in *Madame Bovary* turned it
inside out to exhibit its shoddiness, Gogol never disdained
the dream but regretted having lost it. In fact, the drab
gargoyles of *Dead Souls* stand out against a background of
questioning hope and passion, as Emma Bovary and her as-
sociates do not. Gogol's lyric strain could not be drowned
even in hell. Such celebrated passages, for example, as his
address to Russia are the organ point, the basic accompaniment to the main theme, as it develops through all its variations:

And what Russian does not love rapid driving?
Is it for his soul—that longs to be caught in a whirl,
to lose itself carousing, to say now and then "to hell
with everything,"—is it for his soul not to love it? Not

to love it, when there breathes in it something triumphantly-wonderful? It is as if an unseen force snatched you up on its wing, and you fly and everything flies; milestones fly; in the opposite direction, merchants fly on the coach-boxes of their carriages; on both sides fly the woods with dark rows of spruce and pine trees and the sound of hatchets and the cawing of crows; the whole road flies no one knows where into fading distance; and there is something fearful in this rapid flying-by, with no time to distinguish a vanishing object, when only the sky overhead and light clouds and the moon breaking through, seem motionless. Ah troika, troika-bird! Who invented you? Sure, it is to a bold people only you could have been born—in that land which does not care to jest, but smooth and straight has flung itself over half the earth,—so you can go count the miles, until your eyes grow dizzy. And there is nothing cunning, mind you, in its roads for travel; they are not held down by iron screws but rapidly, hastily put together with but an axe and a chisel by the smart muzhik of Yaroslav. Nor is he in hessian boots, the coachman; a beard, and mittens, and he sits on God knows what; and now he stands up and swings his whip and drawls out a song. Like a whirlwind, the horses; the spokes of the wheels blend into one smooth disc, the road quivers, a passerby screams, stopping in fear,—and there she goes racing, racing, racing! . . . And already in the distance you see how something flings up dust and makes air swirl.

And you, too, O Russia, are you not like a bold troika that cannot be caught? The road smokes beneath you, the bridges tremble, everything retreats and is left behind! The onlooker is left amazed at the God-like marvel: is it not lightning thrown from heaven? What does it mean this horror-bringing motion? And what unseen power is hidden in those miraculous steeds? Ah, horses, horses—what horses! Are there whirlwinds in your manes? Does a sensitive ear burn in your every vein? You have heard from above a well-known song—at once, together, you have strained your bronze chests, and hardly touching the earth with your hoofs, have become lines stretched out, flying through the air,—and the troika races, inspired by God! . . . But whither, Russia, are you flying? Answer me. She gives no answer. The bell tinkles in wonderful music; torn into shreds, the air thunders and becomes wind; everything flies past, everything on earth, and looking askance, other peoples and kingdoms draw aside and make way for her.

Writing of this romantic kind Flaubert tried to eliminate from his work. It was natural to him, as his letters show, but his taste was offended by it; and he spent years of arduous labor in reducing his style to its lean, sinewy contours. Even *The Temptation of St. Anthony*, to which he relegated his gorgeous dreams, he worked over all his life, in an attempt to chasten the original lavish version to something more sober and spare, and in his "realistic" productions he made fun of his dreams. Flaubert hated the dream because it was false to the reality of daily living, and conversely hated reality because it made the dream impossible. Gogol did not hate the dream, but, like Pushkin, was frightened of a state of soul and a state of society which annihilated it.

> Long ago [he writes in *Dead Souls*], in the days of my youth, in the days of my childhood, now vanished forever, I used to enjoy going for the first time to an unknown place; it made no difference to me whether it were a little village, a poor, wretched district town, a hamlet, or a suburb, my inquisitive childish eyes discovered much that was of interest in it. Every building, everything that was marked by some notice-able peculiarity arrested my attention and impressed me . . . I stared too at the infantry officer . . . If a local official walked by, at once I fell to speculat-ing where he was going . . . As I drove up to some landowner's village, I looked with curiosity at the tall, narrow, wooden belfry, or at the spacious old church of dark wood . . .
>
> Now I drive into any strange village with indiffer-ence, and with indifference look at its vulgar exterior; to my cooler gaze it is uninviting and does not amuse me, and what in former years would have set my face working with excitement and roused me to laughter and unceasing chatter now slips by me, and my lips remain sealed in unconcerned silence. Oh, my youth! Oh, my fresh eagerness!

Flaubert succeeded in subduing his romantic cravings, with the result that his *Education Sentimentale* and his *Bouvard et Pécuchet* emit a desiccating flatness. Gogol's problem was not to subdue but to keep alive the wraith of feeling, and the impression he creates is that of a galvanized corpse, magnificent for all its deadness, because the breath that animates it is the breath of genius.

But both Flaubert and Gogol were disillusioned idealists, romantics who wanted to break with romanticism. The great enemy of the dream on which they were both nurtured was, as Flaubert saw it, and as Gogol vaguely felt, bourgeois society with its increasingly dominating standard of accumulation and material gain. The meaning of life, the possibility of art, they saw stifled in a money-grabbing world. Gogol's view of this is most evident in *The Portrait,* where the devil, in the shape of a usurer, corrupts and kills an artist; but soulless acquisitiveness is the dark and deadening power in all his stories, just as with Flaubert it comes out as the disintegrating element of civilization. Bouvard and Pécuchet collect bits of ideas just as Chichikov collects dead souls, and it is not so much the serfs that Chichikov buys as the Russians he deals with and he himself who are the dead souls of Gogol's conception. Even the method of work which these two writers developed, their way of getting down what they had accurately observed, was the result of a desire to deal somehow with their own selves in a hateful environment. Flaubert trained himself to look closely at things and people to cure himself of dreaming, and Gogol to get the better of an engulfing melancholy.

There are, of course, great differences between them, and the chief of these appears in their respective attitudes toward the intellect. What interests Flaubert, in the last analysis, is the nature of mind and the importance of thought, and what he condemns most bitterly is stupidity. But Gogol is concerned with men's actions and their feelings; and what he condemns is moral, not intellectual, deficiency. Flaubert's latent interest is epistomology, Gogol's, ethics; and their work reflects this difference, which, broadly speaking, is a national one. Gogol's realism, more than Flaubert's, is subjective. Flaubert's is a break with himself and a departure from his most intimate experience; Gogol's, a symbolic illustration of it. Flaubert escaped from what troubled him most; Gogol did not: the sordidness he caricatured remained part of himself. Flaubert resented it as an overbearing and oppressive force outside himself, Gogol as a corroding poison within him which he could not ward off. And so Gogol never achieved what he wanted to achieve. What he admired in art, for example, was epic clarity and serenity, like Homer's, Raphael's, or Pushkin's:

> Genuine artistic creation [he wrote] has in it something that is calming, conciliating. In reading, the soul is filled with lofty consent, and after reading, is satisfied: nothing is wanted, nothing desired; the heart is not stirred with indignation against one's brother, there streams through it, rather, the holy oil of all-forgiving love toward one's brother; and altogether it does not strive toward condemnation of others' actions, but toward contemplation of itself.

Such was his ideal, but his gift was in showing the tormented and the damned. Like Flaubert, he loathed the reality he painted best, but, unlike Flaubert, he was always escaping from it. He was more at home with the past and the dead than the living. Except for a few short stories, he wrote not of the city which he knew but of the provinces which he did not know, of the Ukraine which was a childhood memory, or of a historical past about which he knew little. He loved Russia most when he was in Italy, and he loved Rome best of all cities because there was more perished grandeur in it than anywhere else. All these were a refuge from the actual, repositories of heroic ideals and impossible dreams; and his strained observation of reality resulted in tremendous caricatures that had only the features and gestures of ordinary men but, for the rest, the turbulent soul of their creator. Gogol was too tumultuous a being to see himself as clearly as Flaubert saw himself; and so, whereas Flaubert's strength comes of a remarkably lucid introspection, Gogol's depends on a grandiose inventiveness that can create poetic equivalents for chaos.

For sheer inventiveness Gogol has few equals. Even Pushkin must yield to him in power to forge characters and situations out of a given theme. One might, for example, compare *The Cloak* with *The Bronze Horseman* as another in the series of Petersburg Tales in which an insignificant individual is overwhelmed by the enormous city that stands for Russia. With Pushkin one gets the terror of the elemental and the pathos of the victim through suggestion of the man, the city, the flood. The grandeur of the poem depends on its being an outline. It is the situation, the impact of sudden calamity that Pushkin gives. With Gogol the effect comes of his having grasped the situation in minutest details, a minuteness which is, perhaps, the artistic sublimation of *poshlust*. The contours are filled in, as they were even in the themes which Pushkin had provided, with the Hlestakovs, the Chichikovs, the Plyushkins of Gogol's imagination. This makes for a realism that is more a matter of the poet's coming to terms with separate events than of an integrated view of life itself that shapes his attitude toward them. Pushkin's is a realism of intellectual and emotional balance in which intense love of life is tempered by constant awareness of its brevity; Gogol's is a realism of violent hatred which trained perception has been schooled to control. It was real death that Pushkin feared, the death that deprives a vigorous pagan of his joy in the world, and so, as with Shakespeare, this made his images of life all the more beautiful and poignant; but Gogol was afraid of a death in life, which, as a matter of fact, he carried always in himself and of which he tried to be rid by showing it up in objective caricatures.

What Gogol might have done had his mind been formed, like Pushkin's, at a time of national confidence and activity it is probably useless to conjecture. When Pushkin came upon the stagnant hopelessness of the thirties, his poetic gift had already been formed. But Gogol's creative period coincided entirely with the stale regime of Nicholas I; his vague desires had always found a hollow echo in the commonplaceness of his world; he was horrified to see that the emptiness of his own being was all about him, and he took his revenge on both the world and himself. It was, therefore, neither a social conscience nor a gimlet eye to pierce the rottenness of men that made his work what it has always been accounted—a notable record of his age— but an emotional grasp of the disparity between romantic and idealistic notions, and life as it was actually beginning to shape itself in Russia. Pushkin had always been too clear-headed to be disillusioned, whatever his disappointments might have been. But Gogol let himself in for being hurt, and he produced a scathing picture of his country in recording his own hurt.

CHAPTER VI

Ivan Sergeyevich Turgenev

1818–83

TURGENEV DIED IN 1883. "IT IS FROM HIS WRITINGS ALMOST alone," wrote Henry James of him the following year, "that we of English, French, and German speech have derived our notions . . . of the Russian people." It was also from Turgenev almost alone that for a long while readers of the West derived their notions of Russian literature. And yet Turgenev was himself more of a European than other authors of his land. He spent almost half his life abroad, was intimate with the group of writers who gathered about Flaubert, and was in sympathy with the way they thought and wrote. To them he typified Russia, but his compatriots have always sensed something foreign in his work. His prose they recognize as the purest in the language, but his fundamental preoccupations and attitudes do not strike home like those of Dostoevsky and Tolstoy.

He himself was somewhat unhappily divided in his allegiance, unable to settle in his own country but always nostalgically yearning for it, complaining that without it he could not write. "There must be perpetual communion," he would say, "with the environment which one wants to reproduce," and that environment for him was Russia. All his books are about her, even though many of them were written on foreign soil. And it is probably this detachment, this vantage point of an alien civilization, that makes it possible for him to give a clearer picture of his country than that which other novelists present. His work can indeed be taken as a résumé of the social conditions and the intellectual controversies in Russia from the forties to the seventies, but whether it also imparts the "spirit" of the nation, whether it is as deep as it is clear, is another question.

From the first his writing displays a quality familiar to the West but not previously known in Russia. The scheme of his first book, for example, *A Sportsman's Sketches,* was probably suggested by Gogol's *Evenings on a Farm Near Dikanka,* for here, too, we have stories grouped about the life of a country community and held together by the somewhat shadowy personality of a narrator. But to begin with, what a difference between the narrators! The bantering, redheaded beekeeper who invites you to the "evenings" on his farm, and conveys in his invitation such glowing enthusiasm for his neighbors and their jolly times together, is a very different person from the observant huntsman who knows how to ask sympathetic questions and to be intelligent about the people he meets but who is never one of them. Then, what a difference in the descriptions! Take, for example, the one with which the sketch called *Bezhin Prairie* begins:

It was a glorious July day, one of those days which only come after many days of fine weather. From earliest morning the sky is clear; the sunrise does not glow with fire; it is suffused with a soft roseate flush. The sun, not fiery, not red-hot as in time of stifling drought, not dull purple as before a storm, but with a bright and genial radiance, rises peacefully behind a long and narrow cloud, shines out freshly, and plunges again into its lilac mist. The delicate upper edge of the strip of cloud flashes in little gleaming snakes; their brilliance is like polished silver. But, now, the dancing rays flash forth again, and in solemn joy, as though flying upward, rises the mighty orb. About mid-day there is wont to be, high up in the sky, a multitude of rounded clouds, golden-grey, with soft white edges. Like islands scattered over an over-flowing river, that bathes them in its unbroken reaches of deep transparent blue, they scarcely stir; farther down the heavens they are in movement, packing closer; now there is no blue to be seen be-tween them, but they are themselves almost as blue as the sky, filled full with light and heat. The colour of the horizon, a faint pale lilac, does not change all day, and is the same all round; nowhere is there storm gathering and darkening; only somewhere rays of bluish colour stretch down from the sky; it is a sprinkling of scarce-perceptible rain. In the evening these clouds disappear; the last of them, blackish and undefined as smoke, lie streaked with pink, facing the setting sun; in the place where it is gone down, as calmly as it rose, a crimson glow lingers long over the darkening earth, and, softly flashing like a candle carried carelessly, the evening star flickers in the sky. On such days all colours are softened, bright but not

glaring; everything is suffused with a kind of touching tenderness. On such days the heat is sometimes
very great; often it is even "steaming" on the slopes
of the fields, but a wind dispels this growing sultri-
ness, and whirling eddies of dust—sure sign of
settled, fine weather—move along the roads and
across the fields in high white columns. In the pure
dry air there is a scent of wormwood, rye in blossom,
and buckwheat; even an hour before nightfall there
is no moisture in the air. It is for such weather the
farmer longs, for harvesting his wheat.

(CONSTANCE GARNETT)

This is one of those pictures of the countryside for which
their author is justly famous. There is nothing more chaste
in the Russian language. Even a translation suggests something of the delicate sensuousness of this prose, although
it cannot render the grace of its unobtrusive cadences nor
the subtlety of its echoing sounds. And it does transmit
the pictorial quality, the numerous descriptive terms, the
color. The subdued effect is produced directly in the repetition of "soft," "suffused," in such words as "tender,"
"touching," "scarce-perceptible." It is the accurate painting
of a water-colorist who has looked on the scene and enjoyed it. Compare it with a characteristic description from
Pushkin:

He walked on without troubling to keep to the road;
the branches constantly caught at and scratched him,
and his feet continually sank into the swamp—he
observed nothing. At last he reached a small glade
surrounded by trees on every side; a little stream

wound silently through the trees, half-stripped of
their leaves by autumn. Vladimir stopped, sat down
upon the cold turf, and thoughts, each more gloomy
than the other, crowded his mind . . . For a long
time he sat quite motionless, observing the gentle
flow of the stream, bearing along on its surface a few
withered leaves, and vividly presenting to him a true
image of life. At last he noticed that it was growing
dark; he arose and began to look for the road home,
but for a long time he wandered about the unknown
forest before he stumbled upon the path which led
straight up to the gate of his house.

(T. KEANE)

Apart from the fact that Pushkin's descriptions are briefly
and incidentally given, the things he mentions always stand
unique, complete, and meaningful through the sheer poetry
of the way he names them. Turgenev leads them forth
with epithets to stir emotion and create a mood. With
Pushkin all objects are appreciated for what they are independently, with Turgenev, for the purpose they serve.
And Gogol's heavy-laden, incrustated prose also differs
from Turgenev's in a similar way, for though it is highly
subjective, it gives a direct sense of that which is described,
the Ukrainian night, for example, which rouses loving enthusiasm—whereas Turgenev's phrases have reference not
to the thing itself so much as to the impression it invokes.
The sentiment induced in him by the beautiful July night
is more important than the night itself. It is that mood he
would like to render, while Gogol is almost breathless in
wanting to re-create the beauty that had moved him, because for him it is the Ukrainian night, not the state of his

emotions, that matters above all. Turgenev's prose is not so spare as Pushkin's, not so severe, more soft and sinuous, and it has nothing of Gogol's deep-voiced rhetoric. It is the prose of perfect restraint and of perfect taste, where there is not too much to restrain and where the taste is a connoisseur's; and it indicates a peculiar attitude to life that is displayed in other ways also, and perhaps nowhere better than in the sketch of which I have just quoted the beginning.

On the evening of the beautiful July day our hunter gets lost and comes, in the darkness, upon a group of five boys sitting around a campfire. He speaks to them, then lies down under a bush and observes them. They soon forget him and talk freely. Their conversation is, quite naturally in that atmosphere, about various grisly incidents of ghosts and witches, "true" stories which they recount with naïve awe. One of the boys only, Paul, evinces skeptical common sense. He is a calm, brave, practical youngster on whom the others rely and whom the observer especially likes. And the sketch ends: "I regret I must add that Paul died that very year . . . Too bad, he was a nice fellow!" In several ways this story might be taken as a symbol of all Turgenev's work: in the narrator's position as eavesdropper, in his unsympathetic interest in all that is dreamy and superstitious in the Russian people, in his respect for the rational, and in the dismal feeling that what is hopeful for Russia will not survive. We have here, in short, an author who is an analytic onlooker, never identified with his subject.

In another story the hunter, invited to a party at a neighbor's house, spends the night there in the company of another guest, who tells him the story of his life. "In the first place," the stranger begins abruptly when the hunter has turned in, "my French is no worse than yours, and my German even better; in the second place, I've spent three years abroad: in Berlin alone I lived eight months." He announces that he has studied Hegel and knows Goethe by heart, and, moreover, that once he had been for a long time in love with the daughter of a German professor. But, he ventures, in spite of all these worthy attainments, he had not been noticed downstairs. His companion admits that he had not noticed him. That, says the man, is because he stands behind others and behind doors and doesn't raise his voice. He is shy, he says, and not because he is provincial or poor but because he is very egotistic. People call him an "original character" and think they can insult him by calling him that, whereas as a matter of fact, if they only knew it, he is the opposite of what they say. There is not a particle of originality in him. He isn't even stupid in an original way. He lives as if in imitation of what he has read; he even fell in love and married as if he had been doing a lesson. He thought he had married for love, but he never succeeded in making his wife happy, had all but hanged himself the first year of their marriage, and, now that she was dead, could not be sure whether he had ever loved or not. He is a failure. All the hopes that he had raised when he was young had come to nothing. Now everybody realized that he would never amount to very much, and no one paid any attention to him. There has been no real tragedy in his life, he says, but he has experienced something like tragedy. He has known "the poisonous raptures of cold despair; he has experienced the sweetness of lying in bed all morning, cursing the day and hour he was born." Now, although he knew he wasn't welcome anywhere, he lacked the strength to withdraw from people and live alone, and so he went about among his neighbors, intoxicated by the very contempt with which he was treated. At the end of his recital he refuses to divulge his name. A man like that, he says, prefers to remain anonymous; "but call me Hamlet, if you like, Hamlet of Shchigry County." If *Bezhin Prairie* is an epitome of Turgenev's method and of his fundamental philosophical assumptions, *Hamlet of Shchigry County* exhibits his foremost psychological interests. All his life he was to portray the type of man that he sketched here. There are other superb stories in *A Sportsman's Sketches,* such as *The Raspberry Water,* in which a peasant's brief, uncomplaining account of how after the death of his son he had in vain begged to be relieved of the tax he could no longer pay expresses all the hopelessness of the serf's position; or *The Agent,* or *Ermolai and the Miller's Wife,* which give in similar brief conversations further insight into the inhumanity of serfdom; or *The Singers,* the song contest in a tavern that re-creates the peasants' love of music and the dark background of brutality against which their brief festivals take place. Sketches such as these made Alexander II say that Turgenev's book had led him to the Emancipation. But fine as they are, they do not expose so well as *Bezhin Prairie* and *Hamlet of Shchigry County* what is most typical of Turgenev.

In the latter story there is something autobiographic. It is a kind of malicious self-parody, for all his life Turgenev was given to somewhat maundering dissatisfaction with what he did and what he was. He, too, had gone to Germany to study, knew Goethe and Hegel, wondered what Hegel had, after all, to do with real life, and lived, or thought he lived, more by the book than independently.

The story of his life has a dreamlike quality about it, a story of intellectual and emotional attachments wherein he always seems to play a passive role. His will was doubtless broken in childhood by a tyrannical mother, whose portrait he drew many years later in the capricious and domineering landowner of one of his most pitiful tales of serfdom, *Mumu*. When in 1834, at the age of sixteen, he entered the University of Moscow, he became fascinated by German idealistic philosophy, which since the Napoleonic Wars had been replacing French thought in intellectual circles in Russia. The teaching at the university was not, on the whole, very exhilarating; but one of his professors, who, in the guise of physics, was actually teaching Schelling's *Naturphilosophie,* stirred Turgenev's mind. He was not alone in his interest. College students, who were not permitted to speak their minds freely in the classroom, were forming extracurricular groups, soon to become influential in the intellectual life of Russia, to discuss the philosophic notions that were exciting them. And Turgenev made friends with the leader of one of these circles, Stankevich, ardent, selfless, frail, with exalted theories of love and of the importance of art, known to his followers as "the heavenly." His group advocated Slavophile doctrines, which had in common with Schelling's romanticism a love of the irrational, based on the conviction that faith is more important than reason, that "spiritual" rather than material values are valuable in life. Turgenev was attracted to him, as he was always attracted to positive natures, followed him to Berlin in 1838, "threw (himself) head first into the German sea," and the next year traveled with him in Italy, where they wandered together through art galleries and carried on endless conversations. The impression made on him by this severe, high-minded enthusiast was profound. But in 1840 Stankevich died and Turgenev was charmed by a very different kind of man. This was the anarchist Bakunin, who distrusted idealisms of every kind as much as Stankevich had loved them, and believed in reason and the force of economic laws as much as Stankevich had believed in emotion and the power of art. Turgenev saw much of him and was in love for a while with one of his sisters. Next, in 1842, he met Belinsky, the "raging Vissarion" who had also belonged to Stankevich's circle, steeping himself in German idealism, but had then, like many other Russian intellectuals, turned from German idealism to positivism, materialism and atheism, and at the time Turgenev met him was crying down all conventions, including religion and marriage, and advocating, as the most rational, the form of government of the United States. Stankevich had laid all emphasis on the cultural and emotional development of the individual, Bakunin on laws of government and economics, Belinsky on doctrines of humanity and the importance of social service. With an unusually quick and facile understanding, Turgenev absorbed all these theories, in which were represented the divergent philosophic tendencies of his day. In 1848 he met Herzen, who had just come abroad, to remain there in exile for the rest of his life, and Turgenev once more fell under the influence of a socially minded positivist. This friendship lasted a dozen years, but cooled, and when, in 1863, Turgenev was called upon to testify in charges brought against the politically suspect Herzen, he grew frightened and refused to admit that they had anything in common.

Turgenev spent as many years of his life abroad as in Russia. At first he lived in Russia with yearly trips abroad, and for the last twenty years of his life reversed the process, and lived abroad with yearly trips to Russia. The reason for this perpetual vagabondage was mixed. It was partly that European ways of living and thinking appealed to him more than the Russian, and partly that at the age of twenty-five he fell in love with the famous singer Pauline Garcia Viardot and felt compelled to follow her for the rest of his life. Mme. Viardot was happily married, but Turgenev was content to remain a friend of the family; where the Viardots went he went too, and it was in their home he died in 1883. He could not, therefore, have been entirely honest with himself when, in reminiscences he wrote at the age of fifty, he declared that he had done *A Sportsman's Sketches* away from home because he had found the air of Russia "stifling" and had "to move to a distance from (his) enemy, so that (he) might be able from a distance to hurl (himself) upon him with greater impetus." The enemy was serfdom, but after the Emancipation, Turgenev spent even more time in Europe than before. There is something soft and will-less in the story of this life, something that lacks direction and intensity. Both intellectually and emotionally Turgenev was a drifter, moved along by currents of thought and feeling to which he submitted but which he never sought to dominate. George Moore has classed him with Corot, declaring that together they had revealed to him "all that (he) needed to know." "For all things," he said, "are contained in them. He who has seen Corot has seen all the universe, for could we find in the farthest star anything more beautiful than evanescent cloud and a nymph gathering summer blooms by the edge of a lake?" This hits it off, I think. To those who find meat and drink in clouds and nymphs Turgenev can give nourishment. A mournful, homesick note sounds throughout his work, not only in the soft cadence of his sentences but in his characterizations and in his choice of themes.

Painful love affairs are the focus of nearly all his novels. For even though there are other issues involved in them—Russia in relation to the West, the differences between the old generation of aristocrats and the new one of radicals, materialistic and utilitarian ways of thought in contrast to idealist—these topics do not involve him deeply; it is with affairs of the heart that he is most concerned, and he is at his best when he deals with them. This is true of *Rudin*, of *Asya*, of *A House of Gentlefolk*, of *On the Eve*, even of *Fathers and Sons*, *Smoke*, and *Virgin Soil*. All but two of them end sadly, and nearly all of them follow, up to a point, the Tatiana-Onegin pattern. Turgenev's women are usually strong characters; the men nearly always weak, failing either in love or in the tasks they undertake. And those who are strong are killed off, like the little Paul of *Bezhin Prairie*. It is, as Mr. Avrahm Yarmolinsky has remarked, as if Turgenev were envious of success. It is also as if he were perplexed, with the perplexity of a man who was aware of the trying problems which his world faced but could not see how nor through whom they might be solved.

The gist of his perplexity is to be found in the speech he delivered in 1859 on the theme of *Hamlet and Don Quixote*. These characters represented for him two categories of human beings, which today we would probably call "egotists" and "altruists," or "introverts" and "extroverts." Don Quixote was a man who had faith in a reality beyond himself, a difficult ideal which demanded self-sacrifice. He valued his life only in so far as it could be of service to this ideal, was unswervingly single-minded in pursuit of it, and was, for this reason, somewhat one-sided. He did not know very much, and sometimes he seemed mad, and sometimes limited, because he could be light in neither his sympathies nor his enjoyments. But his roots went very deep and his moral strength was great. Hamlet, on the other hand, lived entirely for himself. He was a man without belief, for one so completely self-centered always lacks the intensity requisite for conviction. He doubted everything, had no faith even in his own soul, delighted in watching, examining, denouncing his faults in an exaggerated way; and lived on disdain of himself. He suffered, of course, and his suffering was greater than Don Quixote's; but it did not inspire love. Don Quixote, on the other hand, was both laughable and lovable. The poor, solitary old man who undertook to right all wrongs and to defend the oppressed was a much nobler soul than the rich heir to the throne, who certainly could never have made the silly mistake of taking the barber's bowl for a golden helmet. But was the intelligent Hamlet so right, after all, in his unquestioning assumptions as to what was real and what was not? However bright they might seem, the Hamlets, said Turgenev, were not the great thinkers of the world; they were incapable of making any discoveries. Occupied with themselves alone, they left no trace after they were gone, for great thoughts came from the heart, and Hamlet had no heart. He never loved, not even Ophelia, for whom he had no genuine affection, whom he only pretended to love. His feeling for her was really

only attachment to himself; but who could doubt Don
Quixote's worship of the nonexistent Dulcinea! Hamlet,
the man of the North, was a creature of negation, another
Mephistopheles, the power of self-centeredness; the Southern Don Quixote was all that is clear, naïve, assimilative
in human beings. Hamlet, despite his gestures of independence, scorned the masses of men and was, at bottom, a
tyrant. Don Quixote, respecting established social forms—
kings, knights, the church—was free and respected others'
freedom. It was the Don Quixotes who benefited humanity
through their discoveries; the Hamlets sometimes worked
out these discoveries, but they were for the most part
solitary, useless men.

The novels present· Hamlet and Don Quixote either
singly or in opposition to each other and, in the deepest
characterizations, as mixed within one man. We get
Hamlet notably, not only in the story of *A Sportsman's
Sketches,* but also in *Asya,* in *The Diary of a Superfluous
Man,* and in *Virgin Soil;* Don Quixote in *On the Eve* and
Virgin Soil; the mixture in *Rudin* and *Fathers and Sons.*
It is in love affairs that the Hamlets stand best revealed.
They are sentimental ineffectuals, like N. N. of *Asya,* who
are frightened by love; or amorous men, like Chulkaturin
of *The Diary of a Superfluous Man,* who whine over their
inferiority when they are rejected; or vacillating, mixed-up
intellectuals, like Nezhdanov of *Virgin Soil,* who could be
taken as prototypes for some contemporary presentations
of "fellow travelers" and "defeatists." The Don Quixotes
are men of action, who, like Insarov in *On the Eve,* perish
in a noble cause, or like Litvinov in *Smoke* or Lavretsky
in *A House of Gentlefolk,* whose potential usefulness is
lost in unfortunate affairs of the heart, or like Solomin in

Virgin Soil, the only successful one of them all, and the least convincing as a personality.

But the most interesting are the complex characters, Rudin, who is supposedly a portrait of Bakunin, and Bazarov, in *Fathers and Sons,* whose self-styled philosophy of "nihilism" popularized the label given to the young radicals of the sixties and seventies. Dmitry Nikolaevich Rudin is more a Hamlet than a Don Quixote. He comes in the line of the lost and wandering heroes of Griboyedov, Pushkin, and Lermontov, to all of whom Turgenev's phrase "superfluous men" has come to be applied. But he is neither the fop that Onegin is, nor the cynic that Pechorin (the "younger brother of Onegin" in Lermontov's *A Hero of Our Times*) is, nor the sharp critic of society that Chatsky is. He is more noble and more tragic, and also, in a way, more comic than any of these. And he represents a new, characteristically nineteenth-century problem. For it is neither his world that makes him what he is nor the torments of his conscience, but the incongruousness between his mind's activity and its conclusions. The Superfluous Man had written about himself: "Between my feelings and my thoughts . . . there was a kind of senseless, ununderstandable and unconquerable barrier"—just so with Rudin there is a barrier between what he thinks and what he does, or rather, between what he imagines he feels and what he actually feels; and so, between his idea of what he ought to do and what he is capable of doing. He is all rhetoric, even to his emotions, which, as if cut loose from animal instincts, wander bloated in the artificial vapor of noble intentions; and, as he says of himself, he is destroyed by phrasemaking. A great reader, a brilliant conversationalist, fiery, idealistic in what he says, especially eloquent when he discusses the importance of philosophy, freedom, and the nature of the individual, his elated speech captivates his listeners whether they understand him or not. But the test of action proves him shallow and inadequate. In cowardly fashion he drops the girl whose love he has won, for at the crucial moment—the girl's mother will not consent to the marriage, and it is a question of running away—he finds that he has neither will nor affection enough to act decisively; and although his greatest desire is to be "useful," all his attempts to serve society, like his eloquence, have an element of the fantastic in them; and he approaches his goal only in a last, desperate gesture when, a red banner in one hand and a crooked dull-edged sword in the other, he is shot down on the barricades of Paris on July 26, 1848. Rudin is Hamlet trying to be Don Quixote, a neurotic modern man, longing to be himself but not knowing what he is, and so unable to bring to life the great convictions with which he is on fire. He is, on the one hand, cold, despotic, selfish, ignorant, and, because his words are merely words, not fundamentally honest; but, on the other hand, his empty eloquence is in itself a virtue:

We have all become impossibly rationalistic, indifferent and lethargic, [an old college friend says in speaking of him], we're asleep, we're frozen, and thanks to the man who even for an instant will stir us and warm us. It's time! . . . I once accused him of coldness. I was both right and wrong. That coldness of his is in his blood—he can't help it—but not in his head. He is not an actor as I called him, not a cheat; he lives at another's expense not as a sly intriguer—but as a child. . . . yes, of course, he will die somewhere in poverty and want; but must we sling stones at him for that? He himself will never accomplish anything—precisely because he has no character, no blood; but who has the right to say that he will not, that he has not already done good? that his words have not sown fruitful seeds in young hearts to whom nature has not denied the power of carrying ideas into execution?

To be excited, then, if only by a vision of something noble, is a weapon against stupefying torpor, that *poshlust* which is undermining Russia. Rudin is a subtly drawn portrait of an egotist whom weakness of will—probably connected with sexual impotence—has made what he is: a man so blind to others that he offends when he wishes to be most straight and open, and cannot see that his rhetorical gestures are efforts at self-justification. He is unconsciously hypocritical, and his preoccupation with himself is a perpetual and hopeless endeavor to reconcile what he desires to be with what he is.

In the nihilist Bazarov we have a character who is almost a photographic negative of Rudin; what is black in one is white in the other, but they are both Don Quixotes reduced to tragedy through traits of Hamletism. Bazarov's failure, Turgenev would have us think, is one of intellect rather than of temperament. Unlike Rudin, Bazarov has a will of iron, but the idea for which he fights is, in Turgenev's interpretation, barbarous; he is crushed by the inhumanity of this idea as Rudin is defeated by want of feeling. Bazarov is Turgenev's greatest character, more subtly and deeply conceived than any of the others.

A young doctor, just through with his medical course, he is a man of a new generation. He is a skeptic, a critic, and a scientist; he believes in nothing, he says, and calls himself a "nihilist" from the Latin *nihil,* to express this absence of belief. All sense of beauty, poetry, art he rejects as nonsense. Pushkin is "no earthly use," "Raphael's not worth a brass farthing," Nature is "not a temple but a workshop." Only the "useful" is worth while. Similarly, what is feeling to most people is to him merely sensation. "There are no general principles . . . Everything depends on sensations . . . Why, I, for instance, take up a negative attitude, by virtue of my sensations; I like to deny—my brain's made on that plan, and that's all there is to it! Why do I like chemistry? Why do you like apples?— By virtue of our sensations. It's all the same thing. Deeper than that men will never penetrate." Bazarov has the strength to act on his convictions and, in acting on them, proves them false. He hurts others, running roughshod over their feelings, and he hurts himself, caught in his too rigidly controlled emotions. He is broken by the very strength of will which he denies. But his most serious limitation is that he hates the men to whom he is ready to devote his life. He has a despot's view of people; his treatment of them is domineering. Yet Bazarov is bigger than he shows himself to be. He is fine not because, but in spite, of his views and his actions. His greatness is implicit; what he really is is a contradiction of what he represents himself to be. What is obvious in him is limited and unpleasant; what is hidden is big. He is constantly mistaken about himself; his actions and his words are, without his realizing it, an attempt to screen his real self; even his convictions contradict his unacknowledged beliefs. He is a man of unusual directness, with a hatred of pretense and all mawkish self-interest. He is severe and inflexible as regards both himself and others, innately a democrat, but in practice a tyrant, a reformer of the stuff of which some Puritans are made who are willing to suppress individuality because it is obnoxious to them. But all of this, on principle. He claims that he believes in nothing, but he has the scientist's faith in experiment; he denies the existence of sentiments but he falls desperately in love, against his will, and in spite of what he thinks; he is autocratic and overbearing when he treats men as he thinks he should, but when he is simply himself, people are instinctively drawn to him. His failings are those of a way of thought, not of personality. Just as Rudin's emotional strength evaporates in eloquence and shuts him off from people, Bazarov's theories about people keep him from understanding them. He is a more tragic character than Rudin, who in the last analysis cares only about himself, because it is his very ardor for humanity that, ironically, leads him to disregard too much what is human.

And the story of which he is the center, taking place in 1859, sums up the social and intellectual state of the country just before the Emancipation. The people with whom Bazarov comes in contact, his parents and the parents of his friend Arkady, the peasants who live on their little properties, the advanced "intellectuals" of nearby towns, do not any of them measure up to him in character and intelligence. "When I meet a man who can hold his own beside me," he says to Arkady, his devoted follower, "I'll change my opinion of myself." And he is not merely conceited in saying this; he actually does not meet his match. The tragedy of the book, which is deeper than that of the characters involved in it, is, implicitly, the tragedy of Russia. The country needs saving, we are given to understand: the land is poor, the villages run-down, the peasants ragged and drunken; the new attempt to give them freedom—Arkady's and Bazarov's parents are landowners of advanced views who have liberated their serfs before the Emancipation—does not work. "It can't go on like this," thinks Arkady; "reforms are absolutely necessary . . . but how is one to carry them out, how is one to begin?" To that question there is no answer. The older generation, people rich in affection and devotion, men and women of great personal charm, but quite incapable of vigorous thinking or of managing even their own lives, let alone the lives of others, certainly these ineffectuals cannot be expected to save the country. And as for the younger generation, Russia cannot count on such absurd fops as Sitnikov, or ridiculous intellectuals such as the "emancipated" Mme. Kukshin and her emancipated friends, nor on selfish prigs such as Mme. Odintsov, with whom Bazarov falls in love, nor on sweet and innocent young things like Arkady and Katya. If only the Bazarovs could have some understanding of human beings, the hope of the nation would lie in them. But they do not understand, and even if they did, Turgenev would not let them live. Bazarov dies of an infection which he contracts in dissecting the body of a victim of typhus. He performs the operation out of sheer curiosity, and he dies because the doctor in charge does not know enough to take the most elementary hygienic precautions. There is, therefore, a kind of ironic retribution in Bazarov's death as well as proof that his disastrously inadequate philosophy contains an element of justice. Still, his death is not inevitable. Turgenev kills him off, one suspects, so that the question with which *On the Eve* had ended: "Will there ever be men in Russia?" might be the import of this story, too. The implications of the book, then, are tragic, but the tone of it is not. It is pitying and sentimental, opening on a note of loneliness and expectation and ending on a note of loneliness and resignation.

This is characteristic of Turgenev. It is the voice of one who has no satisfactory answers to the problems life poses. Emotionally there is vague longing and dissatisfaction, intellectually a schematic view of philosophic systems. Turgenev is a liberal and an individualist who believes in the Europeanization of Russia and has no patience with the exclusive, mystic nationalism of the Slavophiles, but who is also critical of the utilitarianism of the West. What appeals to him in Western thought is its rationality, but what he finds among the "reasonable" men of Russia is reason that has lost its balance either through impractical theorizing or through harshness that scorns individuality. In the last analysis, his view is the romantic idealist's. It is for him a man's innate qualities that count, not his actions. He values Don Quixote not for what he accomplishes but for his motives, the manner in which he goes about his work, and the way he feels about people; and he despises Hamlet not for his failure to get things done but for his egotistic unappreciativeness of others. Don Quixote is likely to be more helpful to society than Hamlet, but that is incidental; it is not by their social usefulness that Turgenev judges men.

This interest in the individual is typical of the later nineteenth century in both Europe and Russia, the primary concern, in fact, of all artists and thinkers at the time. But with Turgenev it is limited by his curious predilection for failure. He seems to examine men for the pleasure of seeing them come to grief. He can admire altruism and strength, but he cannot bear to see them succeed; and although he is usually concerned with love, he always presents it, as Mr. Yarmolinsky has noted, at a moment of crisis, tumultuous and brief, never calm, enriching, lasting, fruitful. That, one might say, was also true of Pushkin, but for Pushkin the turbulent moment opens vistas of tragic experience and thereby tinges all life with deeper meaning; for Turgenev it yields only pathos and the remembrance of something sweet. Rootless, wistful, Turgenev is enamored of pathos. In his thought, as in his life, there is something vaporous. It is as if he never faced quite squarely either people or ideas, but wandered about with half-shut eyes, savoring his emotions. Through these half-shut eyes he trained himself to see clearly; but he was always an observer in the realm of ideas as well as of emotions, never a creator nor even a sharer. For despite his interest in philosophy, his was not, like Dostoevsky's, for example, a speculative mind; despite his interest in people, he could not take them with the seriousness of a Henry James; and despite his perpetual dissatisfaction with himself, he had nothing of Gogol's terror and despair nor of Flaubert's merciless knowledge of himself nor of Tolstoy's severity. His common-sense reasonableness has lost that clarity and humor of eighteenth-century enlightenment which shines through Pushkin's work. His is the more troubled rationality of an intellectually confused era when reason is no longer taken for granted and is involved with sentiment, when men no longer think objectively about sentiment, as they did in the eighteenth century, but are likely to be emotional in their thinking, even when they want to be most rational. Turgenev's is perhaps the most beautiful expression of this intellectually and emotionally attenuated view, and in its own way it is perfect, a masterpiece worked out of base material. Like his Rudin, Turgenev remained to the end of his days "steeped in German poetry, in the world of German romanticism and philosophy." German solicitude for sentiment appealed to his self-pampering nature; he was a Lensky, of a later, more hard-headed, though no less troubled generation, come to life in Russian letters.

Pushkin's, Tolstoy's, Dostoevsky's characters are interesting for their strength, Turgenev's for their weakness; and it is remarkable how many of them we can feel sorry for and how few we can love. To get the difference in dimension between modes of taking the same problems, one should compare such a story as *Hamlet of Shchigry County* with Dostoevsky's *Notes from Underground,* that other confessional of an arch-egotist. The difference between them is that Turgenev's individual is flaccid and complaining, that he whines about his fate and feels immensely sorry for himself, whereas Dostoevsky's despises and torments himself, does not complain, does not whine, but analyzes and explains. There is this further difference also, that the Underground man thinks of himself in relation to the outer world, of the effect, that is, he has had and can have on others; he is conscious of the harm he can do, but Turgenev's Hamlet thinks only of adjusting himself somehow to humanity and of slinking away and erasing himself if he cannot come to terms with it. Dostoevsky's man is all anger, passion, and exasperation; Turgenev's, only puerile self-pity. Dostoevsky's is the creature of a mind that has been able to forget itself in an objectively valid symbol; Turgenev's of one that fondles its own hurt and wants to do no more than describe it.

Turgenev neither could nor wanted to identify himself imaginatively with another person, nor did he wish to lose himself in an idea. He liked to be appreciatively aloof, whether people or ideas or things claimed his attention. He had, one might say, an anecdotal view of life, and his method was essentially pictorial, but without the attempted objectivity of a Flaubert to keep himself out of his work. His narratives proceed with the ease and grace of a gentleman talking among friends. That is their great merit. What they lack is that imaginative correspondence between profoundly personal experience and the external world which is what opens prospects on unsuspected visions in Pushkin's work or stirs one with the impact of passionate experience in Gogol. In Turgenev's there seems to be a kind of departmentalization of human faculties, as if emotion, thought, and animal instinct were neither interrelated nor bound one to the other in mutual progress, but happened somehow to collide in their melancholy gyrations. When Marcel Proust, for example, recalls an early love—and this Turgenev delights in doing—he recreates its poignancy and makes one believe in it as something more than a brief occasion, forever lost, and to be recalled only in faint images; it has become part of the grown man and is not to be regarded condescendingly. Turgenev, on the other hand, does not so much present, as discourse about, his early love. For him there is no continuity. The past has been cut off and, from the great distance of a dry maturity, seems encrusted in the aura of bygone emotions. Like the hero of his novelette, *Clara Milich,* who dies in a struggle with the phantom of the woman he might have, but did not, love, until after she had committed suicide, Turgenev's greatness as an artist is killed by the ghost of his ineffectual attachments. The integration of his work is not that of a chemical solution, but of a squirrel cage of sentiment. There is something static and hopeless about it. His variety of realism is new in Russian literature and has more in common with the kind developed in the West, a realism of statement and description that leaves aside as relatively unimportant those possibilities of experience which a clear eye and common sense are incapable of charting.

CHAPTER VII

Theodore Mikhaylovich Dostoevsky

1821–81

DOSTOEVSKY WROTE HIS FIRST NOVEL, *Poor Folk*, IN 1844, when he was twenty-three years old. It is, in main outline, a simple and very pathetic love story, done in the form of letters that pass between a poor government clerk and an equally poor girl, a distant relative of his, who lives across the courtyard from him. The correspondence lasts throughout the spring and summer of a year, six months in which the lonely life of two solitary people is broken by a hope and comes to the inevitable frustration which circumstances impose. It is a tale of extreme pathos because these people ask so little of life and even that little is denied them. The poor clerk feels too humble and too old either to marry the girl or to be her lover, but he becomes attached to her in a kind of fatherly devotion. He denies himself decent lodging, clothes, food so that he may send her gifts; takes care of her when she falls ill; recites to her the whole pitiful story of his life; discusses books with her; makes a fool of himself to avenge an insult to her; and finally, when she decides to marry a rich suitor who turns up, runs errands in preparation for the wedding. She, in the meanwhile, has been grateful and solicitous, has begged him to take care of himself, has told him her troubles, has scolded him, and has felt guilty for being a burden on him. She marries a callous sensualist who frightens and revolts her, because she can no longer bear the torment that poverty forces upon her and her devoted friend. "Unhappiness," she writes, "is contagious. Unhappy people should stay away from each other." Her marriage is a gesture of despair and a form of self-sacrifice. Like his predecessor, Gogol's Akakyi Akakiyevich, the clerk Makar Devushkin is pathetic and laughable, pitifully amusing in his illiteracy, in the absurdity of his remarks about what happens to him, in the rhetoric which he attempts now and then, in his childlike exuberance; and like Akakyi Akakiyevich he is the more lovable for being funny. But there is an important difference between him and his prototype. Akakyi Akakiyevich is only pathetic, but Makar Devushkin is unconsciously heroic. For him it is not physical want but the ego's hurt which is the real suffering that poverty brings. Akakyi Akakiyevich had accustomed himself to his humble position; he wrapped himself in his cloak to keep out the cold of a Petersburg winter, but Makar Devushkin wants tea and decent shoes not for comfort but to preserve a modicum of self-respect among other people. And even this he would sacrifice for his Varenka. That is the important difference between *Poor Folk* and *The Cloak*.

And this difference is shown once more, in another way,

in Dostoevsky's next story, *The Double,* which derives from Gogol's *The Nose* just as *Poor Folk* derived from *The Cloak.* The experience of humiliation is here more destructive than it had been in *Poor Folk;* and Gogol's humorous fantasy is transformed into a realistic study of morbid psychology. Once more we have to do with a humble copying clerk, a Mr. Golyadkin—whose name, from *golyi,* "naked," suggests how unprotected he is, just as Devushkin, from *deva,* "maiden," hints at effeminacy. He goes one night, uninvited, to a party of one of his superiors, makes himself ridiculous there, and is the next morning confronted in his office by an exact replica of himself, a man who not only looks, but behaves, like him, and does not leave him for a moment. There is only this difference between them, that instead of being humble, the Double is a self-assured and dignified creature. At the end he helps Golyadkin into a carriage that takes him to an insane asylum. The Double represents, of course, all that the poor clerk missed in himself. He is the personification of what Golyadkin would have wanted to be had he dared so much as dream of it, and the power of his hallucination is a measure of how much he had secretly desired and how much suppressed. The tragedy of frustration is here shown in its most sad extreme. Makar Devushkin took to drink, felt lost, didn't know where to turn or what to do with himself, but poor Golyadkin, unable to cope even so well as this with his humiliation, goes mad. The reason Golyadkin is doomed to a more disastrous fate is that he lives only for himself, whereas the whole meaning of Devushkin's life is contained in another human being.

When these stories first came out, Dostoevsky was accused of slavishly imitating Gogol. The accusation was unfair and unperceptive, for although he was greatly indebted to Gogol and never denied this indebtedness, he never copied him blindly. He loved Gogol's power of laughter and his flashes of human sympathy. What he could not accept was Gogol's callousness; and even in his earliest productions, when he was most dependent on him, he worked free of the influence and wrote—or so it seems— to contradict him. It is as if he had already understood that it was inappropriate, if not dangerous, to laugh at the kind of experience that he and Gogol were dealing with. It was as if he had already grasped the secret of Gogol's madness. The humor of *The Double*—and it is humorous despite the tragedy—is not unfeeling, and the terror of the story is not fantastic but real, a man's fear of ultimate frustration, that he shall not be recognized as a human being.

The reason that Dostoevsky could understand pain so deeply was that from the first his own experience of it was all but overwhelming. From earliest days he had known cruelty of various kinds. His father was an ill-balanced, suspicious man who tyrannized over his family and was eventually murdered by one of his own peasants; his mother, to whom he was devoted, died when he was sixteen; the engineering school to which he was sent was a torment to him; the years after his graduation were years of poverty and bitter hurt, when he was coldly dropped by the literary circles that had first taken him up and then decided they had exaggerated his importance; then came imprisonment for the crime of discussing socialist doctrines with a group of friends; the famous mock condemnation, brutally contrived to "teach a lesson," when the prisoners were led out to the place of execution and suffered to hear the death penalty read before their last-minute, melodramatic reprieve; exile in Siberia; an unfortunate marriage; a tormenting love affair; bankruptcy—and with all this, a nervous ailment that early in life developed into epilepsy. It was only the devotion of his second wife and the growing development of artistic power that brought a measure of stability and happiness into this tragic life. His mind was able to make a triumph of this suffering. Poetic, philosophic, independent, it forged its own measures and reached conclusions that were far ahead of its generation.

Unjustifiably, Dostoevsky's acquiescence in hardship has been held against him. He has been thought cowardly and even hypocritical for having proclaimed that his imprisonment had been a salutary experience. But however unusual his reaction, it was for him completely logical and certainly not opportunist. Nothing worse can be imagined than the circumstances under which he had been obliged to live:

Imagine to yourself [he wrote his brother] an old tumble-down wooden building which it has long ago been decided to scrap, and which is no longer fit for use. In summer intolerably stuffy, in winter unbearably cold. All the floors rotten. An inch of filth on the floor on which you slip and fall. The little windows frosted up so that the whole day long it is impossible to read. On the panes ice an inch thick. Drips from the ceiling—draughts everywhere. We packed like herrings in a barrel. The stove is fed with six logs; no heat (the ice scarcely melts in the room) and awful fumes—and so it goes on all winter. Here in the barrack the convicts wash their clothes, and the whole of the little barrack is splashed with water. No room to turn round. From dusk to dawn it is impossible to go out to satisfy one's needs, the barracks being locked; a large tub is placed in the corridor and the stench is insufferable. All the convicts stink like swine and say that it is impossible not to behave like swine "since we are living beings" . . .

For five years I have lived under the control of warders in a crowd of human beings, and have never been alone for a single hour. To be alone is a necessity of normal existence, like drinking and eating; otherwise, in this forced communal life you become a hater of mankind. The society of people acts like a poison or an infection, and from this insufferable torment I have suffered more than from anything these five years. There have even been moments when I hated everyone who crossed my path, blameless or guilty, and looked on them as thieves who were stealing my life with impunity.

It is characteristic of Dostoevsky that what should have hurt him most in the hardships he catalogues here was not physical discomfort but estrangement from people. The reason for this alienation was not only the herd proximity he describes, but the fact that he was looked on suspiciously by his fellow convicts because of his education and social position. He managed to break down the barrier and, as a result, was able to write a remarkable book about them when he returned to European Russia. This book, *Memoirs from the House of the Dead,* shows clearly why Dostoevsky considered his period of exile a time of growth, not a break in his development.

Before Siberia his concern for the underdog had expressed his knowledge of himself. He invented symbols for what he knew most intimately—the duality of his humiliated ego. In Siberia he found his own experience objectified and corroborated a hundred times over. There were among the convicts the meek whose meekness harbored depths of violence, and monsters of cruelty who could not tolerate the sickness of a pet dog; mildest, humblest individuals who were guilty of atrocious crimes, and willful bullies who were in essence weaklings and cowards. For years, Dostoevsky found, a man would live quietly, submitting to a harsh lot, then, all of a sudden, something would go wrong and he would stab his neighbor. That, he observed, happened with the quietest, the least noticed of men. And they would give way to crime not in moments of blind passion, but knowing perfectly well that they would be executed in consequence. There was an irresistible thrill in perpetrating such deeds, like that of a man on a high tower who feels he must jump off; he knows he will be killed, but not to jump would be more disastrous. This, of course, is a feeling that comes as the climax of long suppression and accumulated hurt; it is the ego crying out for recognition, ready to extinguish itself for the sake of a moment's self-assertion. Barring certain criminal monsters to whom the rule did not apply, a man would commit a crime just to prove himself a human being in his own right. Even in jail the murderer demanded a certain amount of respect. Without ever forgetting that he was an offender and knowing perfectly well that he was at the mercy of the jailers, he always demanded to be treated as a human being. He would submit to punishment, since he knew it was deserved, but to injustice he would not submit; there was a line in his code of ethics which the keeper would overstep at his peril. Such were the convicts. A man's sense of his own dignity was even more important, Dostoevsky decided, than he had hitherto realized. And, he discovered, this dignity could be destroyed not only by the absence but by an overabundance of power, as was true of the jailers who were always tyrants, often sadists. "A man who has once experienced power," Dostoevsky wrote, "and the possibility of humiliating another creature with the deepest kind of humiliation, somehow loses control over his own sensations. Tyranny is a habit; it can develop, and it does develop, ultimately, into illness . . . The best man in the world can become crude and callous through habit to the point of bestiality." Furthermore, a sense of power was tempting and contagious. It was destructive not only to individuals but to states, and a society that looked on it indifferently was already contaminated in essence. The executioner was to be found in embryo in every modern man. Even those who talked against it had not, all of them, overcome their lust for power. Every factory owner, for example, must experience a kind of irritated joy in the fact that the man he employs, with sometimes his whole family, is entirely dependent on him. But although conditions of society contained elements that favored crime, man himself, and not his milieu, was responsible for it. "It is high time," Dostoevsky wrote, "we stopped complaining about environment which has made us what we are," high time we stopped finding our surroundings responsible for the meanness of our natures. This feeling about material things as relatively unimportant led to that lack of emphasis on prison reform which made readers of the West impatient with the book, especially since they had just been stirred by *Uncle Tom's Cabin*. But Dostoevsky's absence of humanitarianism is not indifference to the fate of man. Only his emphasis is an unexpected one. "Here I am," he writes toward the end of the book, "trying to classify our whole prison camp in categories; but is that possible? Reality is infinitely varied, in comparison with everything, even with the cleverest deductions of abstract thought, and it will not tolerate harsh and broad distinctions." This respect for the individual is both the assumption on which the book is written and its most significant conclusion. It is with the nature of man, not with his physical comfort, that Dostoevsky is concerned. And not only here, but increasingly so in all his subsequent work.

In 1864, five years after his return from Siberia, Dostoevsky published a novelette, *Notes from Underground,* the central point of his work, as Nietzsche was first to point out. It is a monologue by a man who tries to rid himself of a sense of guilt and self-abhorrence by writing down a confession; and it is a disturbing self-portrait that spares neither the man who gives it nor his readers. Hatred is the ruling factor in the nature of the Underground Man. He detests himself and despises others, and this hatred leads him to deny every impulse to good, every manifestation of health, beauty, clarity. He begins by announcing that although he is ill, he will not, out of sheer spite, see a doctor: "My liver is bad—well, let it get worse!" For twenty years—and he is now forty—he has lived in solitude. Long before, when he had a job, he used to take pleasure in hurting people, which he could easily do since he dealt with downtrodden creatures whom it was not difficult to hurt. He was malicious in those days, he says with joy, but corrects himself quickly: had he been malicious, that, at least, would be something to boast of. But he was never anything so positive: neither malicious, nor good, nor a scoundrel, nor honest, nor a hero, nor an insect. He is simply nothing, he asserts; he is utter nullity. He is, as a matter of fact, a hopeless mixture of humility and arrogance, considering himself so ugly, for example, that he has always wanted to conceal himself from people, and yet so different from everybody else and so much more intelligent that all human beings seem to him contemptible, simple-minded creatures who submit unquestioningly to such silly laws of nature as two times two is four. "Good God," says the Underground Man, "what have I to do with laws of nature and arithmetic, if for some reason I don't like these laws and two times two?" The idealism of the Underground Man has reached the stage of solipsism, a rebellious and bold position, with something noble, one must admit, in its wild assertion of individual freedom. But the Underground Man turns his defiance into an infamous joke. He has no faith even in his own skepticism; and it is his spirit of denial, his poisonous suspicion of all values, his refusal to take anything on trust, to accept either himself or others, ideas or beliefs, simply and without question, that makes him a dangerous and evil creature who torments himself and others and finds perverse enjoyment in this torture, a "refined" enjoyment, he explains, which ordinary, active people cannot understand. Just the same, he would like to cure himself of this perversity, but he does not manage to. "Enough," the notes break off, "I don't want to write any more from 'the Underground' . . ."

But, Dostoevsky concludes, "The notes of this paradoxalist do not end here. He couldn't stand it and went on further." The harrowing confessional achieves no more than a loathsome picture of depravity. The Underground Man is an idealist who has been revolted by a materialism which robs the individual of freedom and responsibility and makes of him, as he says, a "piano key," whereas all that man ever wants is to demonstrate the contrary, to prove to himself precisely that he is not a piano key. But his own insights are undermined by skeptical analysis. He is a rationalizing creature, another humiliated Double, like his predecessor Golyadkin, but a philosophical Double with a touchy and finicky consciousness of misery and a strong, though perverted, ideal of morality. It is against the background of a shattered ideal that his notes are written. He cannot put the ideal together again, nor can he even see it clearly; but he knows that it is there. Of this his self-castigation is in itself a proof, and it lends a certain stature to his meanness.

Raskolnikov, the hero of *Crime and Punishment,* written the year after the *Notes from Underground,* is another underground man, who, however, is regenerated, because he has the courage to act on his ideas. A poor student, living in isolation, bothered by metaphysical and moral problems, he wants to find out for himself whether a man is free to act as he wills and whether this freedom is absolute, whether it may extend so far as the deliberate taking of another life. After all, he argues, there are murderers on a large scale, heroes like Napoleon, whose right to kill has never been disputed. There must be, he decides, two kinds of men: the ordinary and the extraordinary. To the ordinary nothing is allowed; they must live according to prescribed rules; the others, the supermen, may do what they please, may even take lives. Like the Underground Man, Raskolnikov despises ordinary human beings and thinks himself intellectually superior to them, but unlike his predecessor, he must have objective proof, and so he determines to find out once for all whether, as he puts it, he is "a Napoleon or a louse." He commits murder not on impulse nor for personal gain, but to test a theory, choosing as his victim an insignificant little old pawn-broker woman whose death will be no loss to society, so that the conditions of his experiment might be uncontaminated by irrelevant factors. But the crime he had planned leads immediately to one he had not counted on, and what Raskolnikov finally discovers is the tragic futility of the question itself. He had not foreseen the punishment he must suffer. He is, of course, sent to Siberia, but the arm of the law is, as a matter of fact, a helpful hand stretched out to him. The real punishment is psychological, the torment of complete isolation from human beings which his guilt imposes and which makes him abhorrent to himself until he has confessed the murder. Raskolnikov comes out of his underground, because his crime is, after all, an act and not a thought. It puts him in touch with other men. Legally it is more serious, but it is less base and less insidious than that of the Underground Man. Raskolnikov learns how infamous are his arrogant views. The Underground Man, stifled in lonely introspection, never emerged from the labyrinth of his hatred; and though he harmed himself more than anybody else, there was possibility of universal destruction in his views.

How this might be is shown in the novel which Dostoevsky wrote next, *The Idiot,* where he had set out to present his "old favorite idea . . . so difficult that for a long time" he had not dared attempt it: "to depict the positively good man." There was, he said,

> nothing in the world more difficult, particularly nowadays. Of all writers (not merely our own, but European writers too), those who have attempted to depict the positively good have always missed the mark. For it is an infinite task. The good is an ideal and that of civilized Europe is still far from having been worked out. In the whole world there is only one positively good man, Christ . . . Of the good types in Christian literature, the most perfect is Don Quixote. But he is good only because at the same time he is ridiculous and succeeds in virtue of this. A feeling of compassion is produced for the much ridiculed man who does not know his worth, and thus perhaps sympathy is evoked in the reader. This rousing of compassion is the secret of humour. Jean Valjean is also a powerful attempt; but he arouses sympathy by the immensity of his misfortune and the injustice of society to him. In my novel there is nothing of this kind, nothing whatever . . .

What Dostoevsky does is to present his positively good man in a negative way by showing, in a kind of ironic cynicism, that all his qualities are the converse of what the world holds good. The Christlike Prince Myshkin is sick and impotent, an epileptic, who has spent the better part of his life in an institution and is, in consequence, supremely detached from the ordinary life of human beings. He is a selfless creature. His judgments are absolutely pure, and people find him almost unbelievable in this, and touchingly amusing. There is, in spite of Dosteovsky's intention, something of Don Quixote in him. But though people laugh at him, they trust him as they trust no one else; and they use him, as such generous people are used by the selfish. He becomes involved in the tumult of their egotistic lives, and since his generosity leaves him not a shred of self-protection, he is broken by all that he endures vicariously and is left, at the end, once more a gibbering madman. The conclusion is, therefore, that Christianity has no longer a place in the world, that it belongs today in the insane asylum, driven there by passionate, self-seeking men. Myshkin's is the story of Christ repeated, with a difference. Christ's compassion had not saved him from the Cross, but his agony redeemed mankind; Myshkin's does not save him from madness, but his suffering remains futile. In a world which the Underground Man has pre-empted, materialist, socialist, nihilist—to Dostoevsky these terms are all one—in which egotistic craving for petty comfort is the accepted standard, the selfless ideal of Christianity has no place.

But Prince Myshkin himself is drawn with great love; there is a good deal of admiration and sympathy for the unhappy, violent souls who destroy him; and even the ordinary, complacent beings who surround the chief characters are treated with much good-natured humor. The hatred from which the book takes rise remains latent. But in the following novel, *The Possessed,* it comes out with exasperated bitterness. This story is based on a notorious incident of which Dostoevsky read in the papers. On November 21, 1869, Ivanov, a student in Moscow, was murdered; and it was discovered that this murder had been committed by a group of young radicals under the leadership of Nechaev, a follower of Bakunin's anarchistic doctrines, who, as the head of a small band of devotees, had dreamed of revolution in Russia. Thinking Ivanov capable of treachery, he arranged to have him murdered. To Dostoevsky this incident confirmed his conclusions about nihilism, of which he had been writing ever since his return from Siberia. An introductory word to *Notes from Underground* had explained that the Underground Man represented the generation of rationalists and skeptics that was beginning to die out in Russia. Raskolnikov's theories were nihilist; Prince Myshkin had socialists and nihilists to contend with. Now something happens that shows up these people for what Dostoevsky had always suspected them to be, murderers and plotters, descendants and heirs of the liberalism of the forties. Pietr Verhovensky and Nikolay Stavrogin, the evil geniuses of *The Possessed,* are the sons of two ridiculous sentimentalists of the old liberal school, one of Stepan Trofimovich Verhovensky, a harmless widower who had at one time cut something of a figure among the liberals of a younger generation, the other, of a wealthy widow, Varvara Petrovna Stavrogina, his good friend, who twenty years earlier had invited him to tutor her son and had kept and dominated him ever since. Their relationship is a somewhat touching and abject affair, a mixture of admiration and secret resentment, a parody of love and friendship, just as their philosophizing is a parody of vigorous and useful thinking. Their sons, young men of the seventies, without a trace of sentiment or dreaming, have learned to adapt the romantic liberalism of their elders to their own use. They are willful men of action who rule others and have no scruples in their dealings with people. Verhovensky is one of the meanest specimens in

Dostoevsky's gallery of depraved villains, an essentially practical, stupid, and cynical lackey, whose one positive trait is his worship of Stavrogin. But even his devotion is base. He adores in blind servility, for with his limited intelligence he cannot understand Stavrogin.

But can anyone understand Stavrogin, the tormented creature of evil, the solitary, daemonic individual who, unlike the other knaves in the book, has a good deal of grandeur in him? The story revolves about him; he enslaves everyone who comes within the range of his influence, and he does so without effort, almost against his will. He is coldly indifferent to people, irritated by their devotion and their exalted view of him. It was probably Dostoevsky's intention that he should not be understood. He is Dostoevsky's version of Satan—and, incidentally, probably a portrait of Bakunin—who must, as the embodiment of Evil, always remain more or less mysterious, even though Evil may, as it does with Dostoevsky, who refused to see it as grand, appear petty in essence. And it is this pettiness of Evil, this *poshlust,* that Gogol had also known and laughed at until it drove him mad, which is the real theme of *The Possessed,* with its miasmal atmosphere of small-town meanness, in which great problems of right and wrong fight out their battles. Not one man but many are stifled in this underground which has now stretched to include the whole of Russia, represented by the vile little town. *The Possessed* is the most savage of Dostoevsky's books. His hatreds are heaped up in it with least restraint, and in point of art it is probably the poorest of his big works.

In his last and greatest novel, *The Brothers Karamazov,* his complex views are best clarified. The murder of old Fyodor Karamazov by one of his sons, the ostensible plot of the book, is, of course, a mere excuse for the real one, which is a theological debate between the eldest brother Ivan and the youngest Alyosha, whose characters and lives exemplify the sides they take in the argument. They are embodiments of their own theories, opposite poles of personality and belief, and their third brother, Dmitry, a simple man of action, is, so to speak, the stage on which their theories are acted out. Early in the story their drunken, lecherous buffoon of a father sets off the argument:

> Is there—he asks Ivan—a God, or not?
> No,—says Ivan—there is no God.
> Alyosha, is there a God?
> There is.
> Ivan, and is there immortality of some sort, just a little, just a tiny bit?
> There is no immortality either.
> None at all?
> None at all.
> There's absolute nothingness then. Perhaps there is just something? Anything is better than nothing.
> Absolute nothingness.
> Alyosha, is there immortality?
> There is.
> God and immortality?
> God and immortality. In God is immortality.

This debate proceeds through various discussions and events which exemplify them and comes to a climax in the most magnificent portion of the book, *The Legend of the Grand Inquisitor,* a prose poem in which Ivan, the rationalist and materialist, formulates his views. It is to Alyosha, his saintly young brother, that he tells his poem. "I want," he begins, "to stick to the fact. I made up my mind long ago not to understand. If I try to understand anything, I shall be false to the fact and I have determined to stick to the fact." His legend has to do with Christ's coming to Spain in the sixteenth century at the time of the Inquisition, of His being recognized both by the people and by the Grand Inquisitor, of the Grand Inquisitor's conversation with Him and his threat to burn Him as a public enemy. The Grand Inquisitor accuses Christ, the greatest lover and greatest benefactor of mankind, of doing man the greatest harm by demanding of him not a forced obedience but the allegiance of his free spirit. Nothing, says the Grand Inquisitor, can make man more unhappy than this demand, the power and the necessity of free choice:

> Thou didst choose what was utterly beyond the strength of men, acting as though Thou didst not love them at all—Thou who didst come to give Thy life for them! Instead of taking possession of men's freedom, Thou didst increase it, and burdened the spiritual kingdom of mankind with its sufferings forever. Thou didst desire man's free love, that he should follow Thee freely, enticed and taken captive by Thee . . . But didst Thou not know he would at last reject even Thy image and Thy truth, if he is weighed down with the fearful burden of free choice?

Only a god can be happy, he says, in the power of free choice. "Thou," he says to Christ, "wert able to resist Satan when he asked for a sign, but the weak, unruly race of men, are they gods?" Man, he says, is a powerless rebel who cannot therefore be happy, unless his rebellion is curbed. His conscience must be held captive for his own happiness; and "three powers alone" are "able to conquer and hold it captive . . . miracle, mystery, and authority." For this reason the function of the Church in ruling the conscience of man is justified. "We have corrected Thy work," says the Grand Inquisitor, "and have founded it upon miracle, mystery, and authority. And men rejoiced that they were again led like sheep." If man had freedom, he would soon realize that he was a rebel, but impotent in his rebellion; he would blaspheme against God for having made him in mockery, and through this profanation would make himself "more unhappy still, for man's nature cannot bear blasphemy and in the end always avenges it on itself." Man must worship: "To find someone to worship . . . is the universal and everlasting craving of humanity." And what he must revere is not what may seem good at the moment, but something that is absolute and unchangeable, something that is "established beyond dispute, so that all men would agree at once to worship it. For these pitiful creatures are concerned not only to find what one or the other can worship, but to find something that all would believe in and worship." The Church, having recognized this need, has made the people happy through a kindly fraud. So that only those who guard the mystery are unhappy. And "How does your poem end?" cries Alyosha. The end is that Christ, without a word, "kissed the man on his bloodless aged lips" and "went away." Christ, that is, has understood the wisdom of the Grand Inquisitor, and has thought it well to let him remain in error.

In the Grand Inquisitor's views Ivan expresses his own. He also believes that man is a weak creature without spiritual freedom who must be told what to do and what to believe, that he must be fed first and then required to be virtuous; and he states his views with such magnificence that some critics have thought they expressed Dostoevsky's own. As a matter of fact, the whole book is a refutation of *The Legend of the Grand Inquisitor*. The answer to it is given in the character of Alyosha, in the biographical notes of the Elder Zossima, the pious monk to whose discipline Alyosha submits, and in the madness of Ivan. The problem that troubles Ivan, as it troubles Dostoevsky, is how sin and suffering—Ivan recites to Alyosha examples of unspeakable cruelty—can exist in a world that is supposedly ruled by a beneficent God. He is willing, says Ivan, to accept the idea of universal harmony, the idea of God, but: "Too high a price is asked for harmony; it's beyond our means to pay so much to enter on it . . . And so I hasten to give back my entrance ticket . . . It's not God that I don't accept, Alyosha, only I most respectfully return Him the ticket."

Ivan's "Euclidian mind," as he himself calls it, cannot solve the problem of the injustice of suffering. And so the most brilliant of Dostoevsky's intellectuals, a noble student of natural science, a man who commands others through the sheer power of his positive and strong beliefs, is shattered by his own intelligence, because, with all its strength and nobility, it is, according to Dostoevsky, shallow and mean. The murder lies heavy on Ivan's conscience, for, having been committed by his degenerate and spiritually dependent half brother Smerdyakov, it is the logical outcome of the theories he had himself expounded. Ivan is lost through this consciousness of guilt and through the realization that his grandest views are, in the last analysis, base. In his madness he is confronted by the devil, in the shape of a shabby little bourgeois, a petty incarnation of evil, who taunts him with the authorship of *The Legend of the Grand Inquisitor,* makes him see his scientific views as a miserable superstition, denies the possibility of grandeur in all things: in belief, in morality, in art, in religion. He is like Goethe's Mephistopheles, the spirit that denies, but there is nothing heroic about him. He is *poshlust* incarnate, Chichikov in his real shape, or, as he himself declares, "Hlestakov grown old." "You are a lie, you are my illness," Ivan cries to him. Yes, replies the devil, "I am your hallucination, your nightmare," but the kind of nightmare that shows you what you really are. Ivan is destroyed by the skepticism and denial on which his scientific rationalism depends.

It is Alyosha's kind of understanding that can cope with the problems which break Ivan, a way of seeing which is as unlike Ivan's philosophy as Alyosha himself differs from his brother. It is a way that opposes human sympathy to rationality, strict individual morality to science, selflessness to egotism; that exalts the early Christian doctrine of good in opposition to modern materialism; and absolves God of the cynic's accusation of His responsibility for evil. Each man, according to the Elder Zossima, in whose doctrines Alyosha had been schooled, is accountable for the sins of all men, a position that, contrary to the Grand Inquisitor's, throws moral responsibility back on man, with a vengeance. All that is unconscious in the world, Zossima holds, is good in essence: trees, flowers, animals, children are good; even savage beasts are good, for their destructiveness is natural and so not morally reprehensible. But on man, who is endowed with consciousness and the ability to choose between right and wrong, a difficult morality is imposed. He cannot proceed with the elemental unconsciousness of nature, although if he sins, he can be regenerated by the primitive. His obligation as a man is to set in his own behavior a standard of conduct so high as to make sin impossible for others. If sin exists, it is that he himself has not been good enough. He has no right to shift responsibility on an unjust God and an evil world.

It is sometimes thought, because his understanding of criminals is extraordinary, that Dostoevsky defends crime. But nothing could be farther from the truth. His is the severe view of individual responsibility which Zossima expounds. If Dostoevsky sympathizes with the wrongdoer it is not through sentimental humanitarianism, but through an imaginative insight into the kind of suffering that leads to felony. His view is almost scientific in its analysis of how humiliation can destroy a man's integrity by way of madness, crime, or intellectual inhumanity. An ego's destruction is for him a terrible and awesome spectacle, and the tragedy of it is the heart of his creation. His characters are not—like Tolstoy's, for example—creatures with an overplus of vital desire; they are marginal souls who are in danger of going under, and whose whole existence is a desperate assertion of their right to be. What seems queer in their actions can be usually explained by this struggle for survival. The pattern of behavior of Dostoevsky's women, for example, always changing violently from friendliness to hostility, which Proust said he had found monotonous, is the behavior of humiliated beings playing the role of courtesy imposed on them by society, until the moment endurance has reached its limit and their real self breaks through the rules of convention. Their pride is a refuge from humiliation and their violence shows strength in contrast to the triviality and falseness by which they are surrounded. Essentially they are not different from Dostoevsky's men, whose individuality must also find devious ways to assert itself: through intellectual dominance, as with Ivan Karamazov, through murder, as with Raskolnikov, through self-abasement, as with all the underground men. But even though there may be much nobility in these people, what they do is not condoned. They are always seen as harmful, hurting not only themselves but others, and thus guilty of the crime from which they themselves have suffered. A lack of respect for the individual has endless repercussions. Tyranny results from humiliation and, as Nietzsche learned from Dostoevsky, divides humanity into masters and slaves. In one way or another all humiliated beings are like the Underground Man, the climax of whose confession is a tale of how he willfully tormented a poor young prostitute who had once felt sorry for him and showed him some affection.

What a man can suffer and what his suffering may lead to is the point of departure in Dostoevsky's understanding of life. The next step is his view that the tyrant and his victim are necessary to each other. Just as Makar Devushkin needs Varenka, through whom he suffers, and as Mr. Golyadkin is not complete without his double, and Raskolnikov must have Porfiriy Petrovich to punish him, and Ivan Karamazov, Smerdyakov to understand himself, so every human being cannot be complete without assimilating his antithesis. The clearest illustration of this is a short novel, *The Eternal Husband,* which was written just before *The Brothers Karamazov.* It is the tale of how a man, after his wife dies and he discovers her unfaithfulness,

deals with one of her former lovers. Lover and husband
are engaged in a psychological duel which is necessary to
them both, for each is the other's double, and each must
confront the other in a realistic way before he can go on
living in any kind of peace. At the beginning of the story
the lover is in a confused, irritated state, sick with a variety
of hypochondriacal ailments and troubled by a worri-
some lawsuit which he considers the cause of his misery.
As a matter of fact, his real trouble is that he cannot decide
whether he had really loved as much as he imagined he
did the woman who had dropped him summarily nine
years earlier. Now he discovers that she is dead and that
she had had a child by him, and the passion with which
he finds himself attached to the little girl shows him that
he had loved not only genuinely but deeply. He is still in
doubt, however, as to how much the husband knows about
all this, and so long as this doubt persists he is in the dis-
traught state of a criminal who has not yet confessed.
Meanwhile the husband haunts him in nightmarish, supposedly accidental, meetings on crowded city streets, taking
a long while to make himself known. Days after he has
been running into him, the lover cannot place him; significantly so, for the husband is the embodiment of his sense
of guilt. It is not for revenge that the husband plays a cat-
and-mouse game with his rival, but to find out what he is
really like. The husband is a weakling, a blindly devoted
man whose wife had held him in subjection and who had
taken to drink after her death. The lover is really his
double, his own successful self, like the Nose in uniform
in Gogol's story or the worthy creature who confronts Mr.
Golyadkin. He must stand up to him to take the measure
of himself. It is for the same reason that presently he in-

vites the lover to meet his new fiancée. He wants to prove to himself that he too can be loved, that he has nothing to fear from this other man, and it is only after he is here once more humiliated that he attempts to murder his rival. Even so the attempt is not premeditated. Up to the last moment he wants to make a friend of him; he fawns on him, nurses him. For, after all, to be his friend would mean that he was on a par with him; it would be a greater victory than to kill him. Psychologically his instinct is right: he wants to understand and accept the most painful experience of his life. But he is too great a coward. His genuine admiration for his rival is too involved with jealousy, suppressed hatred, and self-distrust, and so he must kill him instead of making him a friend; he must cut off the painful experience instead of taking it in. The attempted murder fails, which gives the story a facetious turn. The husband shows himself to the end a pitiful, despicable, and ludicrous sneak, an unsuccessful Smerdyakov, for whom he is probably an early sketch, an Underground Man who misses being sinister because he never manages to do what he sets out to do. He is never "cured," because he lacks the moral vigor for cure, base enough to have no conscience, bothered neither by his attempted murder nor by what amounts to the murder of his wife's daughter. The lover's cure is more successful, but it is not complete. As soon as things have been cleared up, he regains his health and his good humor. The lawsuit also comes out well. Just as at the beginning everything was going wrong, so now everything seems right. But not quite right. At the end he discovers that the husband can still disturb him. For although his immediate problems have been solved, he has not expiated his sin of deceit and so has not achieved salvation. The one through whom he might have gained it, his illegitimate daughter, has died, martyred by the man he had deceived. His guilt returns to plague him, appropriately, in the form of his contemptible victim. The lover is a less intelligent and far less interesting Ivan Karamazov, confronted by his little bourgeois devil.

To trace Dostoevsky's concept of the Double would require a separate study. But I might indicate here a certain interesting series of confrontations. In *The Idiot* the selfless Prince Myshkin and his sensual counterpart Rogozhin stand guard over the body of Nastasya Filipovna, whom each had loved in his own way; in *The Eternal Husband* the husband and the lover face each other over the memory of a woman; and in *The Brothers Karamazov* it is a dead ideal that lies between the devil and Ivan. And this series of doubles who come to grips first over an actual event, then over a memory, and finally over an idea, indicates Dostoevsky's progressive evaluation of what is important for man. First, it is the life he leads and the society on which he depends, as in *Poor Folk, The Double,* and, in fact, in all the early work through *Memoirs from the House of the Dead;* then, beginning with *Notes from Underground,* it is his intellectual rather than his social environment that matters; and, finally, in the big novels, it is a great theory in accordance with which he must either find or lose himself. When he is frustrated, man passes from mere suffering, through madness and crime, to intellectual destructiveness. And, in the last analysis, it is the inhuman theorizers who are for Dostoevsky the most dangerous men on earth. Others can destroy lives, but these can poison souls.

They are the greatest criminals, because their crime is

the crime of sacrilege, of which Dostoevsky's whole work might, without stretching the point too far, be taken as a condemnation. The scientific rationalists of his day seemed to Dostoevsky most guilty of this crime of willfully and maliciously debasing what is holy: human personality, human aspirations, and high reaches of thought. In his *Author's Journal* for 1873 he relates an episode that has a bearing on this matter. One evening some thirty years earlier he had been with Belinsky, whom he had just met and, in his characteristically headlong way, was ready to worship:

> That evening we were not alone; there was also one of Belinsky's friends whom he respected a great deal and agreed with in many ways; there was also a young, budding author, who later won literary fame.
>
> "I find it positively touching to look at him," Belinsky suddenly broke off his fierce exclamations, addressing his friend and pointing to me: "Every time I happen to mention Christ, his whole face changes, as if he wanted to cry . . . Yes, when will you believe, you naïve individual," he jumped on me again, "when will you believe that if your Christ had been born in our day he would have been the most inconspicuous and ordinary man, completely overshadowed by present-day science and present-day leaders of men."
>
> "Well, n-n-n-o," broke in Belinsky's friend. (I remember we were sitting down and he paced back and forth in the room.) "Well, no: if Christ were to appear now, He would join the movement and become its leader . . ."
>
> "Yes, yes," suddenly agreed Belinsky with extraor-

dinary readiness. "He would certainly join the socialists and go with them."

Dostoevsky's work seems to be an elaborate discussion of
this episode. He spent his whole life proving that Christ
would not have joined the socialist movement. Possibly
some barely remembered incident of his unhappy childhood might account for the pain with which all his life
he winced when men of Belinsky's ilk mentioned Christ
or thought and acted in a way that derided Christ's ideals.
That, of course, can be only guessed at. But the ideal of
sacredness, quite apart from any conventionally religious
dogma, was for him the bright norm of existence, twisted
by all that was tyrannous and degraded by the dull cynicism of naturalistic philosophies. Man must have something to worship, he insisted, and those who would deny
him this necessity, taking love as lust, religion as utilitarianism, morality as mechanism, were the most inexcusable
criminals. They always failed, for their attempt to reduce
humanity to the inhuman was a sin against Nature; and
they had to pay the price of suicide or madness or the terror
of the Underground. Dostoevsky's greatest criminals, the
Stavrogins, the Smerdyakovs, the Ivan Karamazovs, are
proud, arrogant men who cannot love even themselves,
or base-minded lackeys, or inhuman theorizers about humanity. They are the lonely ones of the earth, with no
understanding of others nor sympathy with them, incapable of the one kind of relationship which to Dostoevsky
seems good and important, a compassionate identification
of one human being with another. To identify oneself with
others is, for Dostoevsky, not only to love but to understand and to learn; it is not only a moral but an intellectual

act, a way to knowledge as well as to goodness, and it is possible only when egotistic demands are eliminated. The meek, therefore, are for him the really strong and wise. Nor does he, like Tolstoy who also preached humility, present it as another form of power that gives common men the rewards tyrants want. He sees that humility and dominance offer different rewards and that the choice between them is a choice of ends, not of means to the same end.

Man's attempt to be himself in a world of mental and moral conflicts is, then, the problem that concerns Dostoevsky, and because—unlike Shakespeare, for example, with whom he has much in common, but who, in spite of his interest in twisted personalities, can often see a human being as fundamentally integrated and his destiny fulfilled in the natural course of things—he sees integration only as the result of intense and painful effort, his work gives the impression of violence and flux. He is "all struggle," Tolstoy said of him, and said he did not like it:

> There are beautiful horses, but if a trotter, worth say 1000 rubles, suddenly proves restive, then—beautiful and strong as it is—it is worthless. The longer I live the more I value horses that are not restive . . . I have come to love (Turgenev) very much; and, curiously enough, just because he is not restive but gets to his destination—not like a trotter that will not take one to the journey's end and may even land one in a ditch . . . Turgenev will outlive Dostoevsky and not for his artistic qualities but because he is not restive.

Tolstoy expressed the opinion of many who find Dostoevsky too tense and chaotic for their taste. Yet Dostoevsky, in spite of his wildness, is a much more unified being than such comparatively calm authors as Flaubert or Tolstoy himself—to leave Turgenev for the moment out of account. Theirs is an elaborately wrought calm, a frame that sets bounds to chaos. But their minds are perpetually inquiring, and their writing is an experiment to work out questions that bother them. With Dostoevsky the situation is reversed. All his life is carried for him on the current of convictions which his work objectifies. The passionate debates that go on in his novels are means not of solving problems but of presenting answers, arrived at through an intuitive rather than an analytic perception. His work has a unity of lyric statement; but it is more objective than even Pushkin's or Flaubert's, in the sense that his own experience is depersonalized not through artistic creation but before that creation takes place. Ivan's devil, for example, the incarnation of all that is most dangerous for humanity, man's dream reduced to commonplace, holds no threat for Dostoevsky himself. His own strength of passion can annihilate the devil, whereas the petty M. Homais is a living terror to Flaubert, who cannot exorcise him.

It has been said of Dostoevsky that he "felt ideas," and it is this quality of feeling ideas that makes his work different from that of all other novelists. Pushkin's stories, for example, reflect his preoccupations; when his own life becomes involved in envy, greed, and inexplicable machinations, he writes tales that symbolize the malicious and the uncanny; Gogol's are nightmares for which objective analogues have been found; Turgenev's are clear discussions of current problems; but Dostoevsky's symbolize the philosophic meaning of what he has observed and lived through. His is a poetic process that grasps in an intense awareness not only the outline but the philosophic implications of events, and this gives his work unity of the kind that Tolstoy's, for example, lacks. Tolstoy's dramatic presentations and his discourse about them are done artistically on two separate levels, because they come from different and distinct psychological experiences. His reasoning is sentimental compared with the vigor of his drama. But there is no such division with Dostoevsky. His thought is passionate, and the events of his novels are the images in which he thinks. One feels in reading him that he is "all there" as Tolstoy is not. Even his journalistic discussions about the nature and the destiny of Russia are, in a sense, projections of his personal experience; for all events, those of his own life and those of the nation, came to him as instances of meanings that he had grasped emotionally.

His work is so intense, so melodramatic in plot, and so violent in action that its objectivity does not appear on the surface. Yet it is objective, being in essence philosophic. It is realism of the kind in which is implicit the metaphysical assumption that there is a fundamental unity between the man who perceives and the object he perceives, between the *what* and the *that* of awareness; and it proceeds from introspection rigorous and honest enough to yield knowledge not only of isolated beings but of all men. One is always sure that Dostoevsky is no more swallowed up in the chaos of his creations than Shakespeare is in his. There is even something like ironic detachment in his novels. But he is too much a moralist to remain paradoxical, and even his humor is stamped with the almost savage earnestness that suffering had imposed on him. His concentrated passion, his tone of prophetic fervor, make his work seem restive, without the effect of epic quiet that comes of Pushkin's ultimate aloofness or of Tolstoy's hard-won peace.

CHAPTER VIII

Lev Nikolaevich Tolstoy

1828–1910

IN 1852 DOSTOEVSKY WROTE FROM SIBERIA, ASKING FOR information about "the gifted L. N." whose brief novel, *My Childhood,* he had just read in *The Contemporary.* This was Tolstoy's first published work. It was followed two years later by *Boyhood* and, in 1857, by *Youth,* a semi-autobiographical series of novelettes that give the history of a child's development from the infantile self to an independent being.

Tolstoy began working on it in 1851, when he was twenty-three. He was then in the Caucasus, to which he had fled to escape a life of boredom and dissipation. For seven years he had been shuttling back and forth between Yasnaya Polyana, the estate on which he had been born; Kazan, where, at sixteen, he had entered the university, leaving three years later without a degree; St. Petersburg, where he had again made a stab at a university education, passing two of the required entrance examinations to the law school and letting it go at that; and Moscow, where there were relatives and friends. In the city he played cards and spent money on gypsies; in the country he tried to improve the condition of his serfs, got nowhere against the backwardness and suspicion he encountered, went hunting, and fell into intellectual lethargy. The diary which he began to keep when he was seventeen—under the obvious influence of Benjamin Franklin—is a record of failure to carry out prodigious plans for work and for moral reform. The first entry, March 17, 1845, concludes:

> Train your reason to be in keeping with the Whole, the source of everything, not with a part, that is, the society of men; then your reason will be united with this whole, and then society, as a part, will have no influence on you.—It is easier to write ten volumes of philosophy than to put the least rule into practice.

On March 24:

> I have changed a great deal, but have not yet achieved that degree of perfection (in my studies), which I should like to achieve.—I do not accomplish what I prescribe myself; what I do accomplish, I do not do well, do not exercise my memory. For this reason I shall set down certain rules, which, it seems to me, will help me a great deal, if I will follow them.
>
> 1. What you have set yourself to do without fail,—do, regardless of anything.
> 2. What you do, do well.
> 3. Never consult a book for what you have forgotten, but try to remember it yourself.
> 4. Force your mind to work always at its fullest strength.

5. Read and think always out loud.
6. Do not be ashamed to tell people, who are in your way, that they are in your way; first hint at it, but if they do not understand (that they are in your way), then beg their pardon and tell them so outright.

On April 9, at 6 A.M.:

I am entirely pleased with myself for yesterday. I am beginning to acquire physical will power, but the mental is still very weak. Patience and application, and I am sure that I will attain all I want.

But in the next entry, on April 17:

All this time I have behaved not as I wanted to behave. The reason for which was, in the first place, my removal from the hospital [Tolstoy had begun to keep his diary while he was in the university infirmary], and in the second place, the company, in which I have begun increasingly to move . . .

On April 18:

I wrote down a lot of rules all at once and wanted to follow them all, but my strength was too weak for that. Now I shall set myself one rule at a time and add another only when I have become accustomed to following the first. The first rule, which I prescribe, is the following: No. 1: Do everything that you have set yourself to do.—Have not followed the rule.

And the next day, April 19:

Got up very late, and only at two o'clock decided what to do in the course of the day.

Then, June 14:

> Almost after two months I take up pen in hand, to continue my diary. Oh, it is difficult for a man to develop the good that is in him under the influence of only what is bad.

And here is a plan for two years' work, drawn up at a time when he had decided to retire to Yasnaya Polyana:

1. To study the whole course of law necessary to get my degree.
2. To study practical medicine, and to some extent its theory also.
3. To study: French, Russian, German, English, Italian, and Latin.
4. To study agriculture, theoretically and practically.
5. To study History, Geography, and Statistics.
6. To study Mathematics (the High School course).
7. To write my (University) thesis.
8. To reach the highest perfection I can in music and painting.
9. To write down rules (for my conduct).
10. To acquire some knowledge of the natural sciences, and
11. To write essays on all the subjects I study.

In March 1851 [records his biographer, Aylmer Maude] he returned to Moscow after visiting Yasnaya, and he notes in his Diary that he went there with the treble aim of playing cards, getting married, and entering the Civil Service. Not one of these three objects was attained. He took an aversion to cards. For marriage he considered a conjunction of love, reason,

and fate, to be necessary, and none of these was present. As to entering the service . . . he had not
brought the necessary documents . . .

At this juncture his favorite brother Nicholas returned on
leave from the Caucasus and Leo went back with him. He
began writing *Childhood* in Tiflis in November of that
year.

In its opening episode the ten-year-old boy, who is the
subject of the story, experiences, in rapid sequence, sentiments of annoyance, hatred, disgust, affection, love, and
pity for the German tutor who has made him get up, and
is finally reduced to pleasant tears by the old man's kindli-
ness. To explain this shameful and unmanly display of feeling he invents a bad dream: which is that his mother has
died, and now he can sob to his heart's content, assured of
sympathy. At the end of the book the bad dream comes true,
and the truth is not so sentimental as the dream. The boy
stands by the coffin, proud of his grief and privately exulting
in his role of bereaved orphan, quite unable to sense the
reality of his loss, and is shocked to something like awareness of it by the terrible screams of a five-year-old girl who
is lifted up to look on the dead face. Only then does he become conscious of the odor in the room, and is shaken by the
thought that his mother, who had been for him the embodiment of everything that was most quiet, beautiful, and comfortable, had come to be an object that inspired horror. When
Alyosha Karamazov realized that the dead body of the
Elder Zossima was giving off an odor of decay, the shock
he experienced was not due to sudden insight into mortal-
ity. Alyosha was horrified because his beloved saint's body
decayed like any other body; it was in the life of the spirit,

not of the flesh, that he was disillusioned. But to Tolstoy's little girl, putrescence of the flesh is a grotesque insult to life, and to this she responds with the natural reaction of a primitive being—terrible revulsion.

The natural reaction of the primitive being, not only to death but to life, is indeed the substance of the whole book and the core of Tolstoy's speculations throughout his long life. In this early work there are, for instance, quick descriptions that seem to snare and hold the reality of character and landscape. Details of a dull countryside, such as Gogol used for effects of infinite dreariness, are here transformed into something adventurous and bright; and the effect of the whole is of intensity and great simplicity. The book is, in essence, a record of love, such as one finds in no pages other than Tolstoy's—not a lyric, not a symbol, not a dissection of love, but a rational and candid illustration of the basic human need to be accepted in secure affection, and of the primary impulse to reach out for the beautiful and grasp and hold it. It is a very sympathetic picture of egotism at its least complicated and most pure, of passion in its touchingly tender phase, when the window is thrown wide on the flitting scene and the world made one's own. Yet the boy's animal joys are saturated in a desire to get at some meaning of the experiences into which he is thrust by the material world; to be somehow morally united with nature; to loose his restlessness on a spring day, for example, in a sense that he himself is part of what seems to him beautiful, good, and happy in the world. Tolstoy's celebrated "animalism" is here, as always, qualified by his conviction that the animal is a paragon of virtue; and his ability to recapture through the flavor of incidents a process of nature, of life itself as the matrix out of which all lives are formed, makes for a depth without which the story might have been only charming and naïve. Tolstoy was infuriated with *The Contemporary* for having called his book *My Childhood*. *Childhood* was its proper title, he said. It was not himself he had sketched nor anyone else. The circumstances of his little Nikolay Irtenev's upbringing bear certain resemblances to his own, but it is the process itself of growing up which he has here described. This process takes place unemphatically, without soul-shaking crises, through the boy's ordinary relations with parents, relatives, tutors, friends, and in such trivial incidents as getting up, doing lessons, playing games, being punished. Changes come so gradually that one is hardly aware of how childhood has merged in boyhood and boyhood in youth; of how experiences of detachment and loneliness, of being unwanted and disliked, of yearning and hating, of nursing unacknowledged faults in secret shame, have replaced a state of almost undifferentiated identity with others; of how analytic power, developed in adolescence, swells in great waves of moral speculation that come crashing on daydreams and scatter in visions of anger, lust, and vanity.

This ability to get at life itself comes of Tolstoy's longing for some perfect unity in which all things and moments might be brought together, giving the lie to the division of which he was dimly aware in himself. All his life Tolstoy strained for an absolute, impossible identity with people and with things, and suffered endlessly because unshakable partitions separated him from what he loved. In his writing alone he succeeded. His work, which is always autobiographic in essence, represents the lasting attempt of a complex and exacting man to reconcile himself with himself. *Childhood, Boyhood, and Youth* is the first of his autobiographies. It is confessional in impulse and practical in direction but, unlike many confessionals, such as the self-laceration of Dostoevsky's Underground Man, and indeed of all underground men, it is not a vehicle for inverted vanity to be exhibited, but the means for a highly complicated moral consciousness to unfold and explain itself. In recapturing the past, Tolstoy discovers what he is; and the primary point of his discovery is that ready-made schemes will not do for him; that whenever he acts or writes so as to be accepted by the social group to which he belongs on its own terms, he has reason to hate himself; that only independence which breaks through clichés of ethics and of styles is worth the "truth" he sets out to record. Nothing may be taken for granted; and Tolstoy destroys the forms and conventions that stand between his mind and other minds, between his being and nature, between himself at different stages of his existence; he ridicules both his own falseness and that of people behaving in the implicit dishonesty of unscrutinized habit; he describes what everyone knows as if it had never been known before, "making things strange," and uses words in such a way that they seem to obliterate themselves, to be not windows on the world but the air itself through which the world appears.

In 1852 Tolstoy joined the army, took part in the Crimean War, in which he distinguished himself for bravery, narrowly escaping death and captivity on several occasions; and, examining himself in the present as well as in the past, wrote, at the same time as his reminiscent novel, stories of the Caucasus and the war. *The Raid* appeared in 1853, *Sevastopol in December* and *Sevastopol in May* in 1855, and *Sevastopol in August* in 1856. These stories, like those about the boy, give the same impression of robust delight in physical action, which is combined with great susceptibility to atmosphere and, most of all, to nature, people, and events caught at the point of irreducible simplicity. It is to this stage, Tolstoy has already discovered, that one must look for explanations of what appears to be spectacular— like heroism, for example, which is here brought forth as the natural consequence of men's doings in the conduct of their usual business. "If you come to Sevastopol," he writes, "with lofty notions about superhuman bravery, you will be disappointed, for all you will see is ordinary people occupied with ordinary tasks, without restlessness, haste, enthusiasm, or stoic readiness to die." Tolstoy's thoroughgoing materialism, so aboundingly developed in his great novels, is already the primary assumption of his earliest work, where living bodies and inanimate objects are always shown to be the source of the qualities and values with which the mind equips itself.

The success of these productions was immediate. Alexander II had *Sevastopol in December* translated into French, suggested that its promising author be transferred to a position of safety; and when, in 1856, Tolstoy returned to European Russia, he found himself famous. He was lionized; and, in danger of falling once more into a life of dissipation, fled abroad, to study the schools of Germany, France, and England, visiting classes for workingmen and the newly established Kindergarten. He became so absorbed in his new interest that in the course of the next three years he wrote only three or four short stories. In 1859 he established a school for peasant children at Yasnaya and published a monthly magazine that dealt with his theory of education, the chief tenets of which were: that mental development was more important than acquisition of knowledge and not dependent on it, that schooling should be voluntary and pleasant, that information should be imparted only to gratify roused curiosity, and that innate artistic ability should be given a chance for free expression, unhampered by regulations and canons of taste. The school attracted much attention, but Tolstoy grew tired of it and closed it in 1862.

In that year he married. The diaries which he and his wife kept, the letters they wrote, the accounts of friends and visitors have made the story of their years together a notorious one, with blame for the unhappy way it turned out variously apportioned and explained. The tragedy of Tolstoy's family life was probably more harrowing than any described in his work—when he was an old man he said to Gorky: "Man survives earthquakes, epidemics, the horrors of disease, and all the agonies of the soul, but for all time his most tormenting tragedy has been, is, and will be, the tragedy of the bedroom," and as he said this he smiled "triumphantly," with the smile, Gorky thought, of a man "who has overcome something extremely difficult or from whom some sharp, long-gnawing pain has lifted suddenly"—but whatever may have happened subsequently, his first years of marriage were happy, and it was then, between 1863 and 1869, that he wrote *War and Peace*.

This epic of the Napoleonic Wars is one of the most deceptively simple of great novels—the most unhistoric, subjective, and philosophic of historic, realistic, and professedly anti-intellectualist works. Its accounts of the political and military events between 1805 and 1820, with the famous descriptions—of the battles of Braunau, Enns, Schön-

graben, Austerlitz, Friedland, Borodino, of the burning of
Moscow and the retreat of the Grand Army—are accurate,
but it is more than history. Its stories of men and women
in love are absorbing, but it is more than a moving love
story. It is well known that nearly all its characters, both
major and minor, are drawn from life: the Princess Marya
from Tolstoy's idea of his mother, who had died when he
was only two; Sonya, with a good many modifications,
from his auntie Tatiana Ergolskaya, who had brought him
up; the old Prince Volkonsky from his maternal grandfather; Count Ilya Rostov from his other grandfather;
Nicholas Rostov from his father, and so on. Tatiana Behrs,
his sister-in-law, the original of Natasha, tells in her memoirs that an occasion would be made of the great man's
reading from his work while it was still in progress, that
the people present would nod and wink to one another as
they recognized their own traits, and that she herself, quite
aware that she was being closely studied, would beg for
the omission of certain embarrassing episodes in her life.
(Incidentally, they were not omitted, but she has come out
none the worse for their inclusion.) The pages of the book
are filled with portraits of famous rulers, generals, states-
men, and of unknown but actual men. No novel could
have been better documented nor have drawn more immediately on real people and real events. And yet these
men and women and these events are used for a purpose.
They are transcripts of Tolstoy's reading of life—not metaphysical symbols like Dostoevsky's, but exemplars of
morality. The living portraits are fitted into an ethical discourse, while the historic chess game and the military map
have become animated and are seen from the inside. It is
not the results and outline of public activity which inter-

est Tolstoy, but the process itself of action and the motives to it. He analyzes its nature and leaves us with the conclusion that all the fighting and planning, the councils of war, the orders, the attacks and retreats, all the maneuvers that rearranged the face of Europe, had taken place irrespective of what anyone had planned or ordered, and that the decisive and lastingly important element in them was not the outcome of battles recorded in documents, but the private experience and the minds of men on and off the battlefields, that, in short, historic events are only an outward manifestation of what typical individuals make of themselves. And the central character is neither Napoleon nor Kutuzov, but Natasha Rostov, an ordinary woman, the sum total of whose existence is to love, marry, and give birth.

All the other characters are foils to her, and the war itself is a setting to show her off. She stands for what seemed to Tolstoy to be the goal and the meaning of life, and she is, without question, his masterpiece in portraiture. Intense, spontaneous, unaffected, intuitively right in what she does and thinks, responsive to all that touches her, she is an enchanting animal, whom neither science nor philosophy can explain. She is a symbol of Nature, and her beautiful, untutored singing gives voice to the mute life she represents. She is surrounded by women, each of whom, through some deficiency, serves to heighten her brilliance. There is her cold, correct, unloving, and unlovable sister Vera; there is her cousin Sonya, whose natural liveliness and affectionateness are repressed through early experience of estrangement, making her timid, constrained, and solitary, nourished on the spectacle of others' love, and consoled for what she has missed by the consciousness of her self-sacrifice and gratitude—a pathetic "barren flower," as Natasha calls her; and there is her friend and sister-in-law, the Princess Marya, humble, gentle, and unselfish, her whole being expressed in her "luminous eyes," who by mere chance escapes Sonya's fate. These women are not vigorous enough to demand their due of life; and Tolstoy is unmoved by the cruelty of the psychological law they exemplify that to "him who hath shall be given and from him who hath not shall be taken away even that which he hath," for he is not tenderhearted, has more sympathy with fulfillment than with frustration, and prefers to write of success than of failure.

Natasha is the Beatrice of this *Divine Comedy* of the nineteenth century. Who is its Dante? Is it Pierre Bezuhov? Is it Andrey Bolkonsky? The truth of the matter is that, in spite of their distinctiveness and their differences, Pierre and Andrey are really one character, and that, taken together, they are the hero. Prince Andrey is the most consciously unhappy of all the men in the book. A rational being who has lost the ability to act on impulse, he examines himself and is always dissatisfied with what he finds, feeling that there is something better in him than his life expresses, that he is not doing all he might do nor living up to all he might be. Once, when he lies wounded on the battlefield, and once again, when he falls in love with Natasha, he has an intimation of his latent possibilities for good, but no real understanding of them until he is about to die; then he sees himself and all that he has ever done as wholly insignificant. And he is a man who cannot live without understanding—which, no doubt, is the reason Tolstoy dooms him to an early death. We meet him first at the artificial soiree with which the book opens, a bril-

liant young man of whom much is expected by way of a
career. He is world-weary, bored with his touching but
somewhat vapid young wife, exclusive in his friendships
and lordly in his ways, sharp one moment with someone
who has annoyed him, very cordial with someone else the
next. He can be sarcastic and very dry and cold. He is
self-willed, self-assured, self-sufficient, exacting, and extremely just. He inspires confidence, admiration, love when
he wishes, often dislike. In the army, on Kutuzov's staff,
he is considered by the minority of officers "a being different from themselves and from all other men"; by the majority, even though he is thought "sulky, cold, and disagree-
able," he is feared and respected. His moments of anger
and irritability, when he forces obedience, are always pro-
voked by some injustice done. He is severe, proud, and un-
bending, and, on the whole, people do not mean so much
to him as his ideas. He is a noble, gifted, unhappy egotist
who cannot, though he wants to, find anything engrossing
enough to absorb him entirely. The central point of the
epic is the one moment in his life when, wounded on the
field of Austerlitz, he is taken completely out of himself.

At the soiree at which this worldly, polished, handsome,
elegant young man first makes his appearance, we also
meet his exact opposite, Pierre, who is, by contrast on this
occasion, a bull in a china shop, awkward, stout, bespec-
tacled "somewhat bigger than any of the other men in the
room," with a "clever, though shy, observant, and natural
look that distinguishes him from everyone else" who is
there. The hostess keeps an eye on him for fear he may do
something wrong. And he is the only person in that artificial assemblage that Andrey cares for. Andrey is about
seven years older than Pierre but, in experience and in his

views, much older than that. Pierre has the outlook of a very eager young person who finds everything interesting, without the least power to discriminate. He is naïve, with the kind of naïveté that is never lost. He is Tolstoy's version of *"Der reinige Tor,"* the pure fool, the wise idiot, the kind of youth who never grows up but is more mature than those who do. Andrey is proud and knows his worth; Pierre is humble with a kind of self-forgetful humility. Andrey always does what he sets out to do; Pierre does nothing for himself. Things happen to him and he accepts his fate, a little wonderingly. He is married off to the beautiful, depraved Ellen, not knowing exactly how this came about, but feeling that it somehow had to be. He fights a duel that is arranged for him and, having never before held a gun, wounds his opponent by sheer accident. He wanders in civilian clothes on the battlefield, a target for enemy guns, without thought that he might be in danger, and without wondering later that he had not been killed. There is nothing efficient, nothing practical about Pierre. It is characteristic of him that at a time of great unhappiness he should seek refuge in the most mystic and least rational of religious movements—not as Andrey, under similar circumstances, in useful, practical activity. Pierre keeps a diary that is much like Tolstoy's own in his youth, full of self-examination, faultfinding, and plans for improvement, with the same hopeful determination overcome by passions he cannot control. And this self-examination is very different from Andrey's philosophic reasoning. Pierre begins with an intuitive certainty of right and wrong, and his problem is to live according to what he has always known to be right; but Andrey spends his whole life trying to figure out what is right and what is wrong, and the

truth to which he comes, at the very end, is the truth that
Pierre had known from the beginning. Pierre is the "natural" man; Andrey, the worldly man at his best. And
taken together they represent Tolstoy himself, with all the
conflicting elements in his nature. Andrey, the proud, ambitious rationalist, difficult to please, demanding high position, respect, and complete devotion, exclusive, cold, critical, just, capable of hatred, vengeance, scorn, self-controlled
and not easily moved, is the man Tolstoy knew himself
to be among people. The emotional, uncertain, humble, un-
ambitious Pierre, thinking everything good that is not positively harmful, friendly, warmhearted, spontaneous, generous, uncritical, given to momentary dislikes, annoyance,
and anger, but quite incapable of prolonged enmity, im-
petuous, violent, very easily moved, is the man Tolstoy was
in himself and would have liked to be with others. That
Andrey should die but Pierre live on, happily married to
Natasha, is a form of wish-fulfillment on the part of their
creator.

The same distinction between the simple, natural man,
humble and really wise, and the learned, proud, glittering
creature of society extends to the high command of the
army. To Tolstoy the great military leader of the war is
the Russian general, Kutuzov, an unheroic figure as heroic
figures are conceived. Old, feeble, blind of one eye, going
to church service, reading French romances, supporting a
mistress, there is nothing pretentious or grandiose about
him. But he is so true and honest that falseness cannot
stand before him; it shows up glaringly and must turn
tail. There is something amusing in people's feeling of self-
importance in the presence of the great man, when the
great man himself never thinks of the impression he is mak-

ing and behaves with the awkward simplicity of a humble soldier. What is grand about Kutuzov is his complete forgetfulness of himself. He is the only one of the high command who is not moved by desire for personal glory. He is willing to appear weak and stupid, to sacrifice his reputation, only because he cares more about his soldiers and his country than he does about himself. He is never guilty of a cheap gesture, of a show of power, when he knows that a situation is beyond his control. At the council of war before Borodino, when various generals, in a state of great excitement, are proposing contradictory plans for battle, Kutuzov falls asleep and wakes up only in time to dismiss the meeting. And in the course of battle, receiving messengers, accepting reports, he pays more attention to the mood in which facts are brought him than to the facts themselves; lets events take their course, issues few commands, but when he does—often against everybody's opinion of what they should be—his order has the right psychological effect. His example shows Andrey that what he had taken to be patriotism in himself was only another form of self-love. And Tolstoy's own analysis of Kutuzov is a little essay on greatness.

In contrast to him is Napoleon. A puffed-up, vainglorious little man, a caricature of the supposedly great general. Tolstoy looks on him with hatred and sees him as stupid—vain enough to think himself a leader of men, when, as a matter of fact, he is merely a puppet moved about by the force of circumstance, a tiny, troublesome, contemptible, and callous fellow who has not a shred of the dignity that ennobles the common Russian soldier whom at Tilsit he has the presumption to decorate.

The mistake about Napoleon, according to Tolstoy, is

made by all people who believe in "heroes" as leaders of men or creators of events. *War and Peace* is a refutation of the romantic idea, most notably elaborated by Carlyle, that "universal history" is "the history of the great men who have worked in this world . . . the leaders of men . . . the molders, patterns, and . . . creators, of whatsoever the general mass of men contrived to do or to attain." For Tolstoy the great man is the unnoticed, humble, unconsciously heroic individual like those he had known in the Caucasus, or like the little Captain Tushin who, in one of the most moving episodes of the book, reprimanded for having abandoned a cannon in the defense of an impossibly difficult position, finds nothing to say in self-justification for fear of incriminating whatever man had not sent him the ordered reinforcements, and, when Prince Andrey, who had seen the battle, saves him from ignominious punishment, possibly from court-martial, has only this to say to him: "Thanks, my dear fellow, you saved me from a scrape." It is through these little men that momentous events take place, not through those who think they understand what is going on and imagine they can change the course of history.

Theories like Carlyle's, that individual leaders mold human destiny, proceed on the assumption that men are free to act as they please, that a gifted man chooses to lead, and that the masses agree to be led. But, Tolstoy maintains, there is no such thing as absolute freedom; the concept of free will is simply our term for what is unexplained; even simplest actions, like raising an arm, are conditioned by the determining factors of a man's relation to the external world, to time, and to causes leading to the act. Within a group, which is a complex mass of unfree individuals, proceeding, as it must, only in accordance with an implicit law of necessity, there are, even when it seems to be acting in concert, a multitude of contradictory commands, either expressed or implied, and the resultant action will correspond to one of these commands. The man who had been responsible for it will then be called a leader, but actually he is leader only *ex post facto;* it is not through conscious ordering of things that his will has happened to coincide with the "inner necessity of the event." History, then, like the growth of an organism, is a process whereby the nature of events works itself out through the agency of men. Thus, for example, in the burning of Moscow:

The tales and descriptions of that period without exception tell us of nothing but the self-sacrifice, the patriotism, the despair, the grief, and the heroism of the Russians. In reality, it was not at all like that. It seems so to us, because we see out of the past only the general historical interest of that period, and we do not see the personal human interests of the men of that time. And yet in reality these personal interests of the immediate present are of so much greater importance than public interests, that they prevent the public interest from ever being felt—from being noticed at all, indeed. The majority of the people of that period took no heed of the general progress of public affairs, and were only influenced by their immediate personal interests. And those very people played the most useful part in the work of that time.

Those who were trying to grasp the general course of events, and trying by self-sacrifice and heroism to take a hand in it, were the most useless members of society; they saw everything upside down, and all that they did with the best intentions turned out to be useless folly. . . .

In historical events we see more plainly than ever the law that forbids us to taste of the fruit of the Tree of Knowledge. It is only unself-conscious activity that bears fruit and the man who plays a part in an historical drama never understands its significance. If he strives to comprehend it, he is stricken with barrenness.

This philosophy of history, explained in the epilogue, is but an aspect of the fictional plot. Pierre comes, at the end of the book, to the triumphant conclusion that it was not at all necessary for him to have been troubled by the tormenting problems he had posed himself:

What had worried him in the old days, what he had always been seeking to solve, the question of the object of life, did not exist for him now. . . . He felt that there was no object, and could not be. And it was just the absence of an object that gave him that complete and joyful sense of freedom that at this time made his happiness . . . He felt like a man who finds what he has sought at his feet, when he has been straining his eyes to seek it in the distance. All his life he had been looking far away over the heads of all around him, while he need not have strained his eyes, but had only to look in front of him.

In the old days he had been unable to see the great, the unfathomable, and the infinite in anything. He had only felt that it must be somewhere, and had been seeking it. In everything near and comprehensible, he had seen only what was limited, petty, everyday, and meaningless. He had armed himself with the telescope of intellect, and gazed far away into the distance, where the petty, everyday world, hidden in the mists of distance, had seemed to him great and infinite, simply because it was not clearly seen. Such had been European life, politics, free-masonry, philosophy, and philanthropy in his eyes . . .

Now he had learned to see the great, the eternal and the infinite in everything; and naturally therefore, in order to see it, to revel in its contemplation, he flung aside the telescope through which he had hitherto been gazing over men's heads, and looked joyfully at the ever-changing, ever grand, unfathomable, and infinite life around him. And the closer he looked at it, the calmer and happier he was.

What Pierre has learned is to enjoy the moment without philosophic questioning, as Natasha had always enjoyed it; his life has meaning as soon as he stops thinking about it, just as history is made by those who have no idea of the place they hold in it.

Tolstoy's ideal characters, Andrey, Pierre, Kutuzov, Natasha, form a hierarchy with respect to their consciousness of themselves. The most self-conscious is Andrey, the least, Natasha. And Andrey is at his best when he is least self-conscious and Natasha at her worst when she is most self-conscious. What Pierre learns is to forget himself; what makes Kutuzov great is a natural self-forgetfulness. Pierre and Andrey, who cannot live fully until they have understood themselves, come to the conclusion, after thinking a great deal, that the mind will never grasp what really matters, and that they must put a stop to their analyses and questions if they are to experience all that is grand outside and beyond themselves. Their reasoning has been necessary to this end only: that it has shown them the limitations of reason. *War and Peace* has been described as "a tremendous idyl of the Russian nobility." It might also be called, on another level, an idyl of the commonplace. It shows up as false everything in the unusual that passes for magnificent: fruitless passion, intellectual brilliance, display of power; presents as glorious what ordinarily passes for mean; and proclaims all-important that undercurrent of life which reason can elucidate no more than it can explain sensuous and sensual attraction. Tolstoy's passion for unity makes him disparage everything that tends to division: social classes, intellectual differences, historical epochs, even the distinction between men and animals. He wants to see the world as a great, undifferentiated organism, made of living particles, of which each one is a symbol of the whole. The particles that try to be somehow different, like Napoleon, disrupt the organism for a brief while—until they are assimilated or excluded, and the elemental whole, the living process of historical development pursues its determined course.

For all its length and the untold diversity of human experience in it, *War and Peace* is as integrated as a lyric. It is a summary of Tolstoy's own development through early middle age, enlarged and dignified by a philosophy, and made objective in the narrative of others' lives. His childhood craving for affection, his boyhood efforts to be "good," his youthful joy in primitive living, comradeship, and useful labor have been poured into an ethic and a theory of history. Paradoxical as it may seem, Tolstoy is really a lyric poet, whose reason for writing epics is that he considers his private experience worth while only in so far as it is objectively typical of other men's; and he is at his best when he transcends analysis and demonstrates, in enthusiastic simplicity, what he believes and feels. For this reason, *War and Peace* is his supreme achievement; it is more rich and whole than his other works, and as subjective as any of them.

Unhappy times followed its composition: the death of an infant son and of his favorite auntie Tatiana, as well as of other relatives and friends; quarrels with his wife; illness, serious dejection. Tolstoy studied Greek, restarted his school, tried the kumiss cure in Samara. At one point he thought seriously of killing himself. But between 1875 and 1877 he published his second great novel, *Anna Karenina,* and in 1878 *Confession,* in which he recounts the spiritual struggle of these years.

If *War and Peace* is a joyous assertion that, in spite of all disasters, life is good, *Anna Karenina* is a somewhat puzzled and doubting study of everything that had seemed to make it so. It is in every way a more somber work than *War and Peace.* Life seems narrowed in it, and the sense of spaciousness has gone. The children have grown up, their responsiveness to Nature and to each other has given way to despair or resignation; the fortunes of a nation have yielded to household troubles, the battlefields of Europe to the bedrooms of private individuals, a philosophy of history to dogmatic arguments about current problems. The structure of the novel is neatly balanced and enclosed; the scaffolding shows through; and above all, the basic theme is different. The question is no longer "What is death in a process of endless living?" but "What is life to the certainty of death?" In a sense *Anna Karenina* is a continuation of *War and Peace;* Pierre and Nikolay, Natasha and Marya had begun to build their lives on their discovery of what was valuable. Levin and Kitty take up their story, but the idyl of the commonplace is now in danger of fading to platitude. There is the ominous example of the older households: that of Kitty's sister Dolly, with the disruption of which the novel opens, and that of their friend Karenin, whose unfaithful wife is the central figure of the novel.

She is one of the great women of European fiction, but Tolstoy does not forgive her for what he makes her do. Like Levin, he seems to be ashamed of finding her attractive, wants to give his attention to Kitty, and hurries her off the scene, one suspects, because, since he cannot sympathize, he would like to be done with her. For this reason she is not wholly convincing. But that she, and not Kitty, should be the pivotal figure is an indication of the turn Tolstoy's views had taken—for Kitty, like Natasha, is a symbol of goodness and fulfillment, whereas Anna is a tragic failure. Tolstoy's former optimistic faith in the natural and sure reward of virtue has, it would seem, receded to a hope, having given way before too much evidence that evil is more powerful than good; as if, in real life, *War and Peace* had been proved wrong, and Andrey Bolkonsky had survived Pierre Bezuhov. At any rate, the tempest of Anna's and Vronsky's love, which, like war, should have blown over, usurps the day. Tragedy appears no longer as a brief parenthesis, but as the whole sentence. For, though Tolstoy wants us to believe in Kitty and brings Anna to a disastrous end, Kitty's love seems thin and uninteresting by comparison with Anna's terrible, self-abnegating, and yet selfish passion. We are not persuaded, as we were in *War and Peace,* of what Tolstoy would have us believe, for there he expressed his convictions rather than his beliefs, and his daydreams were at one with his philosophy; but here he tries to force belief in what he no longer experiences as true. He is at odds with himself more desperately than he had ever been before; and, sensing the force of what he refuses to acknowledge, he tries, through endless argument, both with himself and others, to come again to some kind of harmony. The struggle is embodied in Levin, who is one of Tolstoy's most unmistakable self-portraits, but it is also shown in the changed method of his narrative and of his characterization. Wonderful though they are, his Anna, Vronsky, Levin, Kitty, and Karenin are no longer remembered, like Pierre, Natasha, and Andrey, as if they were real people. They are not so complex and full, not too real to be fictional characters. They might be segments of the others: Natasha has both Anna and Kitty in her; Pierre, both Levin and Vronsky; Karenin is an angle of Andrey. One suspects Tolstoy of no longer caring for people as he used to care, of having grown more interested in what they represent than in what they are.

The great scenes—such as Anna meditating in the train after her first meeting with Vronsky, Vronsky at the races, Levin's proposal to Kitty, their wedding, and the birth of their first child—come of that extraordinary capacity of Tolstoy to be absorbed in the moment, which endows them with the same qualities of immediacy and drama, as the memorable episodes of *War and Peace:* Natasha's first ball, the hunt at Otradnoe, the sleigh ride, the Battle of Borodino. But the intellectual argument has lost its intensity. Levin's laborious and often tedious discussions are not part of the main action as are Pierre's diary or Andrey's thoughts; they touch it peripherally and have a doctrinaire life of their own, unassimilated to the artistic pattern. Reason is no longer, as it had been in *War and Peace,* an occasionally necessary means to set intuition free of restraints; it now tends to replace intuition altogether. Levin gains no more from it than had Andrey and Pierre, but he expects more and is less aware than they of how much it has failed him. In Tolstoy's development the mind seems to grow both more doctrinal and imperious in proportion as emotion becomes less controllable and more sinister; and this shifting of emphasis represents stages of that discord between strength of passion and respect for all that is quiet and not passionate which was never resolved in his unintegrated nature. The conflict is one with which most writers of the late nineteenth century, with their distrust of the romantic theories on which their tastes and thoughts were formed and with their attempts to retain the stature of idealism in a utilitarian and petty world, were forced to cope. Flaubert settled it by his theory that art was, properly, a passionate record of dullness; Dostoevsky dealt entirely with passion, for there was nothing else he understood. But for Tolstoy passion was restricted to primitive, sensuous, physical, and sensual experience. He began by making it poetic in his early tales of the Caucasus, continued in *War and Peace* by presenting the commonplace as its root and store, and ended in *The Daemon* and *The Kreutzer Sonata* by seeing it as perverse. *Anna Karenina* occupies a middle position, with passion given its poetic due, all the while a somewhat dry analysis tries to show it up as monstrous.

Levin's search for faith is a pale outline of Tolstoy's own spiritual autobiography, the grandly naïve *Confession* in which his capacity for objective self-examination shows at its most honest, ardent, and severe. The underlying assumption of this analysis is that moral perfectibility can be attained through a reasoned detection of sham in both oneself and others, and a will to be absolutely self-reliant, in consonance with an independently evolved ethic. Tolstoy's experience, as he relates it here, begins at a stage of conventionality and moral unconsciousness, the time when as a child, without actually believing what was taught him, he accepted faith on trust and observed the forms of religion as a matter of course and without taking them seriously, when as a young man he tried to perfect himself in both his life and his work, but was moved to do so only by vanity, and wrote for the sake of fame and money in a fashionable tone, treating facetiously and with indifference everything that in reality meant most to him; and then, after his marriage, continued to write for the same reasons, with only this difference, that he now exposed what had become for him the only truth: that one must live so as to have the best for one's self and one's family. Then comes the stage of terrible doubt, when he felt as if somebody had played a bad joke on him, had allowed him to reach the height of his powers only so that he might discover that there was no sense in anything he did. To live, Tolstoy now decided, was possible only while one was drunk with life; with sobriety came knowledge that life was a cruel lie, that nothing in it was either bright or amusing and that the only truth was death. Searching for a way out, he examined sciences and philosophies and discovered that the answers they gave were irrelevant to the only important question: "Why do I exist?" and that those philosophers alone were in the least satisfactory who taught that all was vanity and that non-existence was preferable to existence. The same was true of his acquaintance. They could be divided into four categories: those who either did not understand the problem at all—mostly women, or very young, or very stupid people—and so did not see life as bad; the epicureans, who overlooked the inevitability of disease, old age, and death; those few, who having understood life as evil, had the strength and logic to kill themselves; or, finally, those, like himself, who, though they had understood the wicked senselessness of life, went on living. In the last stage it occurred to Tolstoy that milliards of men lived in accordance with some purpose that escaped his circle of rich idlers; that they came by it through an unreasoning faith which gave them strength to live, and that this faith was really the only meaning life could have. His doubting notions, he decided, were engendered by the class of society to which he belonged, for whom life was vapid and evil, because it was ineffectual, whereas for most men it was neither meaningless nor bad:

> . . . the life of all working people, of all mankind who create life, I now saw in its true significance. I understood that that is life itself and that the meaning given that life is truth, and I adopted it.

One's life, that is, must be good before it can be understandable, and men who think it evil are simply those who live in a sinful and empty way. Animals and birds do what they are meant to do: they feed, procreate, and nourish their families; they are happy, their life is reasonable, and it is a joy to watch them. And yet man's purpose is the same, with only this difference—that he must be responsible for the life of all humanity as well as for his own. Thus, after passing through three main periods, Tolstoy came round to his earliest stage of belief, but he now came to it consciously. His moral search completes a circle and reminds one of Pierre Bezuhov's. In fact, *Confession* is a sequel to and an analytic summary not only of Pierre's spiritual adventures but of little Nikolay Irtenev's also, and of Levin's: and what it yields, especially, is insight into that moral and intellectual radicalism which enabled Tolstoy as a writer to show the distinctiveness of ordinary things and, as a thinker, to squeeze, through force of logic, a plausible doctrine from incredible propositions.

A biographical study of Tolstoy would have to take into account the marital troubles in this epoch of his life, but whether anyone could disentangle with certainty the relationship of cause and effect between his philosophic and his emotional experience is very doubtful. In the course of his life Tolstoy had been attracted to many women, but there is probably only one for whom his passion endured. This was not his wife, but a peasant girl, Aksenya. He had an affair with her before his marriage, and the son he had by her, later served as coachman to one of his younger, legitimate sons. It is she, without question, he had in mind in *The Daemon,* his posthumously published, unfinished novel about a young nobleman's infatuation with a peasant; and it is probably of her, too, he wrote, at the age of seventy, in *Resurrection,* the story of a similar nobleman's attempt to expiate his thoughtless seduction and abandonment of a servant girl. *The Daemon* was written at the same time as *The Kreutzer Sonata,* that exacerbated book of jealousy and hatred between husband and wife; and this fact throws light not only on Tolstoy's emotional involvements at this time but on his ambivalent feeling toward women in general: his traumatic inability to reconcile "reasonable" with "unreasonable" love, and his effort to disentangle what was unintentional and disinterested from what was purposeful and selfish in affection. Gorky thought that Tolstoy hated women. "Woman, in my opinion," he wrote in his *Reminiscences of Leo Tolstoy,* "he regards with implacable hostility and loves to punish her, unless she be a Kitty or Natasha Rostov, that is, a creature not too narrow. It is the hostility of the male who has not succeeded in getting all the pleasure he could, or it is the hostility of spirit against 'the degrading impulses of the flesh.' But it is hostility, and cold as in *Anna Karenina.*" "It is impossible to explain," Tolstoy wrote in *The Daemon,* "why Eugene chose Liza Annenskaya, as it is never possible to explain why a man chooses this, and not that, woman. There were many reasons—positive and negative . . . The chief reason was that his acquaintance with her began at a time when Eugene was ripe for marriage. He fell in love because he knew that he would marry." So Tolstoy might have written of his love for Sonya Behrs, whom he married. But what of his love for Aksenya, whom he did not marry? Teleology might explain certain factors in human relationships, but not all, and perhaps not the most lasting and most strong. In man's emotions, as in the process of history, there was an element of mystery to which the mind must bow. He had said in both *War and Peace* and in *Anna Karenina* that only a love which served the purposes of Nature, and was, therefore, sanctioned by the laws of men, could be considered "right" in more than the conventional sense, that it alone could bring happiness. But he was forced to acknowledge the power and the grandeur of another kind of love which often made it difficult in individual cases to determine equitably who might be responsible for suffering and to vindicate the ways of Nature—and of man—to man. Had Tolstoy been endowed with something of Pushkin's gay, volatile simplicity, he would have been more happy, and his philosophy might have been better integrated. But there was little of the pagan in him. Physical love brought him, probably, more pain than delight. For his relations with women were not adventures which he had joyously undertaken, but compulsions which he resented. He was driven to them by that unappeasable craving of his ego to reach once more its original state of preconsciousness. Sexual intercourse, therefore, seemed degrading to him. He felt guilty, because he could neither accept nor extirpate his desire for it, and his system of ethics was an attempt to justify in terms of Puritanism an experience to which this ascetic doctrine was bound to be irrelevant—or, at least, unequal. It was as if he had tried to explain laughter by means of blueprints or to prove its necessity through geometric formulas—and this in spite of the fact that he knew better than almost any other writer how to make laughter live perpetually, how to reproduce it in all its variousness and in all its stages, from the impulsion to it to its death.

The last thirty-odd years of his life were spent in glaringly public retirement. Trying to live according to his principles, Tolstoy willed his property away to his wife, stripped his personal demands to the barest necessities, dressed and worked as a peasant, published his doctrines in a series of tracts, was anathematized by the Russian Church, and became, unwittingly, the high priest of his special cult of simplicity, with Tolstoyan colonies springing up all over the world, and Yasnaya Polyana transformed into a kind of Mecca, to which his followers made pilgrimages. The imaginative and critical works of these years, of which the most important are the long short story, *The Death of Ivan Ilych,* the tragedy *The Power of Darkness,* the essay *What Is Art?* and the novels *The Kreutzer Sonata* and *Resurrection* are as bold, as free, as sharp in analysis and observation, and as simple in expression, as his great novels, but they do not measure up to them in art, and as psychology and philosophy add little that is new.

From the first, Tolstoy's life is an ethical quest, as fantastic and as strenuous as the search for the Holy Grail, and his imaginative writing is its symbolic history. Art, Tolstoy considered, was an activity as natural and as serious as speech; and he held up to unmerciful ridicule those who permitted affectations and perversions of it to pass in its name. The ferocious description of a rehearsal of an operetta at the beginning of *What Is Art?,* for example, and the pages of *War and Peace* in which an operatic performance is related through Natasha's eyes should have given the genre its *coup de grâce.* In *Anna Karenina* there is a little incident that presents dramatically Tolstoy's views on the nature of artistic creation; and because it is, perhaps, the most subtle, balanced, and complete of his statements on the subject, it may be worth retelling in some detail.

In their travels abroad, Anna and Vronsky stop for a while in a little Italian town, where Vronsky, to occupy

the time, takes up painting. He knows a little about art,
thinks himself gifted, and, having chosen a suitable style,
gets busy on a portrait of Anna, when he hears, by chance,
through a literary acquaintance, that a great Russian artist,
Mikhailov, lives near by and is at work on a canvas which
is talked of as his *magnum opus* and is eagerly awaited
by all devotees of art. It is said that Mikhailov is poor, and
Vronsky feels vaguely generous promptings to play the role
of Maecenas. With Anna and his literary friend, he calls
on the artist. Just before their arrival, Mikhailov had lost
his temper with his wife, had started to work furiously on
a little sketch of an angry man, which had begun to take
on life because an accidental grease spot on the paper gave
the figure a new slant, and, delighted by this unexpected
success, had once more established family peace. When
the strangers are announced, he is in a fairly good humor,
and though he has no illusions about his visitors—he is
acquainted with the general run of patronizing connois-
seurs—is, nevertheless, excited by this visit, for any
comment on his work is important to him. He admits the
trio to his studio and is greatly stirred when they make
appreciative comments, so long as what they say bears on
the meaning of his work; when someone praises his "technique," he grows silent with rage. For he had often heard
that word, and it meant absolutely nothing to him; he
believed that if anyone, a small child or his cook, for instance, had once seen what he himself had looked at, he
could set it down on canvas just as perfectly as he.

The impression he makes on his guests is not altogether
favorable: his appearance is unprepossessing, his manner
is an unpleasant mixture of aloofness and servility, and his
method of expressing himself in conversation is clumsy.

They decide that it is too bad the man is so poorly educated since his talent must be acknowledged as great; and with a touch of magnanimity, Vronsky asks him to do a portrait of Anna. As for Mikhailov, he has rapidly grasped the real character of each of his guests, but the moment they leave, he lets them all pass from his mind; what they had said about his work loses all significance, and he stands before it once more, sure of its excellence, engrossed in improving it. When he begins to paint Anna, Vronsky is amazed that without being in love with her he should have captured the deepest, the most charming traits of her nature, and is quite unaware that Mikhailov has seen in Anna what he himself, with all his love, had never seen. He abandons his own portrait, not at all because he thinks it inferior to Mikhailov's, but because it is now superfluous. In his opinion, indeed, as well as in Anna's and their literary friend's, Mikhailov envies him. Envy must account for his unwillingness to discuss questions of art with them. They do not think of the real reason: that Mikhailov is amused, irritated, saddened, and hurt by their absurd comparisons of his work with Vronsky's.

This little parable on the nature of art has no instrumental bearing on the progress of the novel. It holds the same place in it as all the other discussions—of economic, social, moral, religious questions—which, in a patchwork of intellectual argument, form a kind of homespun backdrop for a drama of unreasoning passion. But it is, in a sense, the author's signature, a miniature self-portrait in the corner of the composition. It is a partial explanation and justification by Tolstoy of himself as artist. Mikhailov does not invent; he discovers and reveals. He is an interpreter, not a creator; and his portrait of Anna is remarkable not as vision but as truth. It has no validity independent of its theme, but the quality it reproduces could have been captured only by an artist. Art for Mikhailov is as unique as his own life; theory and popular opinion cannot touch it; he paints the knowledge he has come by through his natural appreciation of concepts and of people, not through any kind of formal learning. His great canvas, a painting of Christ before Pilate, is a psychological study of the two central figures and an exposition of Christianity, in which is implicit a moral judgment of spiritual and carnal love. Just so does Tolstoy himself draw portraits and interpret Christian dogma, though, of course, had Mikhailov been painting a self-portrait rather than a legend, and if in that self-portrait he had caught the agony of a man's lifelong attempt to cut his way through the forest of his tangled self to a sunny glade of innocence at the heart of it, he would have given a juster symbol of Tolstoy's art.

The record of Tolstoy's struggle is very different from that of the other great Russian writers. The others were obliged to set themselves up in a world that was hostile to them; Tolstoy had to find himself in one that was too friendly. The others were in danger of being killed, or stifled morally; Tolstoy faced the possibility of never having a chance to grow up, however long he lived. He was—in the usual evaluation of such matters—extraordinarily fortunate in the circumstances of his life. Born into a well-established family of landed gentry, he grew up in an atmosphere of simple, genial hospitality, of understanding and solicitous affection. He was physically and emotionally strong; he was intelligent; and, from the first, economically independent and socially secure. Unlike the other great Russian writers, he had neither poverty, nor weakness, nor ill-health, nor indifference, nor absence of love to contend with. The greatest misery of his youth was that he thought himself ugly and inferior to his older brothers; of his manhood, that he could not control his lust for women nor his fits of anger; of his old age, that he found it impossible, in the society of which he was a part, to lead the life he considered good. But he was a Sir Percivale of the nineteenth century—he knew the language of the birds but had to study that of humans— and his writing, whether frankly confessional or ostensibly objective, was a translation into poetry of his adventures in the dark and magic realm of ideals.

There is something touching in the history of this great moralist. In his personal life Tolstoy was accorded the cold admiration of the envious and the exacting disciple-ship of those who did not understand him. His desire for humility was misinterpreted or disregarded. The great-hearted, warmhearted man remained isolated among the people he loved. And we are treated to the strange spectacle, not of the romantic artist emphasizing his aloof-ness, but of an idol trying as best he can to clamber down the pedestal on which he is kept by the adoration of those he himself worships. His writing is at its best in those moments of victory when his own self seems enlarged and divided among the characters he invents. It is at its worst when he explains himself rationally and dictates programs for conduct and schemes of belief.

On the one hand [Lenin wrote of him], an extraor-dinarily powerful, direct, sincere protest against social lies and affectation,—on the other hand, the "Tolstoyan," i.e. a worn-out, hysterical little fellow, called a Russian intellectual, who, publicly beating his breast, says: "I am rotten, I am evil, but I am taken up with moral self-perfection; I no longer eat meat and feed on rice cutlets."

The "sincere protest" comes in concrete drama, the "Tolstoyan" in abstract argument. Tolstoy was an inferior philosopher, through the very fault against which he protested, an intellectualism that cut the living moment from its roots and presented its dead image in abstract pattern. His greatest achievement as artist, an insight into the living moment, such as has been vouchsafed to very few, did not satisfy him, and he obscured it in trying to explain its value. He could do naturally the kind of thing that Flaubert, for example, battled and crawled for. With untold effort, Flaubert managed to keep himself concealed in the wings, watching his play so no one could see him; Tolstoy took all the parts himself, and in such a way that the audience did not recognize him and believed that there were many actors. But his fear that he had only amused, without imparting his convictions, made him step out before the curtain, and then, transported by the enticing consecutiveness of geometric argument, he gave way to lucid fantasy. Thus, when side by side with the unforgettable pictures of Kutuzov falling asleep at the war council before the Battle of Borodino; of Levin working in the fields with the peasants; of Vronsky coming to Frou-frou's stall before the races, that make clear what men are and what they stand for, there are dogmatic protests against "progress" and Western civilization, we wonder whether Tolstoy has not, without knowing it, succumbed to vanity, the sin against which he labored most and which he could not overcome. The reason he could not get the better of it is that it shielded him from an unconquered terror.

Tolstoy feared isolation and extinction more consciously and painfully than most men do. How, having been divided from the world through the natural process of growing up, he might be once more united with it, and how, having established his identity, he might maintain it without exercising tyranny—these were the intolerable questions he could not solve. Through his art he sometimes downed the first of them; he never got the better of the second. He was one of those rare individuals, physically attractive, gay, dazzling intellectually, who subjugate others through the sheer strength of their personalities, and everything in his life served to underscore and develop this native predisposition to dominance. He feared it, and strained to tame his power; there was no one he wished to rule, as there was no man to whom he could submit. And yet submit he must, or be a tyrant. Tolstoy submitted to Nature. Before Nature he could be as humble as animals and children, who were wise, he thought, because they were at one with life, and so, in a measure, vanquished death. Unlike Pushkin, and other pagans, Tolstoy could not be reconciled to death. For Pushkin death was implicit in living; a moment was not spoiled for him by the knowledge that it would pass. But Tolstoy could not love the passing moment, or, rather, he loved it at once too much and not enough to forget its brevity. He had a horror of the ephemeral. Death seemed to him a prodigious unreality, an insufferable fancy of complete and final isolation. He refused to believe in it, and his nostalgia for the primitive was a hankering for the lasting and the real. He was frightened of losing touch with the earth, a dread which he expresses constantly and perhaps most notably in that story of meaningless decay, *The Death of Ivan Ilych*. There was not much more to the conventional and shallow Ivan Ilych than a body subject to decay. But Tolstoy would not admit that this was all there was to life; that death could sum up life; and he granted even Ivan Ilych, at the moment of death, a rather unconvincing glimpse into some bright eternity. But for the genuine, simple man, living in the perfect accord of action and impulse, life, Tolstoy thought, held meaning before it ended; the sheer process of being was its predetermined goal; and the simple man was not troubled by extinction, because without understanding it, he acquiesced in the profound law of history and of Nature, that change is the principle of reality. Tolstoy admired Rousseau extravagantly. At the age of fifteen, instead of a cross, he had worn the image of his adored philosopher about his neck and in the course of his life read everything he had written, "including," he once said, "the musical dictionary," and his love of the primitive had much in common, of course, with Rousseau's doctrine. But this admiration was not so much worship as acceptance and recognition: he found in Rousseau what he had himself experienced independently. His primitivism was not derivative, nor can it be called childish.

Tolstoy humbled himself before processes of Nature, before the course of history, before human passions; and despised all civilized artificialities: abstract schemes for social improvement, committees, "progress" in the Western sense. He had no patience with those whom Freud has described as "civilized hypocrites" who, "psychologically speaking," live "above their means." He could not tolerate Turgenev, for example, for being one of these, and he once became sufficiently irritated with him to challenge him to a duel. For this reason Thomas Mann, who otherwise admires Tolstoy and is influenced by him in no small measure, prefers the more "civilized" Turgenev as a thinker and accuses Tolstoy of nihilism, obscurantism, "pedagogic bolshevism," "orientalism," and "romantic barbarism." Certainly Tolstoy's humility is that of a great egotist, whose self expands over mankind but is not obliterated in it. His conscious, persistent, and vigorous attempt at self-suppression is in itself an act of tyranny—and the extreme dogmatism of his conclusions is proof of it. On the one hand, Tolstoy writes as if he had surrendered to simplicity, achieving in his work that of which he was incapable as a man. He bows before life, which he loves more than his or anybody's notion of it, but regards it with a kind of nostalgia, as if the Golden Age had been known to him personally and somehow lost. He is the grand master of the commonplace. The texture of ordinary things and the pattern of ordinary actions take on with him something of the heroic aspect they have in *The Iliad;* they are the properties of restless heroes, responsible men, whose dignity inheres in the very fact that they are citizens of a quiet world, which, unlike Dostoevsky's, is neither terrifying nor awesome, where God is approachable, love is possible without servility, and the relationship of master and slave need not exist. On the other hand, he lays violent hands on his ideas and makes them serve an ethical but inhuman will. Then the complexity of concrete life drops away, and arguments are marched forth in implacable logic to a moral Olympus on which theories alone can live. The theories are superb, but they no longer belong to Western civilization. Tolstoy loses contact with history in an attempt to explain it, for his genius was the very opposite of Dostoevsky's. His gift was to see the obvious— the full, plain import of usual occurrences. Though he knew how to exemplify beliefs, he could not make philosophic abstractions appear as concrete objects. Thus, by way of illustration, Napoleon in *War and Peace* is a stupid, contemptible, defeated little man, whereas in *Crime and Punishment* he is a poisonous idea that may yet have its triumphs. In *War and Peace* it is the process of history that proves Napoleon wrong; in *Crime and Punishment* it is a poor student's understanding of his own error, which had been engendered by the Napoleonic myth. The difference is of belief in the ultimate importance of events, on the one hand, and, on the other, of reverence for the idea as all-meaningful and all-powerful—the difference, in short, between materialism and idealism.

Tolstoy's greatest failure comes when, in his thinking, he falls prey to his predisposition to play the tyrant. Then, in a lofty way, he makes himself a martyr to his doctrine of simplicity. It becomes impossible for him to belittle the experiences of others by seeing his own as different and better. And so, to justify his ideal of the commonplace as grand, he reduces himself, with an august, blind modesty, to the general run of unimaginative men. Refusing to admit that the extraordinary might also be natural, Tolstoy makes light of his poetic imagination; he wants to give men a religion that will codify what they already know and live by, and so sacrifices his own uniqueness. But the commonplace becomes platitudinous when it struts forth in the panoply of moralistic argument; and Tolstoy seems at the end of his life a giant who, through his love for pygmies, cripples himself to walk in their footsteps. He remains, of course, a giant, even in his martyrdom; and the pygmies have, on the whole, been more grateful to him for his love than for his sacrifice.

CHAPTER IX

Anton Pavlovich Chekhov

1860–1904

CHEKHOV CLOSES THE GREAT PERIOD OF RUSSIAN LITERATURE which begins with Pushkin. What precedes Pushkin is prologue; what follows Chekhov, epilogue—perhaps, also, transition to another period of greatness. And, in spite of differences, these two writers resemble each other. They are realists in a way in which Tolstoy and Dostoevsky are not. They write from an objective view of themselves in relation to the world they know, and this mature objectivity makes their work dramatic. They do not feel, like Tolstoy and Dostoevsky, that they contain the world; they do not present symbolic portraits of themselves. They exemplify even better than Flaubert his theory of impersonality, because they express epochs for which impersonality is more natural than for Flaubert's. Chronologically, of course, all these writers belong to the nineteenth century, but in modes of thought Pushkin is predominantly a man of the eighteenth century and Chekhov of the twentieth, whereas Tolstoy, Dostoevsky, and Flaubert are altogether of the nineteenth.

Chekhov was born in 1860 in the dull little commercial town of Taganrog on the Sea of Azov. His grandfather was once a serf but had bought his freedom; his father was a petty tradesman. When Chekhov was still in school the family lost its money and moved to Moscow in search of better fortune. In due time he entered the university there to study medicine, went through the regular five-year course, and became a practicing physician. But while he was still a student he found that he could make money by writing. He became a regular contributor to a comic paper, then to one that was not exclusively comic, and through these publications managed to be the main support of his family. After college he continued to write, both because he loved to and because he found that writing paid better than medicine. In 1886 some of his stories were collected in a book, which was so popular with the public that it encouraged Chekhov to bring out another collection, while the admiration of the novelist Grigorovich stimulated him to take his work more seriously. The next year his play, *Ivanov*, was produced in both Moscow and St. Petersburg, a success which, added to the others, now made his literary reputation secure and provided him a comfortable livelihood. In 1890 one of his brothers died of consumption, and to discipline himself out of the state of apathy into which this death had cast him, Chekhov set out on a long voyage. He traveled to the prison island of Sakhalin, returning by way of Ceylon, collected material sufficient, in his own words, for "three dissertations," and saw enough to fill a lifetime. The report of his investigations is said to have had some effect on prison reform in Russia, and for his state of mind the trip had important consequences. "I have lived," he wrote upon his return,

"I have had enough. I have been in hell, which is the island of Sakhalin, and in paradise, that is, the island of Ceylon." His life now seemed to him meaningless and dull; whereas formerly the publication of *The Kreutzer Sonata* had been an exciting event, now that kind of thing struck him as funny and senseless. Either he had grown up, he said, or he had lost his mind—he was not sure which. He was in doubt about his writings, as if he had given a patient the wrong powder. He felt alone and useless: if he was a doctor, he ought to have a hospital; if he was a writer, he ought to be with people. In short, after his glimpse of extreme misery and injustice, Chekhov felt the need of some kind of useful social activity; and it was after this that he wrote some of his best things: *Ward No. 6, The Black Monk, My Life, Peasants, The Lady with the Dog, In the Valley, The Bishop,* and the big plays, for there was now added, to his amusement at the world, knowledge of such wretchedness as he had not before imagined.

This knowledge was intensified by his own state of health. In 1884 Chekhov had come down with the first attack of an illness which for some dozen years he refused to diagnose correctly. But by 1897 it became impossible to deny the truth, that consumption was the cause of his frequent fevers, coughing, and blood spitting. He was obliged to leave his little property, Melikhovo, fifty miles from Moscow, where he had lived with his family since 1891, and to regulate his life, for the seven years that remained to him, according to the demands made on it by his bad lungs, living in the Crimea and in health resorts abroad, exiled from the life of the city, from the Moscow Art Theatre—which at its inception in 1897 had acted *The Seagull* and became the chief exponent of his drama—and away for many months of every year from the actress Olga Knipper, whom he met in 1898 and married three years later. He wrote her exquisite letters and the fine plays in which she acted. From 1900 he saw a good deal of Tolstoy and of Gorky at Yalta, the three of them forming, in Mirsky's words, "a sort of sacred Trinity symbolizing all that was best in independent Russia, as opposed to the dark forces of Czarism." He broke a lifelong friendship with Suvorin, editor of *Novoye Vremya,* one of the first to have recognized his gift, by siding with Dreyfus in the celebrated Affair; and he resigned from the Academy when, for obviously political reasons, Gorky was expelled from it. He died in 1904.

Chekhov, then, was a worker, who from his earliest youth had to earn a living, a man ill with a mortal illness, and a scientist. He began by seeing life as a joke, because he was by nature kind and liked to laugh—and also because jokes paid well—then continued to be humorous, from habit, and the conviction that, since there was too much one could not understand, one might as well laugh as cry. He had least patience with the kind of falseness that comes of rhetorical attitudes toward men's ideas and their actions; and he muted the tragedies he wrote with the same kind of smiling, though hardly cheerful, acceptance of human failings, with which, during his final illness, he once spoke to Gorky: to know that one would have to die, not just sometime, but very soon, was, he said, "stupid." Katherine Mansfield, who understood all too well the kind of pain implicit in such understatement, thought his letters "terrible" if one read them intuitively. "It doesn't take much imagination to picture him on his deathbed," she wrote, "thinking, 'I have never had a real chance. Something has been all wrong.'" Indeed, one cannot help feeling the pity of unfulfillment in Chekhov's life, which strikes one as a fragment, a genuine, polished, and beautiful gem, like his writings: the several hundred short stories—some of them but a page long—the many one-act and the few full-length plays. There is nothing long, nothing of which the scope or conception might be called "heroic."

The themes of his tales are so diverse, and apparently so slight, it is impossible to summarize them. Occasionally violent and melodramatic, they are, for the most part, ordinary episodes in the lives of commonplace people. Yet one element seems to unite them—an irony which ranges from simple fun to tragedy and is implicit in nearly everything that happens: two old school friends, for example, meet by chance at a railroad station and are delighted with each other, until they discover their difference in rank— then the less successful of them is suddenly transformed into a tremulous sycophant, and, by contrast to their exuberant greeting, they take leave of each other with the kind of handshake that shows how unbridgeable is the chasm of their inequality; a boy brings his doctor, in payment for saving his life, an obscene old candlestick, the doctor passes it on to a lawyer friend of his, who in turn gives it to someone else, and so on, until the hateful object is brought back by the boy, who is jubilant in thinking he has found its mate; a poor chorus girl is accused by a well-to-do woman of ensnaring and ruining her husband—who, as a matter of fact, had spent his money in some other way —is robbed of the few worthless trinkets the man had given her, and also of the precious objects she had received from others, and is abandoned by him with revolting insults. From behind a door he had watched the scene between her and his wife, and he departs, hissing: "Don't touch me . . . trash! . . . She wanted to get down on her knees . . . and before whom!"—some grim or laughable absurdity is always involved.

In the plays the irony is subtle and elaborate; it is the center of the main idea, radiating to subordinate themes and details of speech and gesture. In *The Seagull,* for example, it is really not Nina who, as she thinks, is symbolized by the waterfowl that has been shot for no good reason, but Treplev, to whom she complains of this; he had killed the bird and thrown it at her feet, as he is later to kill himself, for love of her; and he himself treats Masha the way Nina has treated him, and Trigorin, Nina. In *Uncle Vanya* two goodhearted, loving creatures adjust themselves, at last, to a life of drudgery, for which only their own naïve generosity is to blame. The man they worshiped proves himself to be not only a fraud intellectually but a scoundrel morally; they are cheated by their own mistaken good will, and the real tragedy is that Uncle Vanya's attempted suicide miscarries, since death for him is the only happy way out. In *The Three Sisters* a hope that mere existence might be replaced by life comes to nothing. But the form the hope had taken is itself illusory; one can be fairly certain that even had they reached Moscow, the three sisters would have returned before long to their original condition of misery. It is ironical, too, that Irina should be saved from a fate that might have duplicated Masha's; and that what seems catastrophic at the moment is probably no more than the substitution of one form of unhappiness for another. The central plot of *The Cherry Orchard,* in which old-time landowners are expelled from their domain by a peasant's son who had been dependent on them, is

not more ironic than the circumstance of charming, solicitous, softhearted gentlefolk, full of good intentions, aban-
doning to probable death their helplessly sick, faithful old
servant. So also Lubov Andreevna's attachment to her
ungrateful lover in Paris, about which she talks so much
with such unassuming self-pity, is, one suspects, only
another form of egotism, a masochistic self-indulgence, as
Vanya's frustrated passion is a form of stupidity and the
student Trofimov's mighty views about the future only
repetition of current, liberal ideas, which may, perhaps, be
grasped in outline but neither understood nor acted upon.
Then there are minor touches of irony, on which the
effect of the plays in large part depends—such as the curtain going down on the first act of *Uncle Vanya* with the
complacent toady Telyagin strumming a polka on his
guitar, and Vanya's mother scribbling another note in the
margin of one of her eternal pamphlets, while her son
trails off after the frigid Elena Andreevna, almost beside
himself with love of her; or Dr. Astrow speaking of the
beauty of Elena Andreevna, of the power of her attractive-
ness to move him, and of his own incapacity for love, to the
ugly young Sonya who adores him secretly; or his inter-
rupting himself, in the midst of this, with a shudder at the
sudden memory—that wells up to echo his present frustration and sense of falseness—of how a patient of his, weeks
before, had died under chloroform; or his noticing a map
of Africa and imagining how hot it must be there, at the
moment he has cut himself off from all the human ties that
had given him pleasure and sunk back into the deadly
round of his wearisome life; or Masha, in *The Three Sisters,*
who, in unconscious affinity with fettered creatures and useless motion, cannot rid her mind of the magic lines in the

Prologue to *Ruslan and Ludmila* about the learned cat who, by the curved seashore, walks round and round the oak to which he is held by a golden chain—such touches are countless, and they are superb in psychological penetration.

But the irony in them is cruel—cold, at any rate. This Gorky noted, and it kept Tolstoy from reading *The Three Sisters* to the end. Chekhov insisted that he wrote comedies, not tragedies, that *The Cherry Orchard,* for example, was most certainly a comedy and must be acted as one. "For an ordinary man," replied Stanislavsky, "this is tragedy." Others also accused Chekhov of heartlessness and indelicacy. "Men eat," wrote one critic, "and he makes nasty remarks about food. Men live, and he says nasty things about life." This cruelty, however, comes not of indifference or dislike but of a genuine, though undemonstrative, sympathy with people; and the irony is that of a man who, having accepted the fact that human beings are, in their basic instincts, animals, is always aware of how great is the distance between their "high" notions and their "low" natures.

Chekhov was, first and foremost, a scientist. "The study of medicine," he considered, had "a serious influence" on his writing:

> It enlarged considerably my circle of observation, enriched my knowledge, the value of which for me as a writer only a doctor can understand; . . . and it kept me from making many mistakes. Acquaintance with natural science, with scientific method always kept me on my guard, and I tried, wherever possible, to keep to scientific facts, and where that was impossible—preferred not to write at all . . . To those men

of letters who do not like science, I don't belong; and to those who reach all conclusions by their own wits, —I should not want to belong.

This is not to say that science taught him disrespect for man. On the contrary. Man was the sum and end of all his interests; there was, to his mind, no other ultimate reality; man symbolized nothing beyond himself; and Chekhov was irritated by those who squinted past the human being in search of more important objects to contemplate. In an episode of *The Steppe*, one of his greatest stories—"one of *the* great stories of the world—a kind of Iliad or Odyssey," it seemed to Katherine Mansfield—a little boy, who is taken across the vast Russian plains, listens to a group of peasants as they sit around an open fire, telling fantastic stories. As he listens he takes all they say at face value, but later it seems odd to him that "a man who had seen and known a great deal, whose wife and children had been burnt to death, would so cheapen his rich life that whenever he sat by an open fire, he would either keep still, or talk about what had never been." This might be taken as Chekhov's own credo as an artist. "An ordinary man looks at the moon and is affected by it," he said, "as by something fearfully mysterious and unattainable. But an astronomer looks at it with totally different eyes . . . he hasn't and cannot have such illusions. And I, too, as a doctor, can have very few of them." He saw human beings as not very complex, more or less decent and likable organisms— not magnificent vehicles of passion nor subtle instruments of thought; and so his characters, unlike Tolstoy's and Dostoevsky's, experience easily understandable emotions and expound rather ordinary ideas.

Tolstoy's doctrines were always present to Chekhov's mind. At first he admired them, and then grew disillusioned:

Tolstoyan morality [he wrote in 1894] moves me no longer; in the depths of my soul I am hostile to it and that, of course, is unjust. There is peasant blood in me and you cannot astonish me with peasant goodness. From childhood I have believed in progress . . . But Tolstoyan philosophy moved me deeply, dominated me for six or seven years . . . Now something in me protests; a sense of the practical and justice tell me that in electricity and steam there is more love of humanity than in chastity and abstinence from meat. War is evil and law is evil, but it does not follow that I must wear wooden shoes and sleep on the stove with my laborer and his wife, and so on, and so on . . . Tolstoy has passed from me, he is in my soul no more, he has departed from me saying, "I leave thy house empty." I am tenantless . . . Feverish patients have no appetite but they want something, and they express their vague desire thus: "something a bit sour." So I, too, want something a bit sour. And that is not my case alone, for I see the same mood everywhere. It is as if everybody had been in love, had fallen out of love, and were now looking out for new attractions.

Tolstoy's ideas of abstinence, chastity, non-resistance, seemed to Chekhov trivial, unnatural, and a bit disgusting. We have little travesties of these theories in such stories, for example, as *Good People,* where a woman's fanatical notions about Non-resistance and the Meaning of Life destroy the contentment which she and her brother had gradually built up for themselves and doom them both to loneliness. But criticism of Tolstoy is implicit even when his dogmas are not specifically dealt with. All that constitutes Tolstoy's ideal of happiness and goodness—clarity of conscience, useful labor, simple, "natural" existence—all this is shown by Chekhov to be either false, or harmful, or impossible. He demolishes Tolstoy's idyl of family happiness; and it is perhaps not unintentionally that he calls the predatory, swinish "home-body" of *The Three Sisters* Natasha. There is nothing here of Tolstoy's joy in such natural interests as a mother's caring for her baby, of his sense that small household matters have cosmic importance, and his belief that to gratify one's ego is to grow and become noble. In Chekhov's eyes the ego is usually a monster, a spiritual tapeworm that needs everything and everybody to feed on and gives nothing in return. His people are not grand enough for the commonplace; the prescribed course of daily living dulls both their wits and their feelings, makes crude animals of those who are happy in it, reduces others to lethargy. Nor does he believe in the essential nobility of animals. Tolstoy's Yardstick, that splendid horse, possessing all the moral virtues his masters lack, is given a counterpart in Chekhov's dog, Kashtanka, a creature that, at the most critical moment of his life, gracelessly abandons the man who had befriended and saved her from starvation and runs off to her former, brutal master the moment she hears the sound of his voice.

Men, like animals, are ruled by habit and senseless predilections. And all their fine ideas are absurd if they are cut loose from the simple business of living. Thus, for example, in the story called *The Bet*, a rich banker wagers that a twenty-five-year-old lawyer with whom he had been arguing about capital punishment will not give up his freedom, not even for two million rubles. The young man, who had maintained that life under any circumstances was better than death, takes up the bet and remains in solitary confinement for fifteen years. He is permitted to have a piano, books, and any food and drink he may desire. As time progresses, his tastes become increasingly ascetic: he gives up music, wine, tobacco, light reading. He takes up the classics, learns six languages, studies philosophy and history, from them passes to the Bible and religion, then dabbles in sciences. A few hours before the term expires the millionaire, who has by this time lost his money, creeps into the room of his prisoner, intending to kill him. He finds him asleep at his table, and by his elbow, a letter, which declares that just before his time is up, he will run away, because the wisdom he has acquired has taught him to despise all worldly blessings, since everything is "insignificant, transitory, and deceiving, like a mirage." He has become a skeleton, with long, graying hair and beard; his skin is of an earthy pallor; and the hand which holds his head is so thin that it is frightening to look at. The banker goes away in tears; "at no other time, not even after great losses on the stock exchange, did he despise himself so much as now." Fifteen years before, he had reasoned that the executioner is more humane than the jailer, who, instead of killing you all at once, "pulls life out of you in the course of many years." Now he has himself turned out to be just such a jailer. For the moral of the tale is not that the young man's presumptuous will is a virtue and his asceticism a spiritual triumph. A theory has been tested, and the experiment has led to unforeseeably terrible consequences, for, like Raskolnikov's venture, this too has been proved to be a crime against Nature. Had Chekhov in mind, one wonders, such Tolstoyans as, after years of unnatural seclusion, come to despise the world and decide that all is vanity?

The best of Chekhov's people are those who do useful work, the scientists, the doctors; and it is not their speculations, but their practical activity, which makes them good. The student Trofimov in *The Cherry Orchard,* with his belief that he is in "the front ranks" of a humanity advancing "toward the highest truth and the greatest happiness possible on earth," even Dr. Astrow, in *Uncle Vanya,* cultivating his nursery and feeling, when he hears the wind in his young trees, that he has some small effect on climate and is doing something to save Russia from complete deforestation, are dreamers, who hold onto their dreams with a kind of desperate mournfulness. We, who look on, are made certain that Trofimov will come to nothing and that Astrow will die with no one to take over his nursery; and we know that they, and others like them, have only a will to believe in "progress" and "the good life," but have no clear idea precisely of which elements these splendid objects may be constituted nor of how they are to be attained. Good men and fine ideas are by no means valueless. A wise and educated man, as Vershinin tells Masha in *The Three Sisters,* is not lost, even though his own life may be blotted out. For three such men to every hundred thousand, there will be six in the next generation, then twelve, and so on; and every man must believe that in future, life will be better, he must look forward to it and dream of it. But he should not dream with his eyes closed and his hands folded.

Work, the noble characters keep repeating, is the only way to happiness; and this, it seems, expressed Chekhov's own belief. Gorky wrote of him that he had "never met a man who felt the importance of work as the foundation of culture so deeply and so comprehensively," that Chekhov "loved to build, plant gardens, to adorn the earth," that he "felt the poetry of work." At the same time he also knew that there was too much work without poetry: in *The Three Sisters,* Irina's job in the telegraph office or Olga's in the school only dulls the senses and cannot subdue the pain of perpetual longing for some vaguely perceived blessing that might bring abundance and fulfillment. There are even those who, after years of useful labor, discover that, in spite of fame and the gratitude of many people, their lives have been meaningless—like the Bishop, the sum of whose achievements is to realize that he is entirely alone, that even his mother is afraid of him, and that his eminence has brought him only to pathetic yearning for a bit of companionship; or, like the internationally famous professor of medicine in *A Dreary Story,* who, ill, alone, about to die, sunk in a terrible indifference, meditates, sitting on the bed of a hotel room in the strange town to which he has fled from the tedium of his life at home:

What is it I want? I want our wives, children, friends, students to love in us not our fame, our trade-name, and label, but the ordinary man in us. What else? I should like to have helpers and heirs. What else? I should like to wake up a hundred years from now and take a look, even with but one eye, at what will have happened to science. I would like to live another ten years . . . And then what?

Then—nothing. I think, I think a long while and can think of nothing else. And no matter how much I think and wherever my thoughts may wander, it is clear to me that in my desires some essential thing is lacking, something very important. In my passion for science, in my desire to live, in the way I am now sitting on a strange bed trying to understand myself, in all the thoughts, feelings, ideas that I have about everything, there is nothing general, nothing that might tie everything together into a single unit. Every feeling and every thought lives in me separately, and in all my judgments about science, the theatre, literature, students, and in all the pictures that my imagination paints for me, even the most skilled analyst would not find what is known as 'a general idea, or the god of a living man. . . . When there is nothing in a man that is higher and stronger than all external impressions, then, really, a bad cold suffices to make him lose his balance, to make him see in every bird an owl, to make him hear in every sound the baying of a dog.

Then there are those who find work satisfactory only because it gratifies their vanity: people such as Serebryakov, the retired professor of aesthetics in *Uncle Vanya,* a pompous nonentity, who accepts as his due the sacrifice of others' lives, or the actress Arkadina, in *The Seagull,* and her lover, the second-rate writer, Trigorin, who between them are responsible for the suicide of her son and the broken life of the young girl whom her son loves.

Why is this so? In the first place, because there is no "general idea." In answer to a criticism that his famous story *Ward No. 6* lacked "spirit," Chekhov wrote:

Tell me honestly . . . which of my contemporaries, i.e., of people 30–45 years old, has given the world but a single drop of alcohol? Science and technology are living through a great period at present. But for us authors this is a vapid time, sour, dull; we ourselves are sour and dull . . . Consider that the writers whom we call immortal, or just simply good, and who intoxicate us, have a single very important trait in common: they're going somewhere, and calling you to come along, and you feel, not with your mind, but with your whole being, that they have some kind of goal. . . . The best of them are realists and write of life such as it is, but because their every line is soaked, as in a fluid, in the consciousness of a goal, you feel, apart from life such as it is, also life such as it ought to be, and that tempts you on. But we? We! We write of life such as it is, and beyond that, not a step. Beyond that, we might as well be whipped. We have neither immediate nor distant goals; our souls are empty. We have no politics; we do not believe in revolution; we have no God; we are not afraid of visions; and I personally am not even afraid of either death or blindness. He who wants nothing, has faith in nothing, and is afraid of nothing, he cannot be an artist.

No one, then, is going anywhere; and Russia is a dreary land, where men of promise or of recognized achievement, or simply goodhearted, hopeful men, are destroyed by the overwhelming misery of a perniciously drab, morally stultifying existence. The young man in *The Teacher of Literature,* who marries the girl with whom he is genuinely in love, writes in his diary, at the end of one year: "Where am I, my God? . . . Dull, insignificant people, little pots of sour cream, jugs of milk, roaches, stupid women . . . I must run from here. Run today, or I will lose my mind!" Dr. Yonich, when he first comes to the provincial town where he is to begin his career, is interested in people and even falls in love, but, after a few years, is sucked into the mean environment and ends up fat, rich, self-satisfied, dominating, crude. The man in the story called *Gooseberries* has cherished one fond dream: to have a house with a bit of property and a gooseberry bush. He works, saves, marries a rich girl, and his dream comes true. But his brother, who comes to visit him and tries to eat the sour gooseberries which are exultingly proffered as the sweetest in the world, is overpowered by a feeling that is near despair as he looks on at the sleek, fat, lazy, contented, pompous clod who is entertaining him. The pastoral romance of the epilogue to *War and Peace* and of the Levin ménage in *Anna Karenina* has been repudiated. Chekhov does not think that Natasha and Pierre, Marya and Nikolay, Kitty and Levin can be happy together. He does believe that Anna and Vronsky can be miserable. "He saw life," Gorky said, "as a living struggle of men toward satiety and rest; the great dramas and tragedies of life were buried beneath the thick crust of ordinariness." Masha, in *The Three Sisters,* is an Anna Karenina who is not given the chance to be herself; and the little episode called *The Lady with the Dog* breaks off where the story of Anna and Vronsky begins, the man and woman wondering helplessly what they are to do now they have realized that their illicit love for each other is not transitory but serious and lasting. The strenuous search for ideals, the capacity to be quickly and deeply moved, which with Tolstoy make dullness unendurable and obliterate it, are with Chekhov rare, brief, and mostly nonexistent. For him, dullness is the norm. His people are as torpid as the sleepy towns in which they live; and so the situations in which they might be expected to act with heroic unconventionality come to inconclusive or pathetic ends. As much as to say, happiness and heroism are so unusual in real life there is no point in writing about them.

Like Gogol and Dostoevsky, Chekhov is distressed by pettiness; and sometimes, as in *Ward No. 6,* he shows it up as almost tragic. This story has to do with a well-meaning doctor in the hospital of a provincial town who has found, after many years of effort, that he cannot cope adequately with all his patients and that there is no use in trying to improve conditions. He sinks into indifference and a life of almost complete solitude, reading in the evening, and having an occasional chat with the postmaster, the only man in town with whom he can talk, when one day he discovers that in the insane ward of his hospital there is an interesting young man who has notions about the grandeur of the human mind and the beauty of life and who is bitter about men's meanness and the stupidity and cruelty of those who stifle truth. He talks eloquently, and the doctor finds himself saying over and over: "You're right, you're absolutely right."

He begins to visit him every day, finding himself gradually shaken out of his long stupor—until the young, ambitious doctor, recently sent as an assistant, overhears these conversations, reports them to a higher authority, has the old man examined by an official board of psychiatrists who, on hearsay, have made up their minds about him before the interview, and gets him locked up with his patient in Ward No. 6, where he dies, maltreated by a brutal keeper. But who is to blame here? Should not the doctor have been strong enough to keep his head above water, should he not have seen the maniac's ravings for what they were? Chekhov does not sentimentalize him; he makes him pathetic and a trifle silly.

Or who is to blame in *Enemies*? Here a country doctor, at a moment when he is almost crazed with grief at the death of his only child, is called upon by a wealthy neighbor to come to attend his wife, who is dying. They were having dinner with a friend, he says; his wife had suddenly clutched at her heart and fainted; he had left her prostrate and had galloped over. The doctor is the only one for miles around. There is no one else, the man pleads, to whom he can appeal. After all, he says, as delicately as possible, there is nothing more he can do for his child, but there is a life he might save. Dazed and hopeless, the doctor goes with him; he waits in the richly furnished, perfumed drawing room while the man runs upstairs—where, instead of his wife, he finds a note explaining that the faint had been a ruse and that she was running away with the other man. The doctor cannot understand. "But where is the patient?" he keeps asking. At last, having grasped the truth, he is enraged. These rich men, with their little amours, can drag a poor doctor away like a slave, whenever they please! Both men lose their tempers, insult one another, and part as enemies.

Such stories as these, and the plays as well, deal with great, and apparently inescapable, unhappiness. What keeps them on the brink of tragedy, in a borderland between the grotesque and the solemn? What is the nature of the corroding evil by which they seem to be pervaded? No character in the big plays can be haled before a tribunal to answer for wrongs consciously committed. And yet hopes are killed, wills are smothered, feelings permanently hurt. All four are dramas of frustration; and it will not do to call the personages involved weak, silly, and deserving no more than what they get. The pathos of it is that even the "bad" ones among them do what they can and cannot help what they are. Is Trigorin to blame because his moral and emotional mediocrity destroys a young life that was entitled to something better: according to his lights, he is responsible neither for the infatuation nor the jealousy he inspires; nor is it Arkadina's fault that the only kind of love of which she is capable is greedy and possessive; and who is answerable for the intensity of her son's nature? Should one laugh or shed tears at Uncle Vanya's capacity for hero worship, or at the three sisters' inability to make themselves models of strength and will, or at Gayev's and Ranevskaya's impractical sentimentalism? An evil deed is so much part of the atmosphere in which it was committed that one cannot draw it forth to be examined on its own merits. The beautiful, weird garden in *The Black Monk*, owned and tended by a kind, eccentric, irascible old man, is not just background but part of this story of a psychic illness, which is both "natural" and mad.

There is *The Seagull,* with its carelessly managed estate by the shore of the "bewitching" lake, where it is "hot, quiet, where no one does anything, and everyone philosophizes," and where people invent fantastic dramas and kill themselves for love; or *Ward No. 6,* having read which, Lenin "ran out of the house to get over the impression of being locked up." This art is, somehow, of a radical wholeness. These works are little globes that may, perhaps, be smashed but not divided.

Chekhov never forgot the town in which he was born, and the circumstances of his life made him familiar with various social groups—petty bourgeois, impoverished landowners, struggling artists, country doctors, government clerks, small-town teachers, lawyers, engineers, that unknown and undistinguished mass of humanity which, in Tolstoy's work, seethes vaguely in the background—whom he found drab and petty, but did not hate with the hatred of a Flaubert, for example, because to him they were not symbols of humanity, but just poor souls, who could not always afford the luxury of integrity. Chekhov was identified with their commonplace morality, as Flaubert or Tolstoy, looking on at men from the vantage point of most uncommon freedom, could not be. "I have been terribly spoiled," Chekhov once wrote, "by the fact that I was born, brought up, went to school, and began to write in an environment in which money plays a disgustingly large part." And again:

Write me a tale of how a young man, a serf's son, a one-time shopkeeper, a choir boy, a school boy and a university student, brought up to respect rank, to kiss the hands of priests, to bow to others' thoughts, to give thanks for every piece of bread, often whipped, obliged to go out without overshoes to give lessons, fighting, tormenting animals, liking to dine with rich relatives, flattering both God and men without any need, only through a sense of his own insignificance, —write me how drop by drop, this young man squeezes the slave out of himself and how, having waked up one fine morning, he feels that in his veins there flows at last, not slave but real human blood.

That tale was about himself, but as he emerged from the morass he continued to see everywhere the stupor, the mean servility which had almost sucked him in. There was, he wrote, "pharisaism, stupidity, and arbitrariness" not only among merchants but also among scientists, writers, and mere youths. And he would hold no brief for any group, neither for "policemen, nor butchers, nor scholars, nor writers, nor young men." In this sad Russian mist of superstitions, dreams, hopeless desires, and small brutalities, which holds men as if by wizardry, character neither changes nor evolves, but only shows itself through some inevitable action and, in the little incident of a play or story, is fixed in space and time. Everybody is dissatisfied, and nearly everyone is selfish. There are only degrees of dissatisfaction and selfishness, leading, perhaps, to suicide and tyranny, or stopping at whimpers of self-pity and harmless vanity. Chekhov seems always to be telling jokes, though sometimes melancholy ones, and his meaning is elusive.

Above all [he once wrote] be cheerful; do not look at life so ingeniously; probably it is in fact much simpler. Whether it, namely life, which we can never

know, merits all the torturing reflections with which
our Russian spirits wear themselves down—why, that
is the question.

His own answer to the question was *no,* and he wrote from
a conviction that life was simple.

> I do not remember a single one of my stories [he
> said in a letter to Grigorovich] at which I worked
> for more than twenty-four hours; and *Eger,* which
> you liked, I wrote in the bath house. I wrote my
> stories the way news reporters write their notes about
> fires, mechanically, half-consciously, without the
> slightest concern about the reader or myself.

He was no assiduous Trigorin, applying himself to life as
to a necessary but obnoxious study, in order to make something of it in writing. But neither was he a mere reporter,
as in his modesty he implies. He was a poet, whose tales
were the symbol of what he could not help observing and
of the conclusions to which he came intuitively. He was
very modest, with the humility of a practicing physician
who does his best but knows that he cannot get the better
of death. Mere consciousness of death, of course, does not
explain him. Pushkin, Tolstoy, Turgenev also always felt
themselves in the presence of death, but for Pushkin this
awareness only served to make his joy in the world more
passionate, for Tolstoy it made the problem of the meaning
of life urgent and imperative, for Turgenev it doubled the
sweetness of passing emotions. The important point about
Chekhov is not his consciousness of death but his perpetual, practical attempt to fight it, and, above all, the fact
that he was by nature so self-effacing that he found others

more interesting than himself. To gaze into his own soul did not give him pleasure; and his positive feelings and well-defined convictions were the canvas, not the outline nor the pigments of his paintings. He wrote not from a moralist's anxiety, nor from personal attachments, nor from self-love—but out of a professional understanding of strangers, whom he knew without having to vivisect them.

It was a neurasthenic world he lived in, and his characters are, more often than not, neurotic, always falling in love with those who cannot love them in return, always wishing to be something they are not. When they are on the point of madness, like Andrey Vassilievich Korvin in *The Black Monk*, they may curse those who are well for being unperceptive, but in Chekhov's view they are neither more fine, more noble, nor more helpful than the healthy. They are absurd in the violence of their suffering, which is out of all proportion to its cause, and they are dangerous. Chekhov does not coddle them, but neither does he lecture nor punish them. In a year of famine, when reactionaries were blaming peasants for having brought the disaster on themselves through drunkenness and laziness, he wrote his friend, Suvorin:

To talk now of laziness, drunkenness, and so on, is as strange and tactless, as to preach reason to a man while he is vomiting, or is ill with typhus. Satiety, like every kind of strength, has in it a certain amount of insolence, and this insolence shows itself primarily in that the well-fed man instructs the hungry. If in times of serious grief, comfort is disgusting, then what can be the effect of moralizing and how stupid and insulting must that moralizing seem. . . .

But this was true of more than the year of famine, and Chekhov's tactfulness always prevented preaching. He saw the world as a hospital, not as a schoolroom or a church; and, with neither the vision nor the self-assuredness of a prophet, he was too wise to sermonize and too kind to scold. All humanity was his patient; he did not propose to instruct it while it was ill; his bedside manner was perfect when he reproved it, and when he watched death, of either soul or body, he was thoroughly composed. Above all, he was too good a doctor to be free with quack panaceas, he lacked the smugness to give general advice. He could diagnose diseases, but he did not make the mistake —for which Dostoevsky had blamed himself in *The Memoirs of the House of the Dead*—of classifying men. He did not believe in "trademarks and labels," he said. These were "prejudice," and his "holy of holies" was "the human body, health, intelligence, talent, inspiration, love, and the most absolute freedom, freedom from force and lies in whatever way they might express themselves."

With Pushkin, Gogol, Turgenev, Dostoevsky, Tolstoy, the individual is measured against a background of fate, or of a crushing experience of frustration, or of a love of sentiment, or a concept of good and evil, or a doctrine of ethics—so much so that he stands as a mark or image of values latent in all life. For Chekhov there is no background. If "natural law" to Dostoevsky and Tolstoy is also a law of ethics, to Chekhov it is no more than the command to live with one's feet on the ground and one's head not too far in the clouds. Dostoevsky and Tolstoy strive to get at an ultimately simple moral order; Chekhov is convinced that, although existence may be simple, morality is not—if there is such a thing as morality at all. And so it is a new concept of good and evil that is given in his work. His characters are neither malicious nor passionate, nor are they the victims of a supra-human force. They hurt one another, almost accidentally, simply by being what they are; and these hurts are irreparable, because they are inflicted on the sick. The harm is done imperceptibly, the drama is one of process, and the painful events are swallowed up in the continuous progression of life.

Like Tolstoy, Chekhov was impressed by the steady continuum of living. "Let everything on the stage," he wrote, "be as complicated and as simple as it is in life. People have dinner, just have dinner, and meanwhile their happiness is made and their lives are broken." What happens on the stage in *Uncle Vanya* is but a brief occurrence; the characters had lived before and would remain alive after the final curtain. Life goes on, coursing through individuals; but Chekhov sees in it what Tolstoy did not see: a progressive intellectual development, which is man's hope. History does not evolve without the conscious agency of men, for while the Trofimovs talk and the Gayevs vegetate, the Lopuhins take over. It is in the power of crude, active men to change the course of history; in time, Chekhov thinks, they will become enlightened.

I believe [he wrote a friend] in separate individuals, I see salvation in separate individuals, scattered over the whole of Russia here and there—whether they are intellectuals or muzhiks—strength is in them. No man is a prophet in his own country; and the separate individuals of whom I speak, play an unnoticed part in society, they do not dominate, but their work is seen; whatever may be the state of

things, science is always advancing, social consciousness is growing, moral problems are beginning to
take on a troublesome aspect, etc., etc.,—and all that
takes place in spite of public prosecutors, engineers,
governors, in spite of the intelligentsia *en masse,* and
in spite of everything.

He was not a pessimist, he insisted; he enjoyed life too
much. Stanislavsky tells the story of how at a dress rehearsal one day Chekhov ran up and down the aisle
laughing, to the discomfiture of the actors, who were supposedly engaged in something altogether serious. After
the performance it transpired that he had been laughing
from sheer joy at seeing a thing well done. It was in such
merry enthusiasm that he thought he saw life. That his
stories turned out to be sad seemed almost strange to him.
"The more happily I live," he wrote, "the gloomier do my
stories become."

The reason for this, of course, is that, happy or not,
Chekhov is touched by pathos, which in his work is un-
sweetened and unrelieved because, unlike Turgenev's, the
pathos by which he is moved is that of actual pain, not of
nostalgia—as in that characteristic sketch about the cab-
driver who must tell someone of the son he has just lost
and, because no man will listen to what he has to say, talks
about him to his horse. The pain is sharp because it is felt,
not savored. Chekhov pays man's suffering the homage of
taking it to heart and of conveying it with restraint; but
in this world of woe his own position is rather like that of
Dr. Dorn in *The Seagull,* who hums some well-known
sentimental tune by way of comment on every heart-rending remark, wanders, figuratively speaking, among suffer-

ing souls with a face of perfect serenity and eyebrows
permanently raised, and argues, as it seems to Sorin, "like
a well-fed man." His favorite personage in *The Cherry
Orchard,* he once said, was the ridiculous governess,
Carlotta, the most lonely of all the characters in the play,
the one who has least to look forward to, and also the most
good-naturedly humorous about the dusty end to which
her honest life has brought her. Chekhov's is, perhaps, that
face of saintly charitableness described by Marcel Proust:
*"le visage sans douceur, le visage antipathique et sublime
de la vraie bonté."* And this is so, in spite of the fact that he
often laughs.

> Chekhov *said* over and over again [wrote Katherine
> Mansfield], he protested, he begged, that he had no
> problem. In fact, you know, he thought it was his
> weakness as an artist. It worried him, but he always
> said the same. No problem. And when you come to
> think of it, what was Chaucer's problem or Shake-
> speare's? The "problem" is the invention of the nine-
> teenth century. The artist takes a long look at life.
> He says softly, "So this is what life is like, is it?" And
> he proceeds to express that. All the rest he leaves.
> Tolstoy even had no problem. What he had was a
> propaganda and he is a great artist in spite of it.

Yes. But Chekhov was so troubled because he had no
"problem" that he looked at life, desiring to discover one;
and, though he loved Tolstoy—"he always spoke of Tolstoy," Gorky reported, "with a special, almost imperceptible little smile of tenderness and anxiety in his eyes; he
spoke with a lowered voice, as of something phantasmal,
mysterious, which requires soft and wary words"—he

envied his wholeness of view. It was, of course, the wholeness that mattered; the view itself did not stand the test of his own knowledge of the world, and Chekhov rewrote Tolstoy. Tolstoy's great egotism, with its love of human beings that is, like Walt Whitman's, an extension of his love of himself, shows up by comparison with Chekhov. For Tolstoy, humanity is himself. He is everybody; and when he hates himself, he hates others too; when his own life ceases to be an idyl, he debases emotion, grows jealous of passion, punishes both himself and humanity with a moralizing asceticism, and holds up an ideal for ordinary men that he himself cannot live up to. He is a prophet of sanity, but toward the end of his life there is something insane in his prophecy. Chekhov is neither a prophet nor insane; his view of sanity is not a program but a description; and he shows up Tolstoy's divine ideal as something either more or less than human.

His aloofness is as complete as Pushkin's, and, as with Pushkin, a great unanswered question underlies it—only Pushkin wondered about fate, but Chekhov about ordinary life. Pushkin wrote as if he had accepted terror; Chekhov, as if he accepted nothing but preferred to remain puzzled rather than adopt anybody's ready-made scheme. Pushkin stood farther back from the world, leaving room in the foreground for the sheer joy of lyric play; Chekhov gathered life quickly and shaped it without dalliance. Pushkin loved emotion for itself and liked to emphasize its power; Chekhov was not interested in emotion, but only in emotions as they worked themselves out concretely in the lives of individuals—for romanticism, which was a force in Pushkin's day, in Chekhov's was hardly a memory. Chekhov thought of both present and future in terms of many lives and many deaths, and of the past he did not think at all; Pushkin considered time in the light of man's potentialities, of the crime, terror, and the pity of frustration, and brooded on the meaning of all men's experience throughout the ages. Chekhov culled bits of scattered life and made each one a lovely miniature; he did not achieve, nor did he aim at, the grandeur of Pushkin's sustained, historic sweep.

There is a similar difference between him and Gogol, the two great humorists of Russian letters. They laugh at essentially the same thing: the state of *poshlust* which troubles them both. But Chekhov, in his scientific, twentieth-century way, takes for granted what the romantic Gogol could not tolerate—and that makes his smile almost sedate by comparison with Gogol's laughter. Chekhov sees *poshlust* embodied in his epoch and his country in a way that almost absolves men of blame; and Tolstoy, for whom no social problem seemed too difficult for an individual to solve, could not tolerate the way environment had, in his work, overshadowed men. Even Shakespeare—he did not care too much for him—Tolstoy said, had emphasized people and would indicate a place only by a sign. Now, in *The Three Sisters,* place had become everything. Tolstoy blamed Chekhov for his "cruelty"; but Chekhov did not believe that men could make themselves titans of Tolstoyan self-reliance, nor did the kind of love that demanded the impossible seem generous to him. With all its lack of warmth, Chekhov's view of men seems, beside Tolstoy's, or even Gogol's and Dostoevsky's, lenient, not to say indulgent. His subject is not tragedy, either of fate or of great human flaws, but the pathos of weakness; and when he deals with frustration, which is his central theme, he exhibits, not the crushing of genuine possibilities, which would be terrifying, but the spectacle of men's illusions about themselves, which is ridiculous. For although he says that he believes in the power of individuals to do great things, he never writes as if he had faith in them. They are all like Sorin, who thinks of himself ruefully as *"l'homme qui a voulu,"* or like Uncle Vanya, who is sure that under other circumstances he might have been a Schopenhauer or a Dostoevsky. Gogol would doubtless have made us believe them, but with Chekhov we are only convinced that they are deluded and a little stupid.

Chekhov then, like Pushkin, is amoral by comparison with the great subjective realists Tolstoy and Dostoevsky, who see life either as morality in concrete form or as the outward aspect of metaphysical truth. More cheerful, tolerant, and less troubled, Chekhov and Pushkin can accept even man's doom to ignorance with a smile; they are, in varying degrees, resigned to the impossible. Both are figures of transition, but Pushkin comes at the end of an age which he sums up, Chekhov at the beginning of one he introduces. And for this reason, and also because the eighteenth century was intellectually ordered and well rounded, whereas the twentieth has so far proved to be a chaos of confused assertions, Pushkin conveys a view that is magnificent and whole, but Chekhov presents only very clear, sharp glimpses. Incidentally, one might note, for what it may be worth, that Pushkin is not only himself mature but writes of mature people, compared with whom Chekhov's are children, who know how to endure but have lost the capacity to experience. The spirit of an age, as well as genius, made Pushkin a much greater writer, but Chekhov was no less wise in being able to delimit precisely the boundaries of his understanding and to give his knowledge the form and tone appropriate to its restricted clarity. Pushkin's work represents the triumph, and his life the tragedy, of poetic genius in an unpoetic and unenlightened society; Chekhov's, both the success and the limitations of practical science in art and in thought.

Tolstoy used to speak of Chekhov's work with tears in his eyes, saying it was "like lace made by a chaste young girl," one of those lacemakers who "used to depict all their lives, all their dreams of happiness in the lace-design," dreaming "in designs of all that was dear to them"; and Gorky declared that he himself lacked the fineness and the subtlety to write about Chekhov. Indeed, to give the gist of his sketches is impossible, because the gist is the whole sketch. To explain them is to explain an epigram; to describe his longer stories or plays is like trying to serve up air cut into segments; and to read his letters is to eavesdrop on a heart. Chekhov tempts one to such tender reflections, but to prize the delicacy of his lace is not enough; one should admire also the toughness of the fiber from which it is made.

There was a time after World War I when, especially in England, it became fashionable among intellectuals to think of Chekhov as on a par in greatness with Dostoevsky and Tolstoy. That is as mistaken as it would be to rank Keats with Milton and Shakespeare. Chekhov is, if one likes, the Keats of a positivistic era; and it is more just to see him thus, as it would certainly be more pleasing to his unassuming and fair-minded ghost.

CHAPTER X

Conclusion

EVERY WORK OF ART IS, IN A SENSE, REALISTIC AND
symbolic—realistic in so far as it purports to be a
record of truth (and authors of wildest fantasies may insist
on the validity of their dreams); symbolic, because to whatever extent it may be a record of the actual, the observation from which it proceeds is directed by interest and
usually stands for a belief. But it is not necessarily classical
or romantic. Romanticism and classicism are both forms
of hedonism: romanticism exalts all sources and means of
delight, classicism proceeds on the assumption that to create formal beauty is to afford man the highest enjoyment
of which he is capable. In the case of both, knowledge and
understanding are secondary interests, and, when they are
present, are thought to be attainable by the mind, freely,
without aid from any kind of objective test. For realism,
on the other hand, enjoyment, either as substance or effect,
is almost irrelevant. Delight may be a by-product of a
realistic work of art, but not its aim. Knowledge and

understanding are its primary concerns, so much so that it is always in danger of stepping beyond aesthetic bounds into the realm of the merely useful. If the form in which it is cast has been reduced to triteness, a classical production is a shell; when exaltation turns to bombast and simple emotion to sentimentality, a romantic work becomes laughable and shallow; and when some narrow purpose kills invention, a work of realism becomes pedantic and utilitarian. The danger of each mode is the limitation of that on which its excellence primarily depends: of form for the first, of feeling for the second, of idea for the third. And conversely, whereas the excellence of the romantic depends on overemphasis, on the exaggeration and extension of willfully limited experience, and of the classicist on the subduing to perfect harmony of what might otherwise appear as monstrous and chaotic, that of the realist comes of ability to preserve balance, without exaggeration or exclusion, through a broad and discriminating faculty which reveals the universe to him but shows him, too, the minor place that he himself holds in it.

Even though he must be largely concerned with himself, a great realist cannot be consistently egotistic. His work is a corrective to self-interest in its revelation of where he stands with respect to the world. And this quality of non-egotism (not to be interpreted as altruism) can be taken, I think, as the most characteristic trait of Russian literature. It is displayed in every possible way: in artistic method, in ethical emphasis, in psychological approach, in social implications, even in metaphysical presuppositions and the understanding of history; and it involves an extensive and intricate analysis of the ego.

No one author, of course, may be proclaimed the

spokesman and symbol of his nation, just as no single event may be taken as the summary and explanation of all the others that preceded it in a people's history. The concept itself of nationality is but a label that serves to designate approximately what is, at best, a questionable truth; and it is most justifiably attached not to a separate item but to the recorded aggregate of a development. But as, in a limited sense, whatever happens is the outcome of the past and serves to shape the future, so a great author takes up and carries forward the culture of his land. Thus, although not one of the great Russian writers stands absolutely for his country, taken all together, they form a tradition that one may rightly consider to be representative of it. Even so, there can be no certainty in the matter. All that anyone can do is to interpret, and every interpretation is disputable. In the last analysis, the only question that may be relevantly asked of a work of art is: can one bear to be without it? But when we answer with a categorical negative, it is tempting to search out the reasons for our attachment, to examine the treasured object and talk about it, as lovers long to describe the beauty and the virtues of those they love; and such attempts may even show the supposed blindness of infatuation to be more incisive than the cool outlook of indifference.

Why, then, one asks, is the work of the great Russians loved so much even when it is known in the inadequate medium of translations? Why has it influenced the best modern writers of Europe and America and become part of the tradition of Western civilization much more securely than any of the country's political, philosophic, or economic achievements? The answer is that its voice is that of men, and not of systems, and that the voice of men can be hushed neither by the natural barriers of oceans and mountains nor by the artificial walls of governments and "ideologies."

Perhaps the basic impression it conveys is that of absolute unity between the author and the world he deals with. No theory, no preconception seems to divide him from the object he contemplates. In fact, "contemplation" is the wrong word to describe his experience. He writes not from the analytic curiosity of a scientist, but from the more intimate knowledge of one who has become absorbed in and identified with the person, concept, thing, or theory to which he has been drawn. He writes, to begin with, if he is Pushkin, Gogol, Dostoevsky, or Tolstoy—and these are the greatest—not as a duty, nor from purely intellectual interest, but from an overwhelming attraction to life that craves to be expressed. If he is Turgenev, he yearns for this passionate esteem, of which he is himself incapable; and if he is Chekhov, he is made uneasy by the limitations of his honest scientific position. This going to the world is very different from a man's drawing the world to himself or his seeking to "find himself" through self-surrender. It is a more pagan attitude, wherein the ego remains intact, capable of enjoying external objects and longing to know them. It is an appreciative outlook, which takes many forms, is sometimes troubled, but, being critical, is seldom blind, and is especially attuned to all that is diverse and paradoxical. Thus, Griboyedov's Chatsky, Pushkin's Tatiana, Dostoevsky's Alyosha Karamazov, or Tolstoy's Natasha or Kutuzov are enlarged and brightened by a consciousness of a world peopled by their opposites; Akakyi Akakyievich Bashmatchkin has roused guilt in the heart of at least one kind clerk, even the Underground Man has practiced his knavery on a creature capable of affection; and the satanic laughter of Hlestakov seems to resound in a moral heaven, which he has skirted in his transit through a special hell. Each separate love, that is, is seen in relation to that which is not loved, and every hatred is explained by its negative. Thus also the unilinear sentimentality of Karamzin's *Poor Liza* is given another dimension even by Turgenev, with whom, in such stories as *First Love* or *Clara Milich,* it is enriched by psychological curiosity; in Gogol's *The Cloak* it is deepened to great pity; and with Dostoevsky it grows to the far-reaching compassion of tragedy. Santayana's description of the sympathy which Goethe "felt with things" as "egotistical," that of "a lordly observer, a traveler, a connoisseur, a philanderer," is applicable among the Russians only to Turgenev, who looked to things for the solace and nourishment of his sensibilities. Pushkin, who was, in his way, "a lordly observer, a traveler, a connoisseur, a philanderer," was all of these without solemnity or self-regard. He did not use the world. He admired it, praised it, clasped it to himself from sheer exuberance, and enriched it with a profoundly disinterested understanding. Dostoevsky bowed to the earth in primitive reverence; and Tolstoy struggled to lose himself not in it, but by way of preparation for entering it. Whatever evil qualities the Russians, as a nation, may possess, egotism is not the chief among them. And the ethical ideal, both as it is expounded and implied in their literature, is a severe condemnation of this vice and the praise of its antithetical virtues. From Tatiana to Tolstoy's Natasha, and from Onegin to Chekhov's Trigorin, we are given a series of figures who are admirable precisely because they are not self-regarding, and of villains who are evil because they love themselves more than anyone or anything they know. The whole romantic tradition is damned on the score of egotism in *Evgenyi Onegin;* the whole disaster of the Napoleonic Wars is so explained in *War and Peace;* and the essence of capitalism is shown up in Chichikov's journeys to be a profanation of life itself through the greed of egotistic monsters, whose only aim is to accumulate dead matter.

Egotism in Russian literature appears as petty; and the history of pettiness in it presents an interesting evolution. Pushkin's Olympian playfulness is obscured toward the end of his life by an atmosphere of small oppressions—the kind in which a Mozart can be poisoned by an envious Salieri and a cautious Hoffmann may tempt fate for the sake of money. This Hoffmann of *The Queen of Spades* becomes the evil genius of Gogol, who, partly in emulation of Pushkin, tries to laugh him off but is so bewitched in the magic circle of the evil he portrays that he cannot see through it and finds himself laughing at what Pushkin had not laughed at. Pushkin's smile has turned into a horrifying grin, and the laughter has a savage and tragic sound. Turgenev looks on the issue in a detached and systematic way, but Dostoevsky unfolds its deepest implications. The devil appears to him in the shape of a conventional, bourgeois flunky; the greatest crimes are committed in an environment of gnatlike loves and shallow hatreds; and the noblest doctrines are proved base if they arise from respect for trifling comforts. The great materialist Tolstoy tries to exhibit the divinity of matter and to show how it might be desecrated, and man's happiness sacrificed, by egotistic notions about the mind's pre-eminence. Chekhov deals with a fragmentary world inhabited by powerful little egotists and helpless men with noble theories, and Gorky,

who is the bridge between the literature of czarist and of
Soviet Russia, is concerned with how, through a revolutionary social philosophy of self-abnegation, the Che-
khovian pieces might be fitted into a grand unit of happy
individuals.

Grandeur is possible when the universe is not a spiral
rotating about the kernel of a self, but an infinite vista
that entices the mind and enlarges its horizons. It is to be
found in large-souled beings, such as Pushkin's Mozart
delighting in the music he creates, or Tolstoy's Natasha
who can be herself only when she has a chance to love; in
men and women of great humility like Pierre Bezuhov,
Kutuzov, or Prince Myshkin; in wild, generous souls like
Dmitry Karamazov; in clear-eyed rebels such as Chatsky,
or in staunch but independent upholders of the law like
Ilya of Murom. It is more evident in character and action
than in theory—but theories also may be large of spirit:
the Elder Zossima's views, the belief which Pierre attains,
even Raskolnikov's and Ivan Karamazov's philosophies,
which are mistakes of great magnificence; even the pseudo-
practical visions propounded by Chekhov's well-meaning
but limited Astrovs and Trofimovs; and certainly those for
which Gorky's revolutionists give their lives. There is
grandeur also in the sweep of history as it is sensed, rather
than thought about, by the author of *The Lay of the Host
of Igor,* by Pushkin in his acceptance of the complex fate
of man as an eternal journey from life to death, by Tolstoy
in his deep feeling for the voiceless processes of existence,
by Dostoevsky in his assuredness of a rock-bottom moral
order through which humanity might be guided.

But the magnificent individuals are what they are not
through some transcendental power that by fiat coins

them as static images of virtue. Just to be good or to feel rightly is not enough. Being and feeling must prove themselves in action. All moral qualities have reference to a reality outside the individual who is tested by his relation to it, and whose fulfillment does not come through an enforced or blindly willed capitulation but through an understanding of his own nature, which may indeed lead him to self-abnegation, but only after he is in a position to realize it as experience, not as the force of accident or constraint. That submissiveness which is the supreme virtue of Pushkin's, Dostoevsky's, and Tolstoy's people comes as the result of discovery, not of command—and sometimes the discovery is intuitive and immediate, and sometimes it is rational and of a slow evolution. A man's understanding counts more than any law, principle, or idea to which he submits; and it is his evaluation of someone or something that is important, not his giving himself up, which is but the outcome and the evidence of an independent choice. The ego, that is, is always supreme, and it retains its dignity and wholeness even in surrender.

By the same token, the great theories are not programs for the expansion or the dissemination of the self but for understanding nature; they are such instruments of union between man and the world as permit him to be neither lost in it nor in absolute command. So also the sense of Fate and the views of history come of a secure trust in the reality of man's dual position as both humble component of Nature and prime molder of life. Nothing is more erroneous than the opinion that Russians are fatalists, if by "fatalism" one means belief in an ungovernable power that operates on man without his knowledge or his sanction.

The Russian writers seem to take for granted that men are parts of a universal order and of a temporal process and that it is possible for them to be virtuous because they are by nature moral. And these are instinctive beliefs, since human beings are normally inclined to see evil as perversion of good rather than good as sublimation of evil, and are more readily aware of the present as a limited point between the past and the future than as a self-enclosed moment of eternal duration. These theories are, then, articulations of uninhibited insights, based on suspicion of whatever doctrines and fashions may repress instinct in artificialities. Reason is accredited when it corroborates the knowledge yielded to animal faith, for life—the Russians say—is apprehended by animal faith, while consciousness and observation, however strained, accurate, and close they may be, can arrive at the form and outline of it only. All that does not serve this truth seems arbitrary, therefore, and is condemned as false. So superstition is condemned, and fancy that masquerades as knowledge, and slavish adherence to fact.

With all their love of primitivism, the Russian writers, from Pushkin on, are horrified and disgusted by the superstitions of their countrymen, which, in Pushkin's day, could lead peasants to murder the doctors sent to cure them of cholera and, in Chekhov's time, could make an "enlightened" teacher stir up a witch's brew to serve as a love potion. Occult and supernatural proceedings might be the substance of nightmares, but even so, a Gogol would see their ridiculousness, and no one certainly would accept them as substitutes for knowledge. Russian literature is directed toward discovery, not invention; its aim is to disclose rather than to create. Even Pushkin's Mozart is moved to the forebodings out of which he shapes his "Requiem" by something that actually happens to him; and all the writers look upon themselves as seers of empiric truth or as scientists, at least. They have the humility, the gratitude, and the pride of those who contemplate great matters and are able to unravel something of their mystery. They are not Chauntecleers who believe that the sun obeys their crowing; they do not belong—not even the playful Pushkin—to the company of frolicsome souls, so much in love with themselves and the words they use that they imagine the world as trailing in the footsteps of their jests. But neither are they so overwhelmed by the impact of events as to be imprisoned in the narrowness of the immediate. They are not given to the illusion that they and the world are one and the same, nor are they lulled by the charm of thinking the universe a drama staged for their amusement and edification. They stand in awe before the earth, from which they have come, and which they know to be different from themselves; and their art is a passionate attempt to understand it and to ally themselves with it. They are not tormented by the old philosophic duality of mind and matter, craving to be assured of the reality of the one or the other, for they have seen that this division need not exist, that the arrogance of the dreamer asserting the primacy of illusion and that of the factual observer, scoffing at the presumptuousness of the dreamer, are lost in the recognition that the self, with all its dreams, and the world of which it is conscious are both factors in that primary whole which constitutes experience. They are, in short, materialists and realists in the deepest meaning of these terms; and the earth, it seems, has rewarded their self-forgetfulness by giving up to them some of its secrets.

Their understanding of experience as the unpremeditated adventures of a soul in its search for knowledge has several corollaries. In the first place, since experience, which is the distinguishing characteristic of human life, involves action, that which is static is inhuman; a state of being, an act of willing, a sense of pleasure are unimportant until they have been propelled into a world beyond the one who is, wills, and enjoys, and have returned, not with mirrors of himself, but with reports and messages from realms that are independent of him. It is after Tatiana has dared acknowledge that she loves Onegin, after Raskolnikov has dared to test his theory, after Alyosha Karamazov has become involved with men outside the monastery, and Natasha Rostov has reacted, as best she could, to Andrey Bolkonsky, Anatole Kuragin, and Pierre Bezuhov, only after character, will, desire have proved themselves in action, that life reveals something of its meaning. The motionless world in which Chekhov's people live, as under a glass bell, is the tragedy of the sick, who can only gaze, and long, but never move. That is why Russian literature is dynamic and dramatic. Only the work of the sentimentalist Turgenev turns upon itself without egress, like a dog in perpetually wistful pursuit of its tail; and although a self-pitying whine accompanies the process, one knows that Turgenev delights in it, whereas Chekhov is distressed by this kind of spectacle and does not relish the flat pictures which his own honesty compels him to draw.

Another corollary is that only the simple are capable of great adventures. The soul must be stripped before it may proceed on its quest; and no statement is more emphatic in Russian literature than that affectation is at best absurd and at worst pernicious. It is remarkable how little posing and how little prying there is among Russian writers. They seem to have no desire to act out an ideal role, showing themselves to be other than they are, nor to engage in dissections. They do not pride themselves on systematic inquiries, and the drama which they see everywhere does not appear to them as a design imposed upon the world by clever people. They feel the press of life too much to escape in pretense, and their minds are too involved in knowledge that is immediately given to pursue problems of special research. In short, they accept themselves, are engrossed in being, and glory neither in display nor in analytic perspicacity. They are not given to exaggerated hopes nor to fanciful disillusionments, and are not interested in the kind of truth yielded by post-mortems. It is the actual and the living they deal with; and to those who are used to taking life for granted, their way of thought seems primitive, even at its most sophisticated. Krylov's fable, *The Quartet*—in which a monkey, a donkey, a goat, and a bear, having tried every possible seating arrangement, on which, they think, their music must depend, turn, in despair, to a nightingale for advice and are told that what they need is what they do not and cannot have: namely, ability and a delicate ear—whether it was intended to satirize a certain pompous literary society or a political body, is a witty parable of the truth that form is not a substitute for intrinsic worth and that those who assume that it is make themselves ridiculous. Russian literature abounds in examples of such fools, from Pushkin's Onegin to Gogol's Hlestakov and Chichikov, Dostoevsky's Epanchins in *The Idiot,* Karmazinov in *The Possessed,* or Rakitin in *The Brothers Karamazov,* to Tolstoy's Napoleon or Ivan Ilych, Chekhov's Dunyasha and Yasha in *The Cherry*

Orchard, and Gorky's Klim Samghin. They are silly, pathetic, despicable, or dangerous, as the case may be; and they are what they are either through natural shallowness and stupidity, through cowardice or sentimentality, or by virtue of some more evil perversions of values—but what is common to them all is a predilection for posing and for conventionality. Turgenev alone has such respect for forms that one is left in doubt as to whether his Pavel Petrovich Kirsanov, in *Fathers and Sons,* is intended to be admirable or not.

Russian literature is not antisocial, but the opinion it presents of what is valuable in society is different from that of English or of German literature. In the work of Thomas Mann, for example, the decorousness of social tradition is a heroic element, even when it is satirized. It appears as almost the backbone of cultural history; and the offhand carelessness of the Russian Claudia Chauchat, in *The Magic Mountain,* which first shocks and then entrances Hans Castorp, properly reared in German ways, is intended to symbolize the polarity of human traits represented by the two nations. As for the individuals of English novels, they are invariably formed by their immediate environments. In all their opinions, and in their ideas about themselves, it is impossible to think of them as apart from their social milieu, even when they are isolated or rebellious. But the Russian characters are first themselves, and secondarily members of a group, for although for self-fulfillment they must be placed in direct relation to a reality beyond them, they are obliged to achieve an inward integration before they can establish fruitful contact with others. The substance of their lives comes from outside, but their values are their own.

They cannot prize what they have not themselves created or accepted as freely proffered gifts. They cannot live on borrowed things.

No literature has given a more searching analysis of the human personality, and although none has been more richly introspective and more concerned with the complexities of individuals, Russian authors have not valued introspection in itself nor have been satisfied to tell the histories of an ego's development. The "bildungs-roman" is not characteristic of Russian literature, nor the kind of triumph of imaginative reflectiveness achieved by Marcel Proust. It is understandable that both Proust and Mann should have admired Tolstoy, and also that they should have diverged from him so widely. For Thomas Mann the evolution of an ego is a tale of spherical completeness in which the entire history of mankind is reproduced, and for Marcel Proust life itself is a tissue of images recalled to a mind, whereas for Tolstoy a man's awareness of his own growth is only a step toward shedding his consciousness of it, his coming to know himself, only a necessary stage in forgetting himself. That is true also of Dostoevsky, who sees evil as generated in a festering hell of introspection, to reverberate there in disastrous crescendos. Both Pushkin and Gogol give themselves up so completely to living that they have no time for prolonged self-analyses; they laugh and suffer in a world into which they have flung themselves, like swimmers into a rough sea with which they battle and which they love—while Mann stands on the shore, and Proust is incased at the bottom, watching reflections through translucent depths. Chekhov is impatient with Tolstoy for giving even as much emphasis as he does to the inward view; and only Turgenev—without, unfortunately, the gift of divination—smoothes and fingers the ego as if it were a magic crystal.

Russian literature is serious, critical, and, at once, passionate and aloof. Its seriousness derives from the primary conviction that man is the center of things, and that, because he is infinitely important, everything which touches him calls for an honest and undeviating solicitude. Its frankness has led to the popular misconception of it as morbid. But uncompromising treatment of morbidity does not necessarily show a love of it—and in this literature it serves a deeper purpose than scabrous or exhibitionist pleasure. The lurid pages of Dostoevsky's books, for example—supposedly the chief offenders in this respect—are somehow turned to brilliant white, irradiated, as through a phosphorescent underglaze, by the ever-present belief implied in them, that evil seeks its own extinction. And some luminous feeling or vast concept such as this is always latent, to show up the many facets and the full contours of the dark individual instance. The "pessimism" of the Russians is but a prime ingredient in a kind of hearty effervescence which is more characteristic of them than any variety of gloom—for although they have great sympathy with unfortunate men and spare no one's feelings in describing their misery, they do not insult humanity with pity. Because they see things in the large, they despise coy, mincing, soft, and tinny attitudes that narrow life and belittle man; and because they see themselves in relation to the world, and can examine even their convictions in a discriminating and critical light, they do not sacrifice grace to tragedy, nor fun to seriousness. Their laughter is broad and ironic.

They display, perhaps, too little faith in the sweet reasonableness of rational discourse. They are proud of man's Karamazov passions, of his ability to look on good and evil without squinting. They believe in clean breaks and clear sweeps. They will sacrifice anything to a passionate persuasion, but nothing to a merely comfortable *modus vivendi*. It is because in Western modes of thought they saw too great a readiness to compromise with human qualities for the sake of animal satisfactions that Slavophiles were so insistent in their opposition to them. And it is because they saw not compromise but possibilities of spiritual enrichment in Western progress that such writers as Turgenev, Chekhov, and, later, Gorky, advocated it. The actual conditions of life which one glimpses through the great poetic symbols of the writers are, of course, appalling; in Gorky's work they were to come into the foreground, presenting the raw substance out of which Dostoevsky and Tolstoy had fashioned their grandiose pictures of cruelty and of kindness. But the work of all of them is built on knowledge of a materially crude and brutal existence, on respect for human qualities that remain magnificent in the midst of brutality, and on a flexible but aloof interest in so-called "civilized" conditions of living and thinking.

There are men who fear the inarticulate, for whom even music is terrifying because it is not sufficiently explicit, and who distrust the primitive and recoil from it as from a loathsome and dangerous assault on man's essential humanity. To them respect for the elemental is not an enlargement, but a limitation of civilized living— an insult to man's reason rather than an enrichment of it. Such men are likely to lean on systems and doctrines, to consider forms of government more important than the people for whom they are created, and schools of art more interesting than individual artists. As for the artists themselves, they, too, are divided into those who love and praise the flux of life which consciousness may or may not turn into experience and those who despise and disparage it. Russian writers are so divided, as well as those of other countries. But because in Russia governments and forms of social behavior have usually impressed independent thinkers not as reins held by the people, but as shackles that confined them, her greatest authors have been suspicious of all formulas and systems. Nothing has seemed to them to be ultimately valid but the individual in his most distinctive traits and in his direct relation to the world, nor artistically worth while but the communication of this belief in such a way as might make all men recognize that they are most similar in their uniqueness.

Those who wish to explain the history of a nation by what they understand to be the character of its people, should bear in mind that crimes are sometimes committed in the name of great ideals, that it is important to distinguish between the ideal and the crime, and to determine whether the allegiance of men has been claimed by the one or the other. To this end, the study of a nation's literature may be helpful. And if every great work of art provides a new mode of discourse that gives men means of finding grander ways through their experience, and if the language of a people's art, like their speech, is marked by special qualities, then the Russian is the tongue of those whose faith is given entirely to man, who love him unsentimentally enough to take him seriously, and who see the only hope for the world in his realization of his own complexity, and of both the grandeur and the meanness of which he is capable and for which he is alone responsible.

In Soviet literature this language has undergone some remarkable transformations; it sounds strange at times in paradoxical new tones and accents, but it has not been lost.

171